From Theory to Practice

From Theory to Practice
How to Assess and Apply Impartiality in News and Current Affairs

Edited by Leon Barkho

intellect Bristol, UK / Chicago, USA

First published in the UK in 2013 by
Intellect, The Mill, Parnall Road, Fishponds, Bristol, BS16 3JG, UK

First published in the USA in 2013 by
Intellect, The University of Chicago Press, 1427 E. 60th Street,
Chicago, IL 60637, USA

A catalogue record for this book is available from the
British Library.

Cover designer: Ellen Thomas
Copy-editor: Michael Eckhardt
Production manager: Tim Mitchell
Typesetting: Contentra Technologies

Print ISBN: 978-1-84150-726-2
ePDF ISBN: 978-1-78320-228-7
ePUB ISBN: 978-1-78320-229-4

Printed and bound by Gomer Press Ltd, UK.

To the Hamrins, the Swedish benefactor family
Without your sponsorship this book would never have seen the light

Table of Contents

Introduction

The theory and practice of impartiality in news and current affairs

Leon Barkho

This volume deals with one of the most contentious and controversial notions in journalism. Impartiality has always been difficult to define and even more difficult to put into practice. Philosophers have grabbled with the notion, and so have journalism and communication scholars. Journalists and their organizations normally avoid providing explicit definitions of the term, with emphasis placed on its major components or elements. Practitioners, while shunning philosophical or scholarly deliberations, show a high degree of consistency and unanimity on what elements impartiality should include or exclude. Prejudice, bias and self-interest are traits of partiality. Therefore, practitioners aiming at impartiality say that they do their best not to be prejudiced towards or against any actor or action in their stories. Other important impartiality elements the media highlight include fairness, independence, balance, transparency, accuracy and diversity of opinion.

Impartiality and controversy

Impartiality attracts most attention when news coverage deals with controversial and sensitive issues, where it is rather difficult to keep our own opinions, interests and prejudices under wraps and tell things as they are and not as we see them, or sometimes as our institutions would like us to view them. Impartiality is in danger in a world like ours, in which our discourses shape, and are shaped, by our actions and the social reality of the world we live in. Adherence to one's own discourse and opinion is, for many people in our world, as important as adherence to one's own religion, ethnicity and national identity. The chapters of this volume deal mainly with how impartiality comes into play when news coverage specifically tackles issues and conflicts that drive societies, countries, civilizations, ideologies and religions apart. They attempt to supplement the measures and standards of impartiality in news and current affairs in the age of digitization. Focusing mainly on the coverage of conflicts and impartiality, the chapters address why and how we fail to understand the issues, controversies and conflicts afflicting our world, or in the words of Helen Boaden (2010), director of BBC News, 'the "whys and wherefores" of [...] whatever subject' an impartial reporter is assigned to cover. Impartiality has always been a much sought after goal in journalism; nonetheless scholarly literature on journalism and the stream of complaints from audiences provide ample evidence of prejudiced, bipartisan and opinionated coverage that has increased in intensity and density in our digital world.

Clashes over mentalities and religion, represented in discourse and action, have been intensifying since the September 11 attacks on the US. The attacks and their consequences have produced a discourse whereby politics and religion have been socially and discursively abused to the extent that our best models of impartiality might fail to properly explain the why and the how of controversial events and actions that are driving our world apart (Bernstein 2005). While wars, battles, controversies and clash of mentalities rage in our world, language has become one of the most important tools in the hands of protagonists in their different battlefields. Today, battles over mentalities or religion are not only fought by arms. Words today are as sharp as swords.

Mentalities, religion and impartiality

Religious issues, particularly those with a bearing on the Muslim world, have posed major dilemmas to western models of impartiality and objectivity. Western media have confronted such controversies in their news and current affairs, but their best models of impartiality have failed to provide answers for questions such as whether it is right or wrong to air or print, for instance, the Danish cartoons of the Prophet Muhammad, which many Muslims see as offensive and disparaging to their religion (Kimmelman 2008). Other religious controversies involving Islam and causing widespread anger, and even violence, across the Muslim world include the anti-Islamic video *Innocence of Muslims* (Post 2012); the flushing of the Koran, Muslims' holy book, down a toilet by US troops (The Economist 2012); the burning of the Koran (Sieff 2012); and remarks by Pope Benedict XVI in which he quoted a fourteenth-century Christian emperor as saying that Muhammad had brought the world nothing but 'evil and inhuman' things (Shadid 2006). If impartiality becomes an issue when dealing with controversial and sensitive topics, it is in the tackling of problems like these that impartiality models and standards are challenged.

Religious controversies are part of the clash of mentalities in our current world, and are no longer restricted to holy books or prophets. A good deal of editorial discussions today revolve around religious clothing and insignia, which have become editorially newsworthy. A large deal of discussion in the BBC's impartiality seminar, in which numerous hypothetical questions are raised about assessing and applying impartiality, centre on religion and whether it is proper to wear a hijab, a cross, a cap, a sari, a turban or a flag when reading news (BBC Trust 2006b). The question to raise here is not whether its permissible or not, but whether, for instance, the Koran, the Bible, the Torah (the Jewish Bible), the Muslim hijab, the Jewish cap, the Sikhs' turban and the Indian sari mean the same thing for their followers and advocates. And similarly whether 'holy' men like Muhammad, Jesus, Moses, Sikhs' Gurus or a Hindu Avatars have the same meaning and influence among the different people who follow them. Most importantly, why throwing a copy of the Bible in a dustbin or drawing a cartoon of Jesus or Moses would not lead to violent protests among Christians or Jews, and doing the same thing to the Koran or Muhammad causes widespread disturbances among Muslims. And why wearing religious insignia on-air becomes an editorial issue and a topic that has generated heated debate on impartiality and objectivity.

We live in a sensitive world, and it seems that digitization and globalization, while they have helped in removing geographical barriers, have failed to reduce our cultural differences to the extent that a picture of US President, Barack Obama, holding a baseball bat during a telephone conversation with Turkey's Prime Minister, Erdogan, was about to deal a blow to US-Turkey relations as many Turks interpreted it as carrying a 'hidden message' with a negative 'symbolic meaning' (Jansen 2012). Clash of mentalities and religions in our world is displayed mainly in signs and insignia which are part of discourse, and today even a beard, like the one worn by US Army Major Nidal Malik Hasan, the Fort Hood shooting suspect, delays court's proceedings and prompts a military judge to have it forcibly shaved (Fernandez 2012). Are issues like these related to impartiality? Have we ever thought of the importance some groups attach to their culture and the way their religion, saints and signs are represented? Have we tried to explain to our audiences that, for certain groups, religion is central to their view of themselves and their social and discursive world? How far should an impartial reporter or medium go in explaining and manifesting within discourse the different views different groups have about their religion and its discursive and social representations? Are editorial decisions about wearing or displaying of insignia on-air, or even in the newsroom or in the field, a sign of bias? Are not we committing a potential 'offence' when forcing people, journalists or even suspects not to wear or display their religious or cultural signs? Have we ever considered the point that such signs and insignia might have become part of the individuals wearing them?

We are aware that our world is full of controversies but we lack proper knowledge on how to understand and explain them. Our traditional models of impartiality do not seem to have assisted us in going beyond the surface meaning and structure of the issues facing our world (see Chapter 4). A critical model of impartiality, as the one advocated in this volume, would try to explain, through debate and dialogue, why a turban is so important for a Sikh, why a beard has become an issue in a US court, and why Muslims react violently when someone disparages their prophet or holy book. Impartiality, according to Helen Boaden, 'is not a fixed point [see Chapter 9]. It is a process [...] determined by an open mindedness, a capacity to challenge yourself and challenge your team to bring in views that are not things you thought of, things you find comfortable' (BBC Trust 2006b). One great challenge to impartiality is to challenge the things which a news institution forbids its reporters from saying, while also challenging the things which a news institution tells its reporters to use. This may apply to numerous issues, controversies and mentalities; in avoiding their debate, discussion and explanation, we may mistakenly think of them as a yardstick of impartiality in modern journalism. (For additional details see Chapter 7).

Religious insignia and impartiality

Consider the different religious insignia mentioned above, and how the people adopting them use them as a discursive and social paradigm of how actions can be carried out, and whether such actions are reasonable or not. Also consider how the abuse or humiliation of a religious sign or personality (saint or prophet), discursively or socially, has been used as a paradigm to fuel not only anger and fury, but also violence in several parts of the world. Let us take Pope Benedict XVI's remarks about Muhammad and try to explain how and why someone in his position would publicly cite an obscure fourteenth-century theological treatise, and cause so much chaos at a time the world was passing through a period of religious and political divide probably not seen since the time of the Crusades. Do we have the right explanation for why the Pope said what he said? Do we have the right explanation for the protests and the ensuing violence that followed the Pope's remarks? Or shall we just blame the Muslim world or 'radical' Islam for the chaos? When the Pope made his remarks, he might have thought that doing so would spur Muslims to reconsider their attitude towards what he sees as violent passages in their holy book, the Koran. We can assume that the Pope had thought carefully before using that type of language, and had calculated its consequences. He might have thought within himself that he would say this to show that as the head of the western Catholic Church, he is against Muslim violence, and to win hearts and minds of the 'Christian West', which was then, under US leadership, fighting two ruinous wars in Afghanistan and Iraq against what it saw as Muslim 'terror'. He might have even thought that he was impartial and objective? Or was he merely expressing his own vagaries and whims? What has gone wrong in this context is the failure to understand the meaning of not only what we do, but also of what we say and its implications to a way of life that is different from us. Our speech acts and actions rely on the embedded social forms of our own life. Problems occur when we use our ways to judge other people's social forms of life. The Pope's language seemed 'rational' from the viewpoint of the speaker and probably his audiences, but it was seen as totally 'irrational' to people pursuing different ways of life. The question is whether we are prepared to accept forms of life, expressed through language or action, that we see as 'irrational', and treat them and deal with them not only with 'due impartiality' but also with due respect. (For further details see Chapter 5).

Language and impartiality

Philosophers drawing on language in order to explain human action or communicative action have demonstrated that our speech and writing constitute, and are constituted by, the social realities of our world. They have shown that linguistic analyses and investigations are a useful tool for the understanding of social concepts and for shedding light on human actions and practices (c.f. Wittgenstein 1953; Austin 1962; Louch 1969; Ryan 1970; Grice 1975; Searle 1979). These thinkers believe that linguistic investigations can help us understand the how and the why of our actions. Our beliefs and viewpoints, they say, are part not only of how we see ourselves, but also of our conception of others 'and this conception in its turn, whether conscious or not, is intrinsic' to the picture we have about the world out there (Bernstein 1976: 83). Therefore, one of the objectives of a reporter or a media outlet with a claim to impartiality and objectivity is not to impose their own discursive criteria and standards of ethics, rationality or intelligibility to explain actors and actions outside their own discursive and social contexts. Their task should be to tell us, uncover or dig up the criteria and standards of ethics, rationality or intelligibility from the viewpoints of the actors they cover. The role of impartiality and objectivity recedes when news or current affairs writers see their job as an arbiter with the power to tell what is right and wrong, or true and false. Of course, it is not their business to 'award', for instance, 'murderers', 'terrorists' or human rights violators. But for the sake of impartiality and objectivity, they should relay to their audiences the social and discursive reality of actors and their actions.

Reporters use language to report the events they are assigned to cover. Not all events make news for every news medium. Moreover, different news outlets have their own standards and viewpoints regarding which event to select and which to discard (see Chapter 6). Someone (an individual or an institution) makes the decision for which event is news. Similarly, someone decides which words, phrases and even sentences are the most suitable. The issue becomes clearer when we move from relatively uncontroversial linguistic items to structures with emotive and loaded meanings. Not only adjectives express value. Names of countries can be as emotive too. There are more emotions and sentiments attached to names such as Syria, Iran, Lebanon and Palestine than to Switzerland and Luxembourg. The very use of certain language is a bone of contention and a source of discursive struggle and division. Note the difference in discursive and social attitudes and representations of Syria, and the upsurge in violence there (see Chapter 9). Decisions on how to describe Syria depend on the individual's or institution's view of the world out there. The language selected relays the 'facts' from a special angle or viewpoint that is part of the reporter's or the medium's world. Names of certain countries or regions can even cause a huge range of difficulties for a broadcaster like the BBC, which prides itself on its 'due impartiality'. The word 'Palestine' for the BBC is seen as highly politicized and extremely sensitive, to the extent that it avoids using it across its platforms unless accredited (BBC 2006). Other names like Iran, Gaza and Lebanon, for instance, might cause a 'headache' for certain media outlets if they are asked to issue an appeal for charity on their behalf (BBC Trust 2006b; Hastings & Sawer 2009).

There are serious questions about whether the selection of language on the basis of the conceptions we have about others is based on objectivity or impartiality standards. Such selection can hardly escape ideological bias. When we use our own view of the world as a basis for the formulation of the discursive or social representations of others, we are judging them from our own ethical standards. How can we provide for an objective or value-neutral account when we use our own theories and concepts of the social in representing others? Using language as a vehicle to discursively represent others from our own views denies them the discursive autonomy they deserve as human beings who are worthy and entitled to their own way of life. Hence, there is a need for a critical theory of impartiality and objectivity that seeks to reveal how language can be used as a tool to hide bias, and at the same time how critical language investigations can help bring to surface the hidden and sometimes dubious values of our accounts of others (see Chapters 3 and 5).

Loaded language carries moral and religious overtones, and while some may only object to it, others see it as humiliating and degrading. Those using such language say they 'correctly, neutrally and logically' represent the others, but they forget that the representation is 'correct, neutral and logical' only from their viewpoints. Language provides an almost inexhaustible source of discursive choices, and the possibility is there for the selection of words that are less evaluative or emotive. In the reporting of emotive and sensitive stories, it seems the need arises, and becomes greater, for the use of loaded and evaluative language, which today pervades news discourse. The prevalence of such discourse not only points to partiality and bias, but shows how different we can be in representing our own human actions and the actions of others.

An analysis of the linguistics of the sensitive and controversial issues afflicting our world can be a good measure to assess impartiality and objectivity in our digital age (see Chapters 5, 7 and 9). Language for impartial broadcasters like the BBC, for instance, is seen as crucial for the attainment of balance, fairness, clarity and understanding of the themes and topics news reporters deal with. Language for the BBC 'is an issue at the heart of impartiality', and is not only crucial for 'accuracy, clarity and precision', but also for 'avoiding bias [...] and providing comprehension' (Thomas 2006). Another BBC report urges caution with the use of language because of the impact it 'may have on our reputation for objective journalism among our many audiences' (BBC Trust 2006a). Philosophers (c.f. Wittgenstein 1953; Winch 1972) have critically explored the implications and effects of language, and its role in helping us understand our social world. A critical analysis of the type of words, phrases and discourses reporters and their organizations employ to represent different social concepts and issues can be a good tool to tell us how fair and balanced they are (see Chapter 1). These philosophers tell us that our social actions and the ideas we have in our mind 'are really the same thing'; and therefore the type of language we employ and the social relations we have 'are just two different sides of the same coin' (Winch 1972: 123).

Impartiality and linguistic strata

We can distinguish two linguistic levels, or two 'language strata' (Winch 1972: 13), in assessing or measuring impartiality. Understanding any society on its own terms requires attention not only to (1) causes, but also to (2) 'intentions, motives, and reasons [that] must precede attention to cause'. I shall call Winch's first linguistic level 'the causal strata' and the second 'the explanatory strata'. These are two different conceptual schemes that I believe are necessary for analyzing and operationalizing impartiality and objectivity from a discoursal or linguistic viewpoint. It is a sign of bias, subjectivity and partiality when the discursive or social structures in news and current affairs provide both the 'causal strata' and the 'explanatory strata' for one side, and deny them when representing the other.

The analysis of both strata – causes and explanations – falls within the linguistic framework which Hanna Pitkin calls '[t]he language of action' (1972: 268). According to

Pitkin, the language actors use is not only shaped in the course of performing or carrying out their actions, its vocabulary and grammar describe and represent actors and their actions. But saying how an action is shaped through language is not enough. Our analysis to detect absence or presence of impartiality should not be confined to how language constitutes, and is constituted by, actors and their actions: 'Sometimes we do (what is called) describe an action objectively; sometimes we do (what is called) predict an action; Sometimes we do (what is called) give a causal explanation of an action'.

The analysis of the linguistic strata briefly outlined above is not possible if we restrict our investigation to the discourses and texts actors produce. Understanding must go beyond textual analysis and involve the institutions who have a say in the selection of language, particularly when we deal with sensitive, emotive and controversial issues and topics such as religion, beliefs, social habits and practices, traditions, symbols with emotive and loaded meanings, etc. (see Chapter 2). When we analyze issues like these 'there are difficult conceptual problems both in principle and fact in deciding even what counts as proper interpretation of the phenomenon involved', particularly when the use of language, which is meant to tell or report things, lacks balance and consistency, and privileges one side through the selection of benign and positive linguistic structures at the expense of the other (Bernstein 1976: 71).

Impartiality, transparency and institutions

The resort to loaded language to represent and describe others is part of institutional bias. Many news organizations today have stopped using the word 'terrorist' unless accredited. But there are many other words and expressions with negative representation, which fall into the same category as 'terrorist'. For instance, though less loaded than 'terrorist', the repetitive use of terms like 'militant', 'radical', 'fundamentalist', 'Islamist', 'insurgent', 'special rendition' and 'illegal combatants' indicate a point of view, as is the use of 'martyr' by Al Jazeera Arabic to represent the Palestinians who fall in battle with the Israelis. Decisions to use or discard sensitive or loaded vocabulary are usually taken at the highest institutional levels. For impartiality and objectivity's sake, it is important that reporters and their news organizations avoid language that is a barrier to understanding others and their actions, as they are not from our own institutional viewpoint. One good measure of partiality should be inconsistency in the use of loaded language and terminology. The use of 'martyr' – or any other label – can be cited as a good example of partiality because Al Jazeera Arabic as an institution uses it to represent Palestinians killed by Israel, and not Israelis killed by Palestinians or Palestinians killed by Arabs, Muslims or other Palestinians. The discursive inconsistency and double standard is overwhelming in cases like these.

A lot of light can be shed on the controversial cases mentioned in this chapter and elsewhere in this volume once we become aware of the institutional role. Let us consider the case of Pope Benedict's anti-Islamic remarks within their institutional context. For the Catholic Church and its practicing followers the Pope is 'infallible', but this is not the case for the secular world. The

Pope's 'infallibility' is not something to reckon with in the Muslim world and its media outlets, most of which see strict adherence to Islamic principles as part of defending their religion against a 'Christian' West who, led by the Catholic Church, encroached on 'holy' Muslim territory during the Crusades. Here comes the role of transparency in impartiality. It means that audiences have the right to be informed about the different roles different institutions play in our life. It is part of understanding the world out there. Institutional partiality cannot be avoided, and should not be forgotten when assessing and measuring impartiality. Organizations, whether dealing with news or other things, have their own histories, traditions, cultures and backgrounds, and as such they lean – in practice and language – towards certain issues consciously or unconsciously (Brunninge 2009; see Chapter 8). A good example of institutional partiality is the repetitive use of appellations, labels or clichés to represent certain groups. The BBC, in one of its major debates on impartiality, says coinage or the use of labels or clichés and their repetition 'can be corrosive' and a sign of partiality (BBC Trust 2006b). Single labels coined to malignantly represent one side of a conflict are not easy to explain (Barkho 2010; Philo 2011). They creep into discourse when writers or speakers fail to study and understand people who lie outside their social world and experience. They become discursively almost impregnable when we exclusively rely on our own way of life to explain other people's way of life. The temptation to use and even introduce new single labels occurs when we do not accept other people's way of life, and instead resort to 'discursive force' to change their beliefs and the way they see themselves. When we use our representations from our own discursive world and apply them to others we are essentially attempting to transform them and make them like us – a move they will naturally resist in discourse and action.

Historian Mary Beard warns against negative representations of others – for instance, the malignant terms commonly used by the rich and the powerful to describe the poor and the less powerful in the society – because 'they will quickly become so. There's no surer way to turn a child into a problem then [sic] to relegate him or her to the "naughty step"' (Beard 2012). Needless to say, all discursive attempts to represent others negatively, even when they are accompanied by formidable military campaigns, fail to achieve their ends and the 'War on Terror', as well as the wars in Iraq and Afghanistan, are clear examples. Negative language that describes others from our viewpoint is likely to spur them to adhere tenaciously in discourse and practice to their special way of life, no matter how loud we cry foul about it. Moreover, the use of malignant discourse in such a repetitive way signals an end to dialogue, debate and discussion; the elements that are essential for the assessment and application of impartiality in our modern age (see Chapters 3 and 6).

Impartiality and autonomy

Who decides which view is true? Reporters pursuing impartiality and objectivity, as well as their organizations, claim that issues of who is right and who is wrong must be left to their readers, viewers or listeners to decide. This means that reporters do not trample with truth or the reality of the events they cover; they treat, view and deal with all the communicative events they cover, and the viewpoints of the different actors, on the same level of playing field. They also claim to be detached and unprejudiced in their coverage and have no say in how their audiences arrive at decisions about the events they handle, and that reporting, which they see as void of subjectivity, has no influence on the attitudes their audiences have about world events.

Claims of impartiality and objectivity, particularly in the coverage of sensitive stories, conflicts, controversies and wars, are hard to substantiate. For many media thinkers, objectivity is a dream impossible to realize. The reality of our world is that it is socially constructed, and as such our ideas about social issues cannot be based on the views we have of natural sciences where objectivity or impartiality is not difficult to obtain. As members of human society, our social behaviour and concepts cannot be interpreted and explicated in the same way as natural sciences. There is a difference between the ways we speak and write about nature and the social; natural sciences have their special non-competing and almost unified norms, ways and patterns through which we can interpret and explain natural or scientific phenomena. But there is no one single pattern to explain social issues and events occurring in our social world, where different and competing groups and cultures have their own special accounts of the social reality of their actions (c.f. Berger & Luckmann 1966; Winch 1972; Bernstein 1979 & 2005). Hence discursive dichotomies of black/white, negative/positive and malignant/benign commonly used in today's media in representing actors and their actions are a reminder of how partial and biased we can be, because we are employing language as a scientific instrument, i.e. a thermometer that can tell to the point of perfection the temperature of the air or the body.

Since impartiality and objectivity are part of the concepts of the social, their application must bear in mind that the societies we live in, and their systems, no matter how inefficiently they may function, pursue a 'social order based on respect for men as persons or autonomous agents' (Louch 1969: 239). The concept of 'autonomy' as used by Louch is important for impartiality and objectivity. It tells us that human societies, despite their differences, deserve autonomous discursive and social representations. Language is a barometer of social conditions and Mary Beard (2009), through her linguistic investigation of slurs and nicknames the rich give to the poor, provides a good picture of social behaviour among ancient Romans and Greeks. Her discursive parallels with our modern age show an almost similar trend of how the elites in the society hold themselves to a very different social standard from the poor through the types of linguistic structures they use to describe individuals and families relying on public services, utilities and benefits. This discursive trend, in which the rich or the powerful resort to negative language to represent the less privileged or those who are different, denies others the discursive autonomy they deserve. Instead of explaining and describing others as they are, reporters and their institutions employ discursive structures, mostly with negative or loaded meaning, to represent others as they see them (see Chapters 3, 5 and 9). Applying our own discursive descriptions to an action or an actor opposite their own social or historical contexts is an artificial process because 'social reality and the language of description of that social reality' are mutually dependent: 'The language is constitutive of the reality, is essential to its being the kind of reality it is' (Taylor 1971: 24). Autonomous discursive and social representation is important for impartiality because it tells it the way those who are different from us would like to be seen by us despite our disagreements with them. Violating linguistic autonomy – using our own language to represent others – is tantamount to linguistic invasion because it replaces others' discourses with our own.

Critical impartiality

Our digital world is different from the old analogue world. Our age is the age of plenty, and is different from the previous age of the few in which audiences only had access to a limited number of media voices. It was much easier not only to apply, but also to assess, impartiality rules and standards when there were only a few media players in the world. Today's technological advances have made it possible for users to produce content in which they express their own viewpoints and pay lip service to impartiality issues like neutrality, others' opinions, distance and open-mindedness.

The traditional model of impartiality in the age of plenty is hard to apply even for a broadcaster like the BBC. Georgina Born has found that the BBC has replaced its 'traditional impartiality paradigm' with a new 'post-impartiality' or 'radical impartiality' model (Born 2004). Although Born's 'radical impartiality' refers to what is happening in the editorial corridors of the BBC, the meaning behind it is applicable to our digital and globalized world, where corporate, state, religious, cultural, political, technological and outside pressures are influencing and transforming the world of journalism. Today we are face to face with a range of issues which either were not there or did not play a big role in our life. Issues like immigration, terrorism, political correctness, racial discrimination, multiculturalism and the role of Islam and sharia in western societies are posing difficult questions and challenges to the impartiality and objectivity models we have been dealing with.

The traditional model of impartiality, for instance, calls for adherence to 'fundamental democratic principles' (Simpson 2012). But the impartiality model which advocates 'fundamental democratic principles' is problematic because it should allow Arab and Muslim journalists and their news outlets to pursue their own model of impartiality; one in which attachment to 'fundamental Islamic principles' becomes part of their own paradigm of 'due impartiality'. One may wonder whether one can likewise accept a special model of impartiality for Chinese journalism in which attachment to 'fundamental communist principles' offers a new paradigm of 'Chinese impartiality'. The model of 'critical impartiality' means that there is not one single impartiality paradigm. One country's, one person's or one outlet's impartiality is another country's, person's or outlet's bias (Maras 2013). If we relate impartiality and objectivity to adherence to 'fundamental democratic principles', we risk getting involved in the debate of the rights and wrongs of democracy and its systems.

Even a system like apartheid at a certain point in time was part of a 'rights and wrongs' debate. But is neutrality, as a basic element of impartiality, acceptable with apartheid or racial discrimination, massive violations of human rights and unspeakable tragedies like the Holocaust? This volume gives prominence to dialogue and critical argument as a means to assess and measure impartiality and objectivity. However, a debate of the rights and wrongs of issues only one side sees as acceptable or unacceptable should be encouraged. According to Boaden, the BBC, in line with its new impartiality model, today encourages debate even of issues which the broadcaster as an institution is against, i.e. racism (BBC Trust 2006b). To prove her point, Boaden cites 'the arguments that people put forward on (BBC Radio) 5 Live […] about the intelligence of black people. They were very uncomfortable views that were challenged pretty hard but you can't just say we wouldn't put them on and treat them with a lack of respect […] if we are impartial, that means testing every argument hard and rigorously and that really does mean every argument' (ibid.; see Chapters 10 and 11).

Impartiality and deliberation

One important aspect of impartiality and objectivity in our current world should be deliberation, a concept which media scholars and philosophers discuss but regrettably practitioners normally overlook. Deliberation means it is not enough that I understand someone else's views from the sources that are made available to me as a reporter, i.e. my own world. An earnest attempt must be made to understand someone else's views through deliberation and dialogue within the media organization, and with the actors or sides of the communicative event. Understanding is reciprocal, not one-way, and deliberation and dialogue help us understand each other. A genuine and serious willingness for dialogue and deliberation with those different from us would certainly have helped the public to know the 'whys and wherefores' of the controversial cases raised in this volume. The volume deliberates these issues at some detail, drawing on moral, discourse and pragmatic philosophers and scholars. Most discussions and conclusions about impartiality and objectivity in today's media outlets are the outcome of top-down instructions. To build a learning organization through dialogue, media practitioners will have to learn more from each other and from the people they are writing about (Senge 1990; see Chapter 9).

Deliberation and dialogue require that we become aware of why and how each camp sees its own mentality as 'rational' and the other side's mentality as 'alien' or 'irrational.' This awareness comes through fieldwork or investigation in which intelligent questions are raised about why and how the followers, believers or advocates of a certain religion, ideology, system or mentality say what they say and do what they do. A breach of impartiality and objectivity occurs when we find a pattern in which the reasons and explanations – the causal strata and the explanatory strata – of one side's choice of language and action are given while their opponents are denied such advantage. A pattern means when there is systematic and consistent discursive behaviour over an extended period of time, or after examining a corpus of news material tackling a specific issue. At the research level, media analysts, through their data and methodologies, can look for the correlations these patterns may have with the social world of the actors involved not only in the production of news, but also about who the news is about. Once we have obtained enough evidence to correlate the patterns with the social world, we can then draw our conclusions and predictions, and see how far they can be generalized.

Dialogue is essential for clarity and explanation, and helps us avoid evaluative language. But who is the target of our explanation? This is an important question and a topic on which philosophers, media scholars and practitioners have dwelt at length. Wittgenstein (1953) believes that it is possible to provide a fair and credible account of an event without having to bear in mind who the targets of our explanation are. However, this conceptual framework is contrary to the vision of most media. For instance, the BBC attends to the needs and aspirations of its license-fee payers in the UK. In other words, part of its duty is to use the type of language and discourse that explains events in a way that is easy for its audiences to understand (BBC Trust 2006b). Similarly, Al Jazeera Arabic, according to Wadah Khanfar, Al Jazeera Network's former director general, resorts to the type of explanation that makes it easy for its Arabic-speaking audiences to understand, and its choice of language to explain events is dictated by its audience needs for understanding (personal communication). This might be one of the reasons for the discursive disparity in the use of language between the BBC, on the one hand, and Al Jazeera on the other. Note for instance the terms they use to represent the same communicative event in Syria (see Chapter 9). While it is doubtful that we can have 'a univocal theory of explanation where all explanation consists in bringing a case under a law', we need to remember that it is the choice of language that is a factor behind the heterogeneity of our explanations (Louch 1969: 233; see Chapters 10 and 11)

No single 'hegemonic' model

The emergence of international broadcasting has chipped away at the domineering or 'hegemonic' influence of western media. The digital age has made it possible for broadcasters and newspapers across the world to make their output available in different formats and platforms. Al Jazeera English and Arabic television channels are not made available for most American viewers, but US audiences can access both channels through the Internet, particularly their news coverage. Most nation states, particularly outside Western Europe, are no longer interested in the impartiality regime which broadcasters like the BBC, ABC and CBC are obliged to observe in their coverage (Maras 2013). Even in the UK, where the BBC and other broadcasters still have to abide by a special regime of impartiality, there have been voices calling for the easing of these rules to allow for editorial interference and direction (see Chapter 1). Sources of information have grown exponentially, and today there are so many diversified ways in which news is produced and accessed: Twitter, Facebook and other social media outlets all allow for diversity of opinion. A good case in point is the way many Muslims and their clerics expressed their feelings through Twitter feeds and other social media forums when Hurricane Sandy hit the US. They believed it was a divine punishment for the anti-Islamic film *Innocence of Muslims*, and pleaded with the Almighty to inflict more damage on America (Associated Press 2012). If we relied on major broadcasters and other news outlets of the Muslim world, which are mostly state-financed and controlled, we would never have been able to learn about such anti-US remarks. Twitter and Facebook do not abide by impartiality rules that govern broadcasters in Europe or the objectivity other media outlets proclaim, but the high degree of freedom of expression they allow has enabled us to see at least how many ordinary Muslims and their clerics think about a natural disaster befalling a country many of them see as an adversary. One wonders whether we will ever have had the chance of being aware of these things had we relied solely on mainstream media, where gatekeepers try to make sure that everything we see, read and listen to must pass through certain filters. Media systems have seen tremendous transformations since the time Hallin and Mancini (2004) published their classic comparative study. The systems are converging and becoming more concentrated, with states striving to steer the medium; but at the same time audiences today have greater freedom to express themselves outside these systems (see Chapters 5 and 11).

The case of Hurricane Sandy is a reminder of the challenge we have always had between how far the media should go in allowing individual freedom of expression, the clash between the freedom individuals have to express their opinion and the restrictions institutions have in place to suppress personal opinion. Impartiality and its operationalization in media and journalism is the prerogative of institutions. Media practitioners have to adhere to impartiality guidelines their institutions have agreed upon. But today the distinction between individual and institutional freedom of expression, so clearly outlined by Onora O'Neill (2002), is turning into a grey area as individuals are capable of using powerful institutions – probably as powerful as any global and multilingual broadcaster we know about – to air their own voices, expressing and advancing not only their personal prejudices and ideas, but also their own culture, religion, ethnicity, etc. When pertaining to conflicts, disasters, wars and clash of civilizations or mentalities, these expressions of individual opinion creep into mainstream media, no matter how 'false, silly, irrelevant or plain crazy' (O'Neill 2002: 112). Individual expressions via Twitter, Facebook, YouTube and other social media forums are shaping our world, and their impact in manufacturing opinion is increasing (see Chapter 5).

Production of news and current affairs no longer relies on impartial reporters or impartial news outlets. As John Lloyd of the *Financial Times* (2009) says, 'money' has brought about drastic changes to the way news is produced, disseminated and received. Western broadcasters, for instance, are no longer the domineering factor in news. Investments in media and communication have made it possible for other countries to launch their own channels with their own news-gathering, producing and disseminating mechanisms, and with their own special models of impartiality. A glance at the English and Arabic news broadcasting landscape tells volumes of how countries like Iran (Press TV and al-Alam), the United Arab Emirates (Abu Dhabi), Qatar (Al Jazeera English and Al Jazeera Arabic),

Russia (Rusia Today), China (CCTV America), Saudi Arabia (Al Arabiya) and Venezuela (Telesur), among others, are striving to break up what they see as western monopoly of news and model of impartiality. These countries have their own Arabic and/or English news channels, offering their own models of 'impartiality' (see Chapters 2 and 8).

In summary and in theory, our digital age has made it possible for almost everyone to express themselves the way they see fit, but the profusion of outlets, and the possibilities social media are offering people to express their opinions, have not yet created a social world that offsets the regional or global influence of a few domineering actors – whether groups, organizations or states. Therefore, we know very little about the views and the beliefs other people have about themselves, and know more about the views and beliefs we have about them. As Berlin (1962) notes, the way others think about themselves is not subjective as far as they are concerned, and their actions and discourses constitute each other, and through them they build their life and their institutions. What is subjective and value-laden is the imposition of our own beliefs and way of life on others, and assessing, measuring and evaluating them through our viewpoints. We, as individuals and societies, are dominated by certain models or paradigms of social and discursive structures. The patterns of our behaviour, which may not appeal to others, are the outcome of our social life and discourse. They are not eternal, but changes and revisions to our way of life largely depend on a change in our social and discursive environment, and not through how others would like us to be. Understanding others and their beliefs and views the way they are, mainly through dialogue, should be an essential component of how to approach, assess and measure impartiality in our digital age. Our age is the age of diversified beliefs, where there is not, and there should not be, one dominant model of thinking. This volume pursues this approach of understanding and the dialogue to impartiality, an approach that is not only confined to diversity and variety, but also the causes, the history and the 'the whys and wherefores of' – the causal strata and the explanatory strata – of whatever subject we are dealing with.

The book and its chapters

The volume is not a template on how to assess and measure impartiality. The authors realize that it is easy to talk about the elements or components that are to be present in a news story for it to be impartial and objective, but rather difficult on what exactly needs to be done to translate these traits into reality, particularly when dealing with controversial and contested issues.

The book is divided into three major sections: 'Theories', 'Applications' and 'Practicalities'. The first section – 'Theories' – comprises two chapters: one on philosophical deliberations of impartiality, and the other on interpreting impartiality and plurality. The first provides a synopsis of how impartiality is viewed in disciplines other than media, namely philosophy and law, and how relevant these views can be to journalism practitioners. The second applies 'public value tests' beyond new media, demonstrating how impartiality and plurality can be interpreted in an increasingly competitive market-driven media environment.

The second section – 'Applications' –consists of seven chapters, all of which have a bearing on contested issues and controversies, and the role of impartiality in informing the world about them. The chapters are of a critical nature, and the authors show the different views various media outlets present about the same controversy, albeit adhering to their claims of impartiality and objectivity. The section starts with a study (Chapter 3) of the Norwegian military's use of Psychological Operations (PSYOPS), and critically examines, from an impartiality perspective, NATO forces' use of newspaper and radio broadcasts in Afghanistan. Drawing mainly on a conceptual framework, Chapter 4 shows that there is no one way to view impartiality in the world of journalism, and that the profession's practitioners do not deny how difficult it is to define, describe and practice the two notions. The relations between mainstream media and alternative grassroots discourse is critically examined from the impartiality perspective in Chapter 5. The chapter tackles one of the most contested issues of our time – web hate – in the case of Anders Behring Breivik, who killed 77 people in two attacks in Norway. Chapter 6 dwells on major activities that are involved in news-gathering. Using textual analysis of prize-winning articles and of articles that played a problematic role in the preparations for the 2003 invasion of Iraq, the chapter demonstrates how these activities achieve the best results when applied in an iterative fashion to authenticate facts and eliminate unsupportable allegations. Analyzing the media coverage of a Tunisian man accused of planning an assassination of the cartoonist Kurt Westergaard because of his drawing of Muhammad that appeared in the Danish newspaper *Jyllands-Posten* in 2005, Chapter 7 demonstrates the constitutive role media discourse plays in defining reality, and the social roles and relations within it. It shows that politicians and other public actors do not adhere to the same ideal of objectivity and impartiality. Chapter 8 discusses the notion of autonomy and impartiality, and how difficult it is for countries in a state of transition to democracy to adopt and apply western journalistic standards. The chapter shows that some degree of 'autonomy' in the path of these countries' transition to democracy is required before attaining the objectivity and impartiality regime that is prevalent in western democracies. Chapter 9 examines some of the major lines of thought of pragmatic philosophers, and relates them to issues of impartiality in news and current affairs. Drawing on Hannah Arendt and her deliberations of politics and discourse, the chapter shows how the discursive and social patterns we use exacerbate conditions, drive opposing parties further apart, and hinder dialogue and comprise.

The last section– 'Practicalities' – looks into the notion of impartiality from a practitioner's perspective. Chapter 10, written by the BBC's former executive editor Kevin Marsh, provides a concise history of how the BBC viewed impartiality in its early stages, and how the concept became a complex issue in modern age. The chapter presents how the BBC applies its impartiality rules to numerous controversial and contested cases it has dealt with in its long history. The last chapter in this volume, written by Reuters' editorial innovation director Eric Auchard, gives a detailed account of the rules and measures the

Reuters news agency applies for the reporting, sourcing, verifying, editing and publishing of a social media. The chapter traces how Reuters, one of the world's most influential news agencies, has developed its own notion of impartiality, and the attempts it exerts to apply its traits in the digital age.

References

The Associated Press (2012), 'Some Muslim clerics say Sandy is God's punishment', *The Atlanta Journal*, 1 November, http://www.ajc.com/ap/ap/international/some-muslim-clerics-say-sandy-is-gods-punishment/nStcX/. Accessed 21 November 2012.

Austin, J. (1962), *How to Do Things with Words*, Cambridge: Cambridge University Press.

Barkho, Leon, (2010), *News from the BBC, CNN, and Al-Jazeera: How the three broadcasters cover the Middle East*, Cresskill, NJ: Hampton Press.

BBC (2006), 'Israel and the Palestinians: Key terms', *BBC Newswatch*, 12 October, http://news.bbc.co.uk/newswatch/ifs/hi/newsid_6040000/newsid_6044000/6044090.stm. Accessed 24 September 2012.

BBC Trust (2006a), 'BBC Management's Response to the Independent Panel Report: Impartiality of the BBC's Coverage of the Israeli-Palestinian Conflict', 1 April, http://www.bbc.co.uk/bbctrust/assets/files/pdf/our_work/govs/israelipalestiniangovernors_statement.txt. Accessed 12 November 2012.

—— (2006b), 'Impartiality: Fact or Fiction – Friday 22nd September 2006. Seminar Agenda and Transcript', 22 September, http://www.bbc.co.uk/bbctrust/assets/files/pdf/review_report_research/impartiality_21century/d_seminar_transcript.txt. Accessed 16 November 2012.

Beard, Mary (2009), *Pompeii: The Life of a Roman Town*, London: Profile Books

—— (2012), 'A Point of View: Why the rich look down on the poor', *BBC Magazine*, 9 November, http://www.bbc.co.uk/news/magazine-20235692. Accessed 16 November 2012.

Berger, P. L. and Luckmann, T. (1966), *The Social Construction of Reality*, New York: Doubleday.

Berlin, Isaiah (1962), 'Does Political Theory Still Exist?', in Peter Laslett and W. G. Runciman (eds), *Philosophy, Politics and Society*, vol. 2, Oxford: Basil Blackwell, pp. 1–33.

Bernstein, Richard J. (1979), *The Restructuring of Social and Political Theory*, London: Methuen.

—— (2005), *The Abuse of Evil: The Corruption of Politics and Religion since 9/11*, Cambridge: Polity Press.

Blum, Steven D. (1984), *Walter Lippmann: Cosmopolitanism in the Century of Total War*, Ithaca, NY: Cornell University Press.

Boaden, Helen (2010), 'Impartiality is in our genes', *BBC: The Editors*, 18 September, http://www.bbc.co.uk/blogs/theeditors/2010/09/impartiality_is_in_our_genes.html. Accessed 3 November 2012.

Born, Georgina (2004), *Uncertain Vision: Birt, Dyke and the Reinvention of the BBC*, London: Secker & Warburg.

Brunninge, O. (2009), 'Using History in Organizations: How Managers Make Purposeful Reference to History in Strategy Processes', *Journal of Organizational Change Management*, 22: 1, pp. 8–26.

Buck, Daniel (2008), 'Objectivity in Journalism', *Socyberty*, 19 August, http://socyberty.com/issues/objectivity-in-journalism/#ixzz1U8yHWg4m. Accessed 28 October 2012.

Cohen, Patricia (2009), 'Danish Cartoon Controversy', *New York Times*, http://topics.nytimes.com/topics/reference/timestopics/subjects/d/danish_cartoon_controversy/index.html. Accessed 7 December 2012.

The Economist (2012), 'Why they won't calm down – Mischief, not madness, often underlies Muslim anger', 15 September, http://www.economist.com/node/21562960. Accessed 25 November 2012.

Fernandez, Manny (2012), 'Fort Hood Shooting Suspect's Beard Must Be Shaved, Military Judge Rules', *New York Times*, 7 September, http://www.nytimes.com/2012/09/07/us/judge-in-fort-hood-case-orders-maj-nidal-malik-hasans-beard-shaved.html?_r=0. Accessed 21 November 2012.

Grice, H. P. (1975), 'Logic and conversation', in P. Cole and J. Morgan (eds), *Syntax and Semantics 3: Speech acts*, New York: Academic, pp. 113–27.

Hallin, Daniel and Mancini, Paolo (2004), *Comparing Media Systems: Three Models of Media and Politics*, Cambridge: Cambridge University Press.

Hastings, Chris and Sawer, Patrick (2009), 'BBC maintains Gaza appeal ban despite widespread protest', *Daily Telegraph*, 25 January, http://www.telegraph.co.uk/culture/tvandradio/4333816/BBC-maintains-Gaza-appeal-ban-despite-widespread-protest.html. Accessed 19 November 2012.

Jansen, Lesa (2012), 'Obama speaks with world leader on phone while holding baseball bat', *CNN Politics*, 1 August, http://whitehouse.blogs.cnn.com/2012/08/01/obama-speaks-with-world-leader-on-phone-holding-a-baseball-bat/. Accessed 19 November 2012.

Kimmelman, Michael (2008), 'Outrage at Cartoons Still Tests the Danes', New York Times, NyTimes, 20 March, http://www.nytimes.com/2008/03/20/books/20cartoon.html?ref=danishcartooncontroversy&_r=0 Accessed 5 May 2013.

Lloyd, John (2009), 'The Politics of Impartiality', *Financial Times*, 15 February, http://www.ft.com/intl/cms/s/0/633b935c-f925-11dd-ab7f-000077b07658.html#axzz2Az4Kg4HU. Accessed 30 September 2012.

Louch, A. R. (1969), *Explanation and Human Action*, Berkley, CA: University of California Press.

Maras, Steven (2013), *Objectivity in Journalism*, Cambridge: Polity Press.

O'Neill, Onora (2002), *A Question of Trust: The BCC Reith Lectures*, Cambridge: Cambridge University Press.

Philo, Greg and Berry, Mike (2011), *More Bad News from Israel*, London: Pluto Press.

Pitkin, Hanna F. (1972), *Wittgenstein and Justice*, Berkeley, CA: University of California Press.

Post, Robert C. (2012), 'Free Speech in the Age of YouTube: Barack Obama couldn't censor that anti-Islam film – even if he wanted to', *Foreign Policy*, 17 September, http://www.foreignpolicy.com/articles/2012/09/17/free_speech_in_the_age_of_youube. Accessed 15 November 2012.

Ryan, Alan (1970), *The Philosophy of the Social Sciences*, London: Macmillan.

Searle, J. (1979), *Expression and Meaning*, New York: Cambridge University Press.

Senge, Peter M. (1990), 'The Leader's New Work: Building Learning Organizations', *Sloan Management Review*, 32: 1 (Fall), pp. 7–23.

Shadid, Anthony (2006), 'Remarks by Pope Prompt Muslim Outrage, Protests', *Washington Post*, 15 September, http://www.washingtonpost.com/wp-dyn/content/article/2006/09/15/AR2006091500800.html. Accessed 13 November 2012.

Sieff, Kevin (2012), 'Afghans protest burning of Korans at U.S. base', *Washington Post*, 21 February, http://www.washingtonpost.com/world/asia_pacific/afghans-protest-improper-disposal-of-koran-at-us-base/2012/02/21/gIQAjhBqQR_story.html. Accessed 11 November 2012.

Simpson, John (2012), 'Inside BBC Journalism: Impartiality', http://www.bbc.co.uk/worldservice/specials/1536_impartiality/page2.shtml. Accessed 5 May 2013.

Taylor, Charles (1971), 'Interpretation and the Sciences of Man', *Review of Metaphysics*, 25, pp. 3–51.

Thomas, Sir Quentin (2006), 'Report of the Independent Panel for the BBC Governors on Impartiality of BBC Coverage of the Israeli-Palestinian Conflict', *BBC Watch*, April, http://bbcwatch.org/report-of-the-independent-panel-for-the-bbc-governors-on-impartiality-of-bbc-coverage-of-the-israeli-palestinian-conflict/. Accessed 11 November 2012.

Winch, Peter (1972), *Ethics and Action*, London: Routledge & Kegan Paul.

Wittgenstein, Ludwig (1953), *Philosophical Investigations*, New York: Macmillan.

PART I

Theories

Chapter 1

How mainstream media can learn from philosophical deliberations of impartiality

Leon Barkho

This chapter provides a synopsis of how impartiality is viewed in disciplines other than media, i.e. philosophy and law, and how useful the deliberations in these areas might be for journalists. These deliberations are supplemented with a few cases and stories which the writer believes have a direct bearing on impartiality issues, and the general criteria comprising impartiality as a journalistic concept. The chapter first reviews how impartiality is defined and explained in the media, and whether media broadcasters like the BBC and the ABC rely on philosophical deliberations of the concept in their guidelines. Then it shows how important the concept is for philosophers, especially in their deliberations of the nature of science and social reality out there. Thereafter, it provides some parallels and differences between impartiality practitioners in both the media and the judiciary. Section 5 presents a summary of the major types of impartiality that are the focus of philosophical deliberations. The last section concludes the study, focusing on the major impartiality criteria from a philosophical perspective.

What is impartiality?

Before delving into philosophical deliberations of impartiality, particularly in judicial practices, we need to explain what the concept means in terms of news and current affairs. As we do so, it is important to remember that impartiality as a notion is viewed differently by different scholars, journalists and news organizations, and as John Lloyd (2009) points out, 'No concept in journalism is more contested than impartiality'.

We can start with the dictionary meaning of the term. Although some may see this as unhelpful, the lexicon specifies at least some of the most fundamental elements of what impartiality should include. Being impartial, according to Hornby (2002), does not mean supporting one person or group more than another, nor showing favour towards or against one group of people or one's own opinion for personal reasons, nor making unfair judgments. The closest dictionary definition to the journalistic notion of impartiality is perhaps the definition by *Webster's Revised Unabridged Dictionary* (1913) which states that '[t]he quality of being impartial' means 'freedom from bias or favoritism; disinterestedness; equitableness; fairness; as, impartiality of judgment, of treatment, etc.'

But it is important to note here that media outlets, including broadcasters with a claim to impartiality, fail to give workable definitions. Broadcasters pursuing impartiality suggest several traits for the concept, and then attempt to explain them through specific guidelines and sometimes with examples on how to translate them into news content. Avoiding straightforward definitions, both the BBC and the ABC (Australian Public Corporation) give what they believe are the basic components of impartiality. The BBC's most comprehensive report on the subject, 'From Seesaw to Wagon Wheel: Safeguarding Impartiality in the 21st Century', says impartiality 'involves a mixture' of twelve key elements or labels: 'accuracy, balance, context, distance, evenhandedness, fairness, objectivity, openmindedness, rigour, self-awareness, transparency and truth' (BBC Trust 2007: 5). In practice, however, practitioners make reference to only a few of these components. For instance, in assessing the impartiality of its own coverage of the four UK nations, the BBC focuses on issues of accuracy, context and balance (BBC Trust 2008). While the BBC impartiality report dwells at length on each of these labels, it is important to note that some of them overlap, duplicate and confuse readers as is the case with the broadcaster's effort to distinguish between components like balance and even-handedness, which basically mean the same thing. Other broadcasters attribute fewer elements to impartiality: the ABC, for instance, recognizes only five: 'accuracy, fairness, balance, context and no conflict or pre-judgment' (ABC 2007: 5).

Media practitioners agree that some of the criteria attributed to impartiality do overlap. For instance, Richard Sambrook, director of the BBC World Service and Global News Division, says that notions like 'impartiality or fairness or balance […] all these words are often used as if they were interchangeable' (Sambrook 2004). The difference, in Sambrook's opinion, is that an objective story, besides its being balanced, neutral, fair and impartial, must be supported by good evidence. Corresponding in definition and function are the two pivotal terms: impartiality and objectivity. These terms are often used interchangeably. For instance, Reuters makes no distinction between 'impartiality' and 'objectivity' in its guidelines, using the terms interchangeably (Auchard 2013).

In his *Objectivity in Journalism*, Steven Maras, drawing on Allan (2010), sees objectivity as closely linked to impartiality. Objective reporting, he says, is 'usually linked to other norms (such as neutrality), or replaced by the norm of impartiality with which it is regarded as "synonymous"' (Maras 2013: 5). In his review of the BBC, Maras highlights the close 'link between objectivity and the norm of impartiality promoted by the organization' (2013: 216). In some countries, the term 'objectivity' borders on what 'impartiality' means for the BBC and other European media. In the US and Canada, objectivity is the concept which covers most of the impartiality components, like accuracy, truthfulness, fairness and balance, neutrality, unbiased reporting, value exclusion, disinterestedness, rejection of ideology, detachedness, etc. (cf. Blankenburg & Walden 1977; Anderson 1987; Mindich 1988; Kaplan 2002; Gabriele 2003; Cohen-Almagor 2008). It is worth noting that impartiality as a regime played almost the same role in the United States as that in Europe until the 1980s when the so-called 'fairness doctrine' – a regulatory government body that required broadcasters to provide balanced and objective coverage – was dissolved (Fiss 1990). (For further details see Chapters 2 and 4).

But not all European broadcasters and media proprietors are happy with the impartiality regime they are required to pursue. There has been serious lobbying by media moguls like Rupert Murdoch and his son James Murdoch who see the European broadcasting impartiality regulations as 'an impingement on freedom of speech and on the right of people to choose what kind of news to watch' (Murdoch 2009: 12). Both have been lobbying to persuade governments to scrap the European ideology of public broadcasting and make room for the 'market forces of ideas' to rule in broadcasting as they do in print and online media. It is not clear whether European public broadcasters themselves are happy with the impartiality regimes they work under. James Harkin (2011) of *The Independent* says that even within the BBC there are voices who would want to get rid of the rulings. Harkin points to a 'remarkable admission' by the BBC's former director general, Mark Thompson, in which he calls for the relaxing of impartiality guidelines governing public broadcasters like the BBC, ITV and Channel 4 in Britain. Thompson, according to Harkin, even goes a step further by calling on the British government to free commercial broadcasters like Sky from its traditional impartiality rules, and allow them to air opinionated and partisan news. Thompson, adds Harkin, would even not mind having a channel like News Corp's Fox News, owned by Rupert Murdoch, in Britain.

But the divergent views, concepts and practices should not stand as a hindrance to research, and there should be an investigation into what it takes for the coverage of a communicative event to be called impartial. While generalizations are hard to obtain due to the divergent forces and powers affecting today's media environment, our job as researchers should not be confined to the unpacking and criticizing of the social and discursive realities of news and current affairs discourse. In order to provide social, cultural and discursive options to improve the reporting of communicative events, our research must have some practical implications arrived at through dialogue, debate and inquiry, and covering actors from different sectors (Habermas 1973; Dewey 1981; Peirce 1992). Philosophers, media scholars and media practitioners concerned with the issue would usually agree that all, or at least some, of the impartiality components should be there for a standpoint to be impartial. The impartiality components philosophers dwell on are not so much different from the elements media scholars and practitioners talk about. For philosophers, impartiality hinges on four basic elements: consistency and universality, transparency, disinterestedness and equality (Stark 1997: 487). But before moving to what philosophers say about impartiality, let us first examine whether the media have ever considered leaning on philosophical deliberations in their discussions of the concept.

Media impartiality and philosophy

The media which value impartiality and strive to practice it across their platforms have their own sets of guidelines and procedures, which they believe will help their practitioners shun biased coverage, and produce what they see as impartial and objective content. But an examination of these guidelines will show that these media rarely make reference to philosophical deliberations of impartiality. The ABC (2007), for instance, believes that impartiality should only be explained within the media context, and without having the concept and its components grounded in law, where most of philosophical deliberations of impartiality take place. The only reference to philosophy is confined to a footnote where the ABC cites an investigation by the Australian Communications and Media Authority (ACMA) into its flagship program, *Four Corners*, and specifically the one broadcast on 16 February 2004 entitled 'Lords of the Forests'. In it, the ABC cites the authority as saying that philosophical deliberations, particularly of how impartiality is applied in judicial cases, 'do contain useful models for formulating tests for impartiality, so long as they are properly adapted to the very different setting of media decision-making' (ACMA 2004: 8).

In its investigation, the ACMA leans on the judiciary's definition of ordinary audiences and their views as a measure to assess whether the ABC had made or failed to make a reasonable effort to be accurate, impartial and balanced when presenting the program. Similarly, the BBC takes into account its ordinary listeners, i.e. license fee payers, in assessing and measuring the impartiality of its news output. BBC guidelines highlight the role of 'ordinary reader', or 'our audiences', in examining whether news and current affairs programs are impartial. Audience research is part of all the reviews the BBC has conducted to assess its own impartiality. The BBC Trust 'represents license fee payers in its oversight of the BBC. It listens to their opinions and expectations and uses them to inform its own decisions' (2008). However, the corporation rarely leans on issues of judicial impartiality and related philosophical deliberations in its numerous impartiality reviews, of which it has done four so far: BBC coverage of business (2007); the devolved UK nations (2008); science (2012a); and coverage of the events known as the Arab Spring (2012b).

Another important aspect of ACMA investigations, and with relevance to this study, is the authority's reliance on the dictionary meaning of the word 'impartiality'. The authority does not have its own interpretation of impartiality. It adopts the explanation *The Macquarie Dictionary* provides for the word. It is worthwhile to compare ACMA's stand on what impartiality means with that of the BBC Trust in its 2007 impartiality report: 'Fortunately this Report is not required to provide an elaborate definition. That is best left to philosophers' (BBC Trust 2007: 23). The BBC makes no effort in its more than 80-page report to shed any light on what philosophers think of impartiality and whether their deliberations can be of any use.

Subjective and objective impartiality

What is the social reality of journalism? Is there one journalistic social reality or several? Are there differences between the way, for instance, the social reality of journalism is viewed in North America and Europe? Scholarly debates about the social reality of journalism, as is the case with other social disciplines, revolve around notions of subjectivity versus objectivity, fact versus value, prescriptivism versus subjectivism, and positivism versus interpretivism. Aiming at objectivity and impartiality in reporting news and current affairs has traditionally placed journalism, particularly among its practitioners, as if it were part of natural sciences, where observers are given the capacity of separating fact from value while at the same time preventing personal or institutional influences from interfering in their work. This view has roots in North America, and especially among thinkers, analysts and practitioners for whom the application of positivist tendencies on social sciences will hopefully 'display a development comparable to that manifested by the physical sciences in the age of Copernicus, Kepler and Newton' (Hull 1943: 400). In this sense, reporters' news output has to be accurate and precise because '[p]recision is an integral element of the criterion of testability' (Merton 1949: 94). The inscription over the door to the journalism building at Stanford University that says, 'Tell it as it is!' is a reminder that objectivity or impartiality in journalism, in the positivistic sense, is possible, and that observers (reporters) and their institutions can shun their values, prejudices and outside influences and concentrate only on the 'facts' of the communication event they deal with.

But today there is an increasing number of thinkers who would question the foundations of a social science or journalism practice built on natural science principles, and would raise an eyebrow over Stanford University's motto. For these thinkers, 'There are no uninterpreted or brute facts that are simply "out there," unaffected by our theoretical and conceptual schemes' (Bernstein 1979: 20). Saying that we can report facts and nothing but facts borders on 'hyperfactualism' that sees collection of data as a means to arrive at 'moral and prescriptive' generalizations. The literature on media and journalism abounds with well-founded empirical generalizations, but they have proved insufficient to help us and our subjects to 'tell it as it is'. Sticking to theory to uncover 'facts' of social reality will not alleviate the risk of investigators – researchers and journalists – advancing their own ideologies (Ryan 1972: 86).

'Tell it as it is!' from the view of philosophers who think that the realities or 'facts' of our world are 'socially constructed' is a 'myth'. What journalists see as 'facts' are in fact 'viewpoints' and not universal truths. For instance, Heinz von Foerster, a top authority in social constructivism, commenting on 'Tell it as it is!' in a lecture at Stanford University, told his audience that there was nothing like 'Tell it as it is!' in the social world of journalism, but rather 'It is as you tell it!' (Foerster & Poerksen 2002: 99). But saying that objectivity in the positivist sense is hard to achieve does not mean that the social reality of journalism is the opposite in the solipsist sense (Thornton 2006). There is a lot in journalism which is not the creation of wildly fanciful imagination or the product of the individual mind. We cannot deny that many media outlets and their reporters work hard not to imagine things through their minds. But at the same time, there is evidence that the role of the individual observer is receding at the expense of a rise in personal and corporate influences, as well as institutional power, to the extent that we are steadily moving from 'Tell it as it is!' or 'It is as you tell it' to 'It is as I want you to tell it' (Barkho 2010). These are the three major concerns that are at the centre not only of today's media research and the discussions that are taking place on the pages and screens of newspapers, but also in philosophical deliberations about impartiality. There is evidence that social and discursive reality is sometimes designed for reporters, particularly when covering sensitive issues and crises where interests of different sorts are involved. The epistemological perspective 'It is how I want you to tell it' defies all the notions we have about objective and impartial reporting since it no longer depends on how the observer sees the world, but how the institution or corporate body views it. The analysis of news, particularly at times of crises, has shown that institutions, through a set of rules, controls, guidelines and gatekeeping mechanisms, can steer the social reality of a communicative event in a way that is contrary to the social reality that unfolds before the observer's eyes (cf. Deborah White 1950; Breed 1955; Bernstein 2005).

Judicial and journalistic impartiality

Is impartiality the same for both the media and the judiciary? It is wrong to say judges and journalists have exactly the same view of impartiality, but at the same it will be also wrong to assume that the two have nothing in common. On close examination, in fact, one can find a lot of common ground in the deliberations on impartiality, whether by thinkers, journalism scholars or practitioners. The conception of impartiality has a bearing on the conception of justice. Reporters are not judges or lawyers, but they are aware of how each party to a conflict consider themselves in the right through the justifications they present to buttress their cases and stands. To arrive at justice, judges deliberate the cases before them, investigate them thoroughly, and then pass their judgment in light of arguments presented by lawyers, statements by witnesses, police reports, medical investigations, legal codes, precedence, reason, etc. Impartial reporters do not pass judgments. Their job is to balance the information they gather through their investigations, interviewing and being on-site witnesses.

One important criterion which is not sufficiently discussed in journalism literature and practice, but amply talked about in philosophical and judicial deliberations, is independence. Independence of the judiciary is a precondition for impartiality. To be impartial in judicial parlance means to be free from political, institutional and other influences. That is of course not the case with all media; some media survive because they evolve within the sphere of outside influences. In judicial practice, as Chief Justice Ruth McGregor points out, independence and impartiality mean that the judiciary can 'operate as a separate and co-equal branch of government' (cited in Judicature 2006).

There is no impartiality without independence, and even in philosophical deliberations the two concepts are sometimes treated as ultimately linked and intimately related (Baar 1991). If the media cannot hold those in power to account, they cannot claim to be independent or impartial. If the media cannot make those holding the reins of power angry and think carefully before acting, they cannot claim to be independent and impartial. Judges would lose their independence and impartiality if they fail to question, challenge and hold to account the other two branches of the government – the executive and the legislative. Perhaps no one clarifies this equation in better terms than Justice Sandra Day O'Connor:

> Our effectiveness as judges relies on the knowledge that we will not be subject to retaliation for our judicial acts [...], we have the power to make the president or Congress or, at the

state level, a governor or a state legislature really angry. In fact, if we don't make them mad some of the time we probably aren't doing our job. (cited in Judicature 2006)

But it is not always so easy to defy power even by the most independent of judges. Driving the executive or the legislative powers 'mad' or making them 'angry' is an effort many, whether journalists or judges, might under certain circumstances not be willing to take as has been the case in the United States following the events of September 11. Despite the serious questions raised about Guantanamo Bay as a detention centre, and the things that happened to the detainees there, the US judiciary has not seriously challenged the legislature (Congress) that made it possible for the executive branch to use it as a prison that bypasses legislation and that makes it possible for the US administration to violate human rights. The 2003 US invasion of Iraq was illegal and resulted in massive human rights violations. Despite its illegality and horrendous consequences, the judiciaries in the invading countries, i.e. the United States and the United Kingdom, have failed to seriously question the leaders who ordered it. The legislative and executive powers can collude to promulgate statutory provisions to circumvent the power of the courts, or undermine it by citing their own concerns about national security, for instance.

Personal and corporate partialities

Whether judges or journalists, we are all affected, to differing degrees, by at least two major types of biases, which Griffith (1991) identifies as personal and corporate. Personal bias, Griffith says, is related to individuals and their background (education, religion, sexual orientation, race, etc.). But even if we claim to have no personal bias in an event or case, it might be extremely hard for us to deliver ourselves today from what Griffith calls 'corporate bias', a concept which I find very useful if studied and analyzed within the context of news and current affairs. Griffith says:

> When people like the members of the judiciary, broadly homogeneous in character, are faced with [...] political situations, they act in broadly similar ways [...]. Behind these actions lies a unifying attitude of mind, a political position, which is primarily concerned to protect and conserve certain values and institutions. (Griffith 1991: 19)

The citation from Griffith, though related to the judiciary, is broadly true when applied to the media, where, for instance, major broadcasters, driven by powerful ideological, social or political orientations, adopt opposing discursive and social practices in their representations of the sides to a conflict – negative/positive, benign/malignant, etc. Institutional power and hegemony is not confined to the media. We can draw on philosophical deliberations in regard to judicial impartiality, where light is shed on the role institutions, as well as personal and corporate influences, may play in steering the course of justice. Lazarus (1999) mentions several cases passed by the United States Supreme Court with a majority of five–four, and in which the decisions by individual judges were rather based on their own stands and ideological preferences rather than impartiality or law. The disputed 2000 US presidential election between George Bush Jr. and Al Gore and the Supreme Court's settlement can be viewed within the same framework (Justia.com 2000). Both judges and journalists can sometimes openly work to advance their own causes and those they stand for. While subjective and biased discourse emanating from particular stands with particular social or political propensities is not uncommon in the media, subjective and biased judicial stands and decisions are not hard to come across. One particular case is that of the justice of the US Supreme Court William Brennan. In an editorial on his retirement in 1990, *The New Republic* wrote:

> Over the thirty-four years of Brennan's Supreme Court service THE NEW REPUBLIC often shared Brennan's politics, but sometimes took issue with his jurisprudence. His passionate judicial activism was unafraid, in a pinch, to leave constitutional text, history, and structure behind. When liberals like Brennan held sway in the courts, judicial activism often led to liberal results; now that 'conservatives' are the ones ignoring legislative history and congressional intentions, Brennan's legacy makes it harder for liberals to cry foul. (*The New Republic* 1990)

Clarence Thomas

The literature on ethical impartiality abounds with judicial cases, hearings of judges and their sayings. One oft-cited case is the US Senate Judiciary Committee's hearings on the nomination of Clarence Thomas, the second African American to serve as the Associate Justice of the United States Supreme Court. The deliberations between the committee members and Thomas have been used as a basis for the conditions many philosophers see as necessary for an impartial judge (Minow 1992).

Pressed to give his own interpretation of impartiality, Thomas' notion of an impartial judge applies to what journalists would emphasize when asked about their interpretation of impartiality in journalism. Thomas says: 'You want to be stripped down like a runner [and] shed the baggage of ideology' (Minow 1992: 1201). In response to statements that he might be influenced by his upbringing in a poor black family that suffered from racial discrimination, Thomas maintains that suffering like that would 'enrich his experiences' and make him more 'attentive to the concerns of the disadvantaged people' (ibid.).

Thomas' focus on 'the concerns of the disadvantaged people' is for some critical thinkers one of the yardsticks of impartiality. But who is going to decide who 'the disadvantaged people' are? In a world like ours, fraught with crises and clash of religions, cultures and mentalities, our notions of 'the disadvantaged people' might differ: '[O]ur baggage of ideology' drives us to pay more attention to relational characteristics than justice and impartiality. Many of us would agree that millions of Palestinians languishing under an Israeli military occupation for more than six decades are 'the disadvantaged people', but the issue is whether we are more attentive to their concerns. Similarly, we know that the innocent people of Iraq are the ones who have borne the brunt of the 2003-US invasion of their country, but one wonders whether western media have been more attentive to their concerns or the concerns of the invading troops.

Another good case in point is the controversy over the BBC's decision to reject a broadcasting appeal for aid for the victims of Israel's 2008 war on Gaza. Mark Thompson, the BBC director general at the time, leaned on the corporation's concept of impartiality not to issue the appeal despite a barrage of criticism. Writing on the BBC's *The Editors* blog, he says:

> The danger for the BBC is that this could be interpreted as taking a political stance on an ongoing story. When we have turned down DEC appeals in the past on impartiality grounds it has been because of this risk of giving the public the impression that the BBC was taking sides in an ongoing conflict. (Thompson 2009)

The dispute over the Gaza appeal reflects that impartiality is at stake mainly in the coverage of controversial subjects and highly politicized and charged conflicts like the struggle between Israel and Palestine. The aid appeal had not only split the British society, but also the British media and politics. While Channel 4, ITV and Five broadcast the appeal on humanitarian grounds, and in response to the urgent needs and 'concerns of the disadvantaged people' of Gaza, the BBC and Sky thought broadcasting it would compromise their impartiality.

Impartiality images and mottos

Both the media and the judiciary resort to images and symbols to illustrate their impartiality. Many courts have the image of the blindfolded goddess with scales and sword, which is taken as an allegorical display of the ideal of justice and moral force the courts and their decisions exercise. Journalists employ symbols and images too, though they may not be portrayed in such vividness as that of the blindfolded goddess. Their imagery of what they see as 'ideal impartiality' or 'due impartiality' are mostly discursive – sayings that have almost gone proverbial. Students of the prestigious Stanford University's School of Journalism have the motto 'Tell it as it is!' inscribed on their building. Al Jazeera brags about its own motto of 'Opinion and the Other Opinion', which is inscribed in decorative Arabic calligraphy on the walls of the studios and offices of the Arabic channel's headquarters in Qatar, and is frequently shown and read on its screen. Mottos like CNN's 'We are Always First' and 'The Most Trusted Name in News', the BBC's 'Nation shall speak peace unto nation', ABC's 'Always Better Service', and NBC's 'More Colorful', have not only come to categorize their outlets, but also assume some of the commercial potential their logos have. Fox News Channel first raised the motto 'Fair and Balanced' before replacing it, following a legal battle about it being 'misdescriptive', to 'We Report, You Decide'. Imageries, mottos or slogans like these might not be quite representative.

Types of impartiality

Philosophers distinguish different types of impartiality. Like the labels journalists attach to impartiality, the different versions of impartiality philosophers talk about may overlap. For instance, the impartiality essay in the *Stanford Encyclopedia of Philosophy* (Jollimore 2011) distinguishes three different, but overlapping, types of impartiality: moral, consequentialist and deontological. This section starts with ethical or moral impartiality and lumps the last two under utilitarian impartiality. The section introduces critical impartiality as the third version.

Ethical impartiality

In terms of ethics, philosophical deliberations present a variety of viewpoints. One important viewpoint is related to interests, and whether the interests of others have the same degree of ethical value as my interests or our interests. The major line of thinking in relation to ethical impartiality is that 'my own interests cannot, simply because they are my interests, count more than the interests of anyone else' (Singer 1979: 12). Disinterestedness is a major issue in philosophical deliberations of impartiality, and one of its fundamental components. If we want our decisions and propositions to be ethically impartial, we should not give ourselves, our interests or our own societies preferential treatment. An impartial decision or proposition within a government, organization or institution means that:

> [W]e ought not to give any special weight to our own desires and interests; instead of giving preferential treatment to ourselves, or to members of our own particular social group, we should try to adopt a neutral standpoint, detaching ourselves as far as possible from our own special desires and involvements. (Cottingham 1983: 84)

Literature on ethics and impartiality draws a lot on the Kantian dichotomy or distinction between the 'is' and the 'ought'. For example, Phillip Meyer says reliance on this Kantian distinction is important if we want to safeguard journalism from threats to its independence. According to Meyer, this distinction can be carried out by creating 'social, moral and ideological barriers that define news people as a race, apart, distant, detached, and uninfluenced by anything but a dogged desire to discover and impart the truth regardless of its consequences' (Meyer 1995: § 7 and 8). Thinkers like Richard J. Bernstein view the distinction in terms of discourse; a notion which I feel has a relation to the practice of impartiality and objectivity in the media. Bernstein relates the 'is' to scientific discourse, and the 'ought' to moral discourse grounded in 'pure practical reason' (Bernstein 1979). But the 'ought' in Kantian terms sees moral judgments as autonomous and universal; in other words, we can have moral judgments or values that border on the objectivity of scientific fact and they 'ought' to be applicable everywhere. The Kantian view has been met with scepticism, and no philosopher has been as critical of Kantian themes on morality than Nietzsche. Thinkers advocating a subjective view of moral discourse take Nietzsche as the foundation for their argument of the subjectivity of moral discourse (Bernstein 1979: 46–47).

'Right or 'wrong' moral propositions

Morality has a bearing on whether a viewpoint is 'right' or 'wrong'. The question is how far should considerations of what we see as 'right' or 'wrong' interfere in our discourse? Social science thinkers deliberate 'considerations of right and wrong' at great length, and the mainstream line of thinking is that it is hard to see a discourse that is not at least implicitly affected by such considerations. These considerations intensify during crises and conflicts with religious, historical and ideological backgrounds. Human beings exhibit' 'strong moral zeal' at times like these, clinging tenaciously to their religions, ideologies, histories and strategic interests (Bernstein 1979: 39). For some philosophers it is a fallacy to say that we can produce discourse that is immune from our values and interests. Nagel writes: 'It is surely beyond serious dispute that social scientists do in fact often import their own values into their analyses of social phenomena' (1961: 488).

Discourse has values and so does journalism, but there is a difference between 'value propositions' and 'wrong and right propositions' (Bernstein 1979). We can relate the former to the application of impartiality and objectivity criteria in news discourse, and the latter to the instances where our discourse exhibits explicit or implicit traces of our approval or disapproval of subjects or their actions – a task which the media claim they leave to their audiences to decide. Shunning value in reporting means providing as much description and explanation as possible of the facts on the ground. Showing value and avoiding facts means going for what 'ought' to be, presenting a prescription of how the situation should be seen by our audiences.

Victimizer or victimized

The ethical view of impartiality is operationalized differently, particularly when the matter concerns ethical grounds for how impartial and objective we need to be in our coverage of 'the oppressor' and the 'victimizer'. The elements that go into making a piece of news or current affairs impartial might be the same, but the way of practicing them may diverge. Al Jazeera Arabic would still see its coverage of the conflict in Syria as impartial despite evidence of bias towards the anti-government rebels. The Arabic broadcaster will go to lengths in defending its impartiality on what it sees as 'ethical grounds' of standing with what it considers 'the oppressed' against 'their oppressors' (see Chapter 9). But surprisingly, there are many 'Islamists', 'jihadists' or affiliates of the terror group al-Qaeda among what Al Jazeera considers the 'oppressed' and describes as 'revolutionaries' (Fisk 2012; Qassemi 2012).

It may not take many of us a lot of effort to see who the 'oppressed' and 'their oppressors' are, but we still have to be fair, neutral and balanced when talking and writing about both. No matter how disgusted and disdainful 'the oppressors' are in our eyes, many of us would still like to hear what they say. The other important issue is that our notion of the 'oppressed' and the 'oppressors' should be built on open debate and dialogue with all actors from different sectors (Habermas 1970; Peirce 1992) in the light of the independent and verified investigations, and not because of pressure exerted by those sponsoring and owning the media and their inclinations. If one bases a particular stand regarding a communicative act on the type of relationships one has, the discourse one produces to represent the event will not only be 'logically incoherent' but also 'morally unsound'. We ought, morally, 'to discriminate between people only on the basis of intrinsic (non-relational) characteristics – that is, the kinds of characteristics that would appeal to the detached and disinterested observer' (Cottingham 1983: 89). (See Chapters 5 and 7).

Impartiality from a moral viewpoint is not always possible and some ethical theorists reject the notion that 'what is mine' is equal to 'what is yours' or 'what is theirs'. For instance, the media in the US do not treat a fallen US soldier in Iraq or Afghanistan in the same social and discursive manner as they would have represented dead Iraqis or Afghanis, who might have been killed by the same soldier. An Israeli soldier taken captive is not treated discursively equally as the thousands of Palestinians, among them women and children, imprisoned by Israel. Ethical impartiality as an ideal transmutes into something else when put to practice. This is why we may come across different categorizations of the same groups or states not on the basis of morality, but in the light of how far or close they are to us, and whether their activities harm our own interests or those of others.

Utilitarian impartiality

In the reality of our world, many thinkers believe that impartiality as an ethical ideal is 'utopian' and impractical, suggesting other impartiality versions; most of these draw on utilitarianism, a concept which assesses issues of morality and ethics in the light of the consequences, purposes, benefits and the general well-being they generate (c.f. Sidgwick 1907; Williams 1973; Kekes 1981; Railton 1984; Friedman 1993).

Most deliberations about utilitarian impartiality start with William Godwin (cf. Don 1980; Vetlesen 1998; Lamb 2006) and include references to his famous 'fire cause'. However, it is important to mention that utilitarian impartiality has different interpretations and should not be confined to the Godwinian version, although I take it as the centre for the discussion in this section. Utilitarian impartiality may treat people or societies equally, but at the same time it weighs their merits and values, and the consequences or purposes their actions, decisions or discourses might have. For the proponents of this type of impartiality, the significance of 'things' or 'people' emanates from how important and valuable they are to the general well-being. This aspect of linking utility to impartiality is widely discussed in the literature, and its point of departure has been the ethical and moral dilemmas Godwin raises in his *Enquiry Concerning Political Justice* (1969).

The 'fire cause'

The 'fire cause' is in fact a scenario by Godwin in which two people are trapped in a burning building: one of them happens to be an archbishop, who is also a philosopher, and the other his valet. The scenario makes it only possible to save one of them and, according to Godwin, that person should be the archbishop and not the valet, not only because justice entails that, but because the philosopher's writings and achievements have contributed to the welfare and happiness of the society, and his survival is very likely to augment that happiness. The archbishop is the one to be delivered even if the valet happened to be 'my brother, my father or my benefactor. This would not alter the truth of the proposition [...]. [J]ustice, pure unadulterated justice, would still have preferred that which was most valuable' (Godwin 1946: 127). Utilitarian impartiality does not take decisions on the basis of what belongs to 'me'; decisions are taken on the basis of their consequences and how good, advantageous and beneficial they are to the general well-being of the society regardless of our personal interests. Impartiality traits like fairness, equality or balance should not be the primary causes for our actions, but rather the 'duty to do everything possible to promote the general weal – together with a rather crude notion of just what it is to do so' (Baron 1991: 842). Thus, impartiality in this sense is also teleological – events in our life happen and develop to achieve a special purpose. As human beings we are equal, but our significance, even in terms of morality, is related to what purposes we can achieve. Therefore, from a Godwinian or utilitarian viewpoint, rescuing the archbishop is the right decision because the purpose behind saving him is certainly going to make a better contribution to the 'general weal' than the valet.

Lessons to be learned

What can we, as media analysts and practitioners, learn from the Godwinian version of impartiality? In terms of coverage, what narratives or discourses are we going to employ to represent the sides in a conflict? Will those who we believe have contributed or will contribute to our 'general weal' be given more space and preferential discursive and social treatment? We can extend Godwin's 'fire cause' scenario to other situations in which the president of a country and one of his bodyguards are trapped under the debris of a building struck by an earthquake. Are we going to represent both of them equally in our coverage? Who are we going to save first? On a personal level, what if I have the alternative of saving one person in a situation in which my wife and another woman are in danger. But what we normally expect from journalists is different. We expect them not to give preference in light of relations characteristics. Self-interest in journalism and the notion of biased and prejudiced observer is not recommended, and newspaper or broadcaster style books and guidelines present, sometimes in minute detail, the rules and standards on how and when to avoid self-interest.

We simply cannot gloss over the rule of utilitarianism, which says that we base our decisions and actions regarding the cases we face in light of how beneficial or valuable people or things are to us. It is extremely hard to base an impartial decision on the Christian ideal of love or the Platonic ideal of a utopian situation where we are all equal and happy, a concept which even Aristotle (1920) criticized. No theory of impartiality is capable of providing a convincing argument to refute the critique lodged at the notion that we as human beings have the ability to produce discourse that is completely unbiased and impartial (c.f. Mill 1861; Bales 1971; Williams 1973; Reed & Brown 1984; Powers 1993; Stark 1997). Hare (1981 & 1984) distinguishes between two types of impartiality in his discussion of the Godwinian version of the concept, which I see as useful in assessing impartiality in news and current affairs. The first is the critical approach, which requires a careful study and investigation of the parties to an issue or conflict via the selection of some appropriate guidelines; the second, which Hare calls the intuitive approach, depends on the application of a set of principles and rules. In news and current affairs we need some form of critical impartiality, albeit not exactly akin to Hare's, but based on at least some of its most important elements. (For an expanded discussion of critical impartiality, see Chapters 3 and 9).

Critical impartiality

There is no doubt that many of the crises we face today are due to the special way we view the world, stemming from our deeply-rooted ideological, religious, historical or political stances that we have come to take as incorrigible 'facts'. Crises and controversies occur and exacerbate when we tenaciously cling to our convictions and beliefs, and react negatively if they are questioned or resisted (Bernstein 1979 & 2005). Thus, critical as well as phenomenological thinkers do not believe in categorical distinctions of descriptive versus prescriptive, fact versus value, empirical versus normative, subjectivist versus objectivist, and positivist versus constructionist that have characterized mainstream social science. These opposing categories, critical thinkers maintain, no longer provide reasonable interpretations of our world where different sides, driven by their own views of life, defend their viewpoints so tenaciously and violently, even to the extent of committing atrocities on the horrendous scale of the September 11 attacks on the US, or the atrocities attributed to the wars in Iraq, Afghanistan, Chechnya, Serbia, Libya, Syria and scores of other conflicts afflicting our world. We need 'reason' to understand our world rather than normative or prescriptive foundations of natural science (Husserl 1970).

Critical thinkers associated with the line of Frankfurt School share phenomenology's criticism of positivistic and prescriptive views of social and political life. Both find that social sciences cannot be understood properly by the application of positivistic standards of natural sciences, where we specifically deal with a type of life that is largely based on reason and rationality. The foundations of critical philosophy as expounded by Frankfurt School were formulated by Horkheimer (1972) and specifically in his 'Traditional and Critical Theory', the essay which has become a classic in critical literature. In it, Horkheimer illustrates the gap separating the traditional theory, which has served as the ideal for the natural sciences, and his own critical theory, which calls for action and practice in response to the crises of our time. Expounding his own views of critical science, he writes:

> By criticism, we mean that intellectual, and eventually practical effort which is not satisfied to accept the prevailing ideas, actions, and social conditions unthinkingly and from mere habit; effort which aims to coordinate the individual sides of social life with each other and with general ideas and aims of the epoch, to deduce them genetically, to distinguish the appearance from the essence, to examine the foundations of things, in short, really to know them. (Horkheimer 1972: 270)

The 'disinterested' observer

The positivistic notion of 'disinterested observer' is no longer valid. For the Frankfurt School and its proponents, the observer has to take a stand, a position that supports and defends 'the vulnerable and the oppressed in the society' in the hope of making them aware of their conditions, and giving them the means to liberate and emancipate themselves. This is at least how today's major proponents of critical discourse studies have come to understand the Frankfurt School's critique and they have attempted to apply it in their investigations, particularly of the media (c.f. Van Dijk 1991, 1998 & 2000; Fairclough 1995, 2000, 2001 & 2003). Horkheimer was a proponent of 'change' for the better in the lives of 'the oppressed', but his call, contrary to the view in the majority of critical discourse studies, had to include some elements of 'dynamism' and some distance from 'concrete historical' interpretations. Most critical studies of the media and news today gloss over these two essential elements in Horkheimer, namely 'dynamism' and 'distance'. The presence of the two elements does not mean that one should be disinterested and work to hide and suppress all subjectivity. Horkheimer's theory does not feign neutrality and absence of action and practice. Nonetheless, the critique should form 'a dynamic unity with the oppressed class, so that [...] presentation of societal contradictions is not merely an expression of the concrete historical situation but also a force within it to stimulate change' (Horkheimer 1972: 215).

Like any other conception, Horkheimer's notion of a critical theory for social science, particularly as applied in media studies, is not without problems. Most of the criticism lodged against critical studies, whether those tackling news or other social disciplines, stems from the fears Horkheimer himself expressed when formulating his theory. Although what Horkheimer had in mind then was related to what he conceived would be the reaction of traditional theorists advocating natural science principles, criticism of the theory has come even from within the circle of its practitioners. Today it is not only the positivists who view critical theory as 'subjective and speculative, one-sided and useless' as Horkheimer

(1972: 138) believed they would. There are voices, some from within the discipline, expressing major concerns (see Blommaert & Bulcaen 2000; Blommaert et al. 2003; Blommaert 2005, Verschueren 2001; Philo 2007; Breeze 2011).

Habermas and impartiality

Habermas is the philosopher who is not satisfied when a critical investigation aims at being merely 'practical' or starts with an attitude. He raises numerous questions about critical studies with a 'bias' right from the very beginning; questions I feel critical discourse scholars have not taken seriously. What is practically possible from my viewpoint does not mean it is 'objectively possible'. Practice has to have some 'rigor of the scientific knowledge' because it will be naïve to determine what is right in the absence of providing some objective orientation to our practice. Habermas believes that what the 'emancipation' and 'liberation' thinkers following the Frankfurt School call for, as well as their calls for ideological demystifications, may not be attainable if we totally disregard positivistic foundations of natural sciences (Habermas 1973).

If we pursue some form of impartiality based on Habermas' critical conceptions, we should be 'inclusive' rather than 'exclusive': in other words, we should remove barriers and hurdles that isolate not only a specific sector of the society or side to a conflict from our deliberations, but also certain epistemologies or methodologies. For Habermas, attempts at isolating others, or building fences between us and others, or considering ourselves, our ideologies and even epistemologies 'good' and 'practical' and those of others as 'impractical', are all bound to fail. Habermas is against pitting one epistemology against the other: 'I regard as abortive, even reactionary, the attempts which characterized the old methodological dispute, namely, attempts to set up barriers from the outset in order to remove certain sectors altogether from the clutches of certain type of research' (1974: 33).

Decisions and actions based on critical impartiality, as well as findings and interpretations based on critical news analysis, should be the result of interaction and cooperation among all 'inquirers' from sectors with an interest in the issue regardless of their divergent and opposing ideologies, values and conceptions, and not merely the outcome of one single inquirer representing one sector and advocating one special ideology or epistemology. This, in my opinion, is what Habermas means by notions as 'system of inquirers' and 'interaction'. Habermas is 'concerned with knowledge-guiding interests which in each case form the basis for a whole system of inquirers' (1974: 33). This means that Habermas sees 'interaction' as communicative action or symbolic interaction (1970: 92). It is governed by binding consensual norms, which define reciprocal expectations about behaviour, and which must be understood and recognized by at least two acting subjects.

Impartiality, as outlined above, is at stake mainly when reporters are involved in covering conflicts where parties have conflicting claims to what is 'truth' and 'justice', and where each party believes they are on the right side of the fence. It is mainly in circumstances like these where we can draw on Habermas' notions of a critical approach to impartiality in news and current affairs. Since it is hard for us as human beings to distance ourselves from our institutions, outside influences, our own prejudices and the cultural implications of our religions, societies and histories, we are bound to lean on our emotions and sentiments at the expense of reason in our attempts to understand a conflict. Once our emotions and sentiments come into play, we exacerbate the conflict or work to dispute it rather than solving it or relaying it in a fair and balanced manner to others (Popper 1962). Like Habermas, Popper is the philosopher who underscores that the best way to approach a conflict is through 'the use of reason' (1962) and reasonable compromise.

Conclusion

To conclude, I would like to stress that the presentation of the philosophical deliberations of impartiality in this chapter is sketchy as it lacks the rigor, the sophistication and the depth of philosophical studies. However, the writer hopes to have given readers a synopsis of these deliberations, as well as some ideas and suggestions on how relevant and useful they can be to both scholars and practitioners of journalism. The issues impartiality thinkers deal with – particularly the cases they mention, although many of them are hypothetical – have a relation to the social reality of journalism. The three journalistic epistemologies identified in this chapter – 'Tell it as it is!' 'It is as you tell it' and 'It is as I want you to tell it' – surface in philosophical deliberations of the concept, albeit in different ways. Philosophers' reflections on these epistemologies, as shown in this chapter, centre on the four major components of impartiality they deal with – universality or consistency, transparency, disinterestedness and equality – the elements which are among the most talked about in the corridors, guidelines and style books of news organizations and their practitioners (Taylor 1978).

Universality, which in philosophical deliberations is closely related to consistency, is of paramount importance for philosophers, particularly those advocating an ethical approach. An impartial stand assumes universality when it is not affected by our own interests, our own ideologies and those of the groups we belong to. There is no place for 'I' and 'we', and what applies to us should be made applicable to others (Rawls 1971).

The other element is transparency. For instance, while the BBC is open about its financing and carefully covers its own financial difficulties, the sources of its income and how they are spent, little is known of how Al Jazeera as a network is financed apart from the fact that it is owned and funded by the royalty in Qatar. In fact, the BBC is under duty in light of its impartiality guidelines to write about itself when it becomes the story. Journalists normally report news affecting others, but impartiality requires them to cover their own outlets, their sponsors and their proprietors when they become a story.

The third impartiality component in philosophical deliberation is disinterestedness, which philosophers employ to refer to state or quality of being just and unbiased. Law scholars (Taylor 1978) also take disinterestedness as a main demand for a judge to be impartial. The absence of the trait of disinterestedness may lead to accusations of hypocrisy and double standards because it puts interests of certain individuals, people, nations or organizations above the interests of others. But philosophers are in disagreement here, particularly those advocating the Godwinian or utilitarian approach to impartiality where benefit, advantage, value or well-being come first in the actions and decisions we take.

The last impartiality trait that is highlighted in philosophical deliberations is equality. Stark, drawing on Friedman (1993: 62), says equality is the 'most prominent theme one finds' (1997: 489) in the philosophical debates on impartiality because it deals with people and issues of moral equality. Philosophical debates focus on whether all human beings should be treated morally equal under all circumstances. Are the interests of all people, from a utilitarian viewpoint, equal and the same, and should they get the same degree of significance? Can we, in our real world, bestow equal moral consideration to everyone?

Impartiality is and will remain one of the most disputed concepts in journalism. Recourse to philosophical deliberations in journalism studies will not dispel disagreements about the concept. However, as this chapter has demonstrated, there is something for journalism scholars and practitioners to learn from philosophers and their discussions of impartiality. As we have seen, media and news organizations rarely make references to philosophical studies in their guidelines. It is time that they and journalism scholars analyzing their discourse revised their position and paid more attention to what philosophers say about the concept.

References

ABC (2007), 'Discussion Paper: Elements of Impartiality', *ABC Editorial Policies*, http://www.abc.net.au/corp/pubs/edpols.htm. Accessed 12 June 2012.

Allan, S. (2010), *New Culture*, Maidenhead: Open University Press.

Alterman, Eric (2010), 'What Liberal Media? The Truth about Bias and the News', *Sacred Heart University Review*, 22: 1, http://digitalcommons.sacredheart.edu/shureview/vol22/iss1/2. Accessed 22 July 2012.

Anderson, Douglas (1987), 'How Managing Editors View and Deal With Ethical Issues?', *Journalism Quarterly*, 64, pp. 341–45.

Aristotle (1938), *Politics* (trans. Benjamin Jowett; introduction, analysis and index by H. W. C. Davis), Oxford: Clarendon Press. Electronic version available at: http://trove.nla.gov.au/work/1071848?q&l-availability=y%2Ff&sort=holdings+desc&_=1343578627844&versionId=166790973. Accessed 16 December 2012.

Auchard, Eric (2013), 'What are the new rules for reporting, sourcing, verifying, editing and publishing a social media world?', in Leon Barkho (ed.), *From Theory to Practice: How to Assess, Measure and Apply Impartiality in News and Current Affairs*, London: Intellect.

Australian Communications and Media Authority (2004), 'Investigating Report Nos. 1418, 1474', www.acma.gov.au/webwr/_assets/main/.../lords%20abc%20tv.pdf. Accessed 3 June 2012.

Baar, C. (1991), 'Judicial independence and impartiality in the aftermath of the Marshall case', *UNB Law Journal*, 40: 260.

Bales, Eugene R. (1971), 'Act-Utilitarianism: Account of Right-Making Characteristics or Decision-Making Procedure?', *American Philosophical Quarterly*, 8, pp. 257–65.

Barkho, Leon (2010), *News from the BBC, CNN, and Al-Jazeera: How the three broadcasters cover the Middle East*, Cresskill, NJ: Hampton Press.

Baron, Marcia (1991), 'Impartiality and Friendship', *Ethics*, 101, pp. 836–57.

Batty, David and Adam, David (2010), 'Climate emails review panellist quits after his impartiality questioned', *The Guardian*, 12 February, http://www.guardian.co.uk/environment/2010/feb/12/climate-change-climategate-nature-global-warming. Accessed 13 January 2013.

BBC Trust (2007), 'Impartiality of BBC business coverage', *BBC* 25 May, http://www.bbc.co.uk/bbctrust/our_work/editorial_standards/impartiality/business_news.html. Accessed 25 May 2012.

—— (2008), 'BBC network news coverage of the four UK nations', 11 June, http://www.bbc.co.uk/bbctrust/our_work/editorial_standards/impartiality/network_news.html. Accessed 10 June 2012.

—— (2011), 'Trust launches impartiality review of BBC coverage of the "Arab Spring"', 26 October, http://www.bbc.co.uk/bbctrust/news/press_releases/2011/arabspring_impartiality.html. Accessed 14 April 2012.

—— (2012a), 'Review of impartiality and accuracy of the BBC's coverage of science', 21 May, http://www.bbc.co.uk/bbctrust/search/?source_url=/bbctrust/search&term=science+coverage. Accessed 14 June 2012.

—— (2012b), 'Trust report on the impartiality and accuracy of the BBC's coverage of the events known as the "Arab Spring"', 25 June, http://www.bbc.co.uk/bbctrust/our_work/editorial_standards/impartiality/arab_spring.html. Accessed 30 June 2012.

Beinart, Peter (2012), 'The U.S. started the bloodshed in Iraq. Time to own it', *The Daily Beast*, 30 July, http://www.thedailybeast.com/newsweek/2012/07/29/the-u-s-started-the-war-in-iraq-it-s-time-to-finish-it.html. Accessed 25 August 2012.

Bernstein, Richard J. (1979), *The Restructuring of Social and Political Theory*, London: Methuen.

—— (2005), *The Abuse of Evil: The Corruption of Politics and Religion since 9/11*, Cambridge: Polity Press.

Blankenburg, William B. and Walden, Ruth (1977), 'Objectivity, interpretation, and economy in reporting', *Journalism Quarterly*, 54, pp. 591–95.

Blommaert, J. (2005), *Discourse: A Critical Introduction*, Cambridge: Cambridge University Press.

Blommaert, J. and Bulcaen, C. (2000), 'Critical discourse analysis', *Annual Review of Anthropology*, 29, pp. 447–66.

Blommaert, J., Collins, J., Heller M., Rampton, B., Slembrouck, S. and Verschueren, J. (2003), 'Introduction', *Journal of Pragmatics*, 13: 1, pp. 1–10.

Breed, W. (1955), 'Social control in the newsroom: A functional analysis', *Social Forces*, 33, pp. 326–35.

Breeze, Ruth (2011), 'Critical discourse analysis and its critics', *Pragmatics*, 21: 4, pp. 493–524.

Cohen-Almagor, Raphael (2008), 'The limits of objective reporting', *Journal of Language and Politics*, 7: 1, pp. 138–57.

Cottingham, John (1983), 'Ethics and Impartiality', *Philosophical Studies*, 43, pp. 83–99.

Crupi, Anthony (2010), 'Fox News Channel tops USA in cable ratings', *Reuters*, 27 January, http://www.reuters.com/article/2010/01/28/us-cable-idUSTRE60R0F720100128. Accessed 30 March 2011.

Cutler, J. (2004), 'Judicial codes of conduct and the First Amendment', *Georgetown Journal of Legal Ethics*, 17: 733.

Dewey, J. (1981), 'The need for a recovery of philosophy', in J. J. McDermott (ed.), *The Philosophy of John Dewey*, Chicago, IL: University of Chicago Press. First published 1917.

Don, Locke (1980), *A Fantasy of Reason: The Life and Thought of William Godwin*, London: Routledge.

Fairclough, Norman (1995), *Media Discourse*, London: Edward Arnold.

—— (2000), *New Labour, New Language?*, London: Routledge.

—— (2001), *Language and Power*, London: Pearson & Longman.

—— (2003), *Analyzing Discourse*, London: Routledge.

Fisk, Robert (2009), 'How can we trust the cowardly BBC?', *The Independent*, 16 April, http://www.independent.co.uk/opinion/commentators/fisk/robert-fisk-how-can-you-trust-the-cowardly-bbc-1669281.html. Accessed 16 March 2011.

—— (2012), 'Syrian war of lies and hypocrisy', *The Independent*, 29 July, http://www.independent.co.uk/opinion/commentators/fisk/robert-fisk-syrian-war-of-lies-and-hypocrisy-7985012.html. Accessed 22 August 2012.

Fiss, Owen M. (1990), 'Why the state?', in Judith Lichtenberg (ed.), *Democracy and the Mass Media*, Cambridge: Cambridge University Press, pp.136–54.

Foerster, H. V. and Poerksen, B. (2002), *Understanding Systems: Conversations on epistemology and ethics* (trans. K. Leube), Heidelberg & New York: Carl-Auer-Systeme Verlag; Kluwer Academic/Plenum Publishers.

Friedman, Marilyn, (1993) *What are Friends For?*, Ithaca, NY: Cornell University Press.

Gabriele, Sandra (2003), 'Politics and the American Press: The Rise of Objectivity, 1865–1920', *Canadian Journal of Communication*, 28: 2, http://www.cjc-online.ca/viewarticle.php?id=793. Accessed 15 January 2013.

Godwin, William (1969), *Enquiry Concerning Political Justice and its Influence on Morals and Happiness*, Toronto: University of Toronto Press. First published 1946.

Greenslade, Roy (2003), 'Their Master's Voice', *The Guardian*, 17 February, http://www.guardian.co.uk/media/2003/feb/17/mondaymediasection.iraq. Accessed 15 August 2012.

Griffith, J. A. G. (1991), *The Politics of the Judiciary*, 4th edition, UK: Fontana Press.

Guthrie, Marisa (2008), 'Fox News Channel Leads in 2007 Cable News Ratings', *Broadcasting Cable*, 4 January, http://www.broadcastingcable.com/article/93247-Fox_News_Channel_Leads_in_2007_Cable_News_Ratings.php. Accessed 24 June 2012.

Habermas, Jürgen (1970), *Toward a Rational Society* (trans. Jeremy J. Shapiro), Boston, MA: Beacon Press.

—— (1973), *Theory and Practice* (trans. John Vietel), Boston, MA: Beacon Press.

—— (1974), 'Rationalism divided in two: A reply to Albert', in Anthony Giddens (ed.), *Positivism and Sociology*, London: Heinemann Educational Books, pp. 50–55.

Hare, R. M. (1981), *Moral Thinking*, Oxford: Clarendon Press.

———— (1984), 'Rights, Utility and Universalization: Reply to J. L. Mackie', in R. G. Frey, (ed.), *Utility and Rights*, Minneapolis, MN: University of Minnesota Press, pp. 106–20.

Harkin, James (2011), 'The BBC is fighting the wrong battle', *The Independent*, 1 January, http://www.independent.co.uk/opinion/commentators/james-harkin-the-bbc-is-fighting-the-wrong-battle-2173387.html. Accessed 10 February 2012.

Horkheimer, Max (1972), *Critical Theory*, New York: The Seabury Press.

Hornby, A. S. (2002), *Oxford Advanced Learner's Dictionary of Current English*, 6th edition, Oxford & New York: Oxford University Press.

Hull, Clark L. (1943), *Principles of Behavior*, New York: Appleton-Century-Crofts.

Husserl, Edmund (1970), *The Crisis of the European Sciences and Transcendental Phenomenology: An Introduction to Phenomenological Philosophy* (trans. David Carr), Evanston, IL: Northwestern University Press.

Jollimore, Troy (2011), 'Impartiality', in Edward N. Zalta (ed.), *The Stanford Encyclopedia of Philosophy (Summer 2011 Edition)*. Available at http://plato.stanford.edu/archives/sum2011/entries/impartiality/. Accessed 11 December 2012.

Judicature (2006), 'A conversation about judicial independence and impartiality', 89: 6 (May–June), https://docs.google.com/viewer?a=v&q=cache:OnR2TrlmdlMJ:www.ajs.org/ajs/publications/Judicature_PDFs/896/Transcript_896f+A+Conversation+About+Judicial+Independence+and+Impartiality&hl=en&gl=se&pid=bl&srcid=ADGEEShHNAGk cgnuiCBFtU9nOTuGq9l6ism6l0GFBWL8qesmSVdvLyndE1B3FacG6GVzDP6KaYsLG41iF0 YipaCsXOtdz2Ni6oMwSaUHf_YYURANUCVJD-olchpOcBKzoyKXPOUtlhdB&sig=AHIE tbTLSVdNcuBix8yCGQUPnaccMVOzAA. Accessed 8 July 2012.

Justia.com (2000), 'U.S. Supreme Court Center: Bush v. Gore', http://supreme.justia.com/cases/federal/us/531/98/. Accessed 15 December 2012.

Kant, Immanuel (1964), *Groundwork of the Metaphysic of Morals* (trans. H.J. Paton), New York: Harper Torchbooks.

Kaplan, Richard L. (2002), *Politics and the American Press: The Rise of Objectivity, 1865–1920*, Cambridge: Cambridge University Press.

Kekes, John (1981), 'Morality and Impartiality', *American Philosophical Quarterly*, 18, pp. 295–303.

Kumar, Deepa (2006), 'Media, War, and Propaganda: Strategies of Information Management During the 2003 Iraq War', *Communication and Critical/Cultural Studies*, 3: 1, pp. 48–69.

Lamb, Robert (2006), 'The Foundations of Godwinian Impartiality', *Utilitas*, 18: 2, pp. 134–53.

Lazarus, Edward (1999), *Closed Chambers: The Rise, Fall and the Future of the Modern Supreme Court*, New York: Penguin Books.

Lloyd, John (2009), 'The politics of impartiality', http://www.ft.com/intl/cms/s/0/633b935c-f925-11dd-ab7f-000077b07658.html#axzz2SVzTPhuE. Accessed 5 May 2013.

Maras, Steven (2013), *Objectivity in Journalism*, Cambridge: Polity Press.

Merton, Robert K. (1949), *Social Theory and Social Structure*, Glencoe, IL: The Free Press.

Meyer, Philip (2005), 'Public Journalism and the Problem of Objectivity', http://www.unc.edu/~pmeyer/ire95pj.htm. Accessed 17 July 2012.

Mill, J. S. (1861), *Utilitarianism*, Indianapolis, IN: Hackett Publishing.

Mindich, David T. Z. (1998), *Just the Facts: How 'Objectivity' Came to Define American Journalism*, New York: New York University Press.

Minow, Martha (1992), 'Stripped Down Like a Runner or Enriched by Experience: Bias and Impartiality of Judges and Jurors', *William and Mary Law Review*, 33: 4–5, pp. 1201–218, http://scholarship.law.wm.edu/wmlr/vol33/iss4/5. Accessed 24 November 2012.

Murdoch, James (2009), 'The Absence of Trust', *Edinburgh International Television Festival, MacTaggart Lecture*, 28 August, http://image.guardian.co.uk/sys-files/Media/documents/2009/08/28/JamesMurdochMacTaggartLecture.pdf. Accessed 10 November 2012.

Nagel, Ernest (1961), *The Structure of Science*, New York: Harcourt Brace Jovanovich.

The New Republic (1990), 'What Brennan wrought. (Justice William J. Brennan Jr.) (editorial)', *Highbeam Business*, 13 August, http://business.highbeam.com/4776/article-1G1-9332403/brennan-wrought. Accessed 6 July 2012.

Peirce, Charles S. (1992), *The Essential Peirce*, vol. 1 (ed. Nathan Houser and Christian Kloesel), Bloomington, IN: Indiana University Press.

Philo, G. (2007), 'Can discourse analysis successfully explain content of media and journalistic practice', *Journalism Studies*, 8: 2, pp. 175–96.

Popper, K. R. (1962), *The Open Society and Its Enemies*, London: Routledge.

Powers, Madison (1993), 'Contractualist Impartiality and Personal Commitments', *American Philosophical Quarterly*, 30, pp. 63–69.

Qassemi, Sultan al (2012), 'Breaking the Arab News: Egypt made Al Jazeera – and Syria's destroying it', *Foreign Policy*, 2 August, http://www.foreignpolicy.com/articles/2012/08/02/breaking_the_arab_news. Accessed 25 August 2012.

Railton, Peter (1984), 'Alienation, Consequentialism and the Demands of Morality', *Philosophy and Public Affairs*, 13, pp. 134–71.

Rawls, John (1971), *A Theory of Justice [TJ]*, Cambridge, MA: Harvard University Press.

Reed, T. M. and Leigh Brown, Alison (1984), 'On the Rational Rejection of Utilitarianism and the Limitations of Moral Principles', *Journal of Value Inquiry*, 18, pp. 227–32.

Ryan, Alan (1972), 'Normal Science or Political Ideology?', in Peter Laslett, W. G. Runciman and Quentin Skinner (eds), *Philosophy, Politics and Society*, vol. 4, Oxford: Basil Blackwell, pp. 86–100.

Sambrook, Richard (2004), 'The Poliak Lecture given at Columbia University: America – Holding on to Objectivity', *BBC Press Office*, 27 October, http://www.bbc.co.uk/pressoffice/speeches/stories/sambrook_poliak.shtml. Accessed 30 October 2012.

Schutz, Alfred and Luckman, Thomas (1973), *The Structures of the Life–World*, Evanston, IL: Northwestern University Press.

Sidgwick, Henry (1907), *The Methods of Ethics*, Chicago, IL: University of Chicago Press.

Singer, Peter (1979), *Practical Ethics*, Cambridge: Cambridge University Press.

Sokoloff, William (2007), 'Impartiality in Televised News and its Influence on Youth Audiences', *PS115 – Public Opinion and Survey Research*, 13 December, ase.tufts.edu/polsci/faculty/portney/studentSokoloff.pdf. Accessed 9 December 2012.

Stark, Cynthia A. (1997), 'Decision Procedures, Standards of Rightness and Impartiality. NOÛS 31:4 (1997) 478–495', http://onlinelibrary.wiley.com/doi/10.1111/0029-4624.00057/pdf. Accessed 29 November 2012.

Taylor, Paul. (1978) 'On Taking the Moral Point of View', *Midwest Studies in Philosophy* 3: 35–61.

Thompson, Mark (2009), 'BBC and the Gaza appeal', *BBC News: The Editors*, http://www.bbc. co.uk/blogs/theeditors/2009/01/bbc_and_the_gaza_appeal.html. Accessed 14 January 2013.

Thornton, S. P. (2006), 'Solipsism and the problem of other minds, in J. Fieser and B. Dowden (eds), *Internet Encyclopedia of Philosophy*, http://www.iep.utm.edu/s/solipsis.htm. Accessed 25 November 2012.

Van Dijk, Teun (1991), *Racism and the Press*, London: Routledge.

—— (1998), 'Opinions and Ideologies in the Press', in A. Bell and P. Garrett (eds), *Approaches to Media Discourse*, Oxford: Blackwell.

—— (2000), 'New(s) Racism: A discourse analytical approach', in S. Cottle (ed.), *Ethnic Minorities and the Media: Changing cultural boundaries*, Buckingham: Open University Press.

Verschueren, J. (2001), 'Predicaments of Criticism', *Critique of Anthropology*, 21, pp. 59–82.

Vetlesen, Arne Johan (1998), 'Impartiality and Evil: A reconsideration provoked by genocide in Bosnia', *Philosophy & Social Criticism*, 24: 5, pp. 1–35.

Webster's Revised Unabridged Dictionary ([1928] 1913), http://machaut.uchicago.edu/?resource =Webster%27s&word=impartiality&use1913=on&use1828=on. Accessed 7 November 2012.

White, David Manning (1950), 'The Gatekeeper: A Case Study in the Selection of News', *Journalism Quarterly*, 27, pp. 283–96.

White, Deborah (2012), 'Iraq War Facts, Results & Statistics at January 31, 2011: 4,487 US Soldiers Killed, 32,223 Seriously Wounded', http://usliberals.about.com/od/homelandsecurit1/a/ IraqNumbers.htm. Accessed 19 October 2012.

Williams, Bernard (1973), 'A Critique of Utilitarianism', in J. J. C. Smart and Bernard Williams (eds), *Utilitarianism: For and Against*, Cambridge: Cambridge University Press, pp. 77–150.

Chapter 2

Assessing, measuring and applying 'public value tests' beyond new media: Interpreting impartiality and plurality in debates about journalism standards

Stephen Cushion

Introduction

In today's crowded media marketplace, public and commercially-driven broadcasters across Europe have found it increasingly difficult to coexist. Where once many public service broadcasters enjoyed either monopoly status or market dominance, in a multichannel and online media environment they face considerably more commercial competition and undermine the neo-liberal logic of free-market economies. While many countries have embraced the expansion of market-driven media by deregulating their broadcasting industries (Baker 2002; Trappel et al. 2011), the shift from analogue to digital in the online era has also triggered confrontations between competing media systems national governments have struggled to reconcile. Many public and commercial broadcasters have entered into turf warfare, jostling with each other to make use of the latest technology and be first to supply the cutting-edge services of the twenty-first century.

In doing so, both media regulators and legislators have been forced to respond to the fast and fluid media environment, considering the role public service broadcasters should play in increasingly market-driven democracies (Lowe & Jauert 2005; Lowe & Bardoel 2008; Iosifidis 2010; Lowe 2010). It is in this context that the European Union (EU) sought to establish a commitment to public service broadcasting amongst members as new media quickly evolved. A 1997 Amsterdam Protocol put it bluntly that all EU countries were able to determine the level of funding of their public service broadcast systems without affecting 'trading conditions or competition'. Subsequent EU accords reinforced this position. Public service broadcasters were not, in other words, confined to the broadcast era. Like their market-driven counterparts, they were free to innovate and expand as public service media.

At the same time, over the last 15–20 years commercial media rivals have lobbied hard about what they see as unfair EU State Aid rules, since they allow public service media to operate outside of the competitive market conditions in other industries (Danders & Pauwels 2010; Michalis 2010). The European Commission's (EC) Directorate for Competition has sought ways to evaluate the supply of publicly-funded new media and, moreover, whether it impacts on commercial competitors. What emerged in an update of the State Aid rules was the introduction of public service value tests that were designed to formally assess new media launched by public service broadcasters or if any significant changes were made to existing services (Moe 2010; Danders & Moe 2012).

Public service value tests, then, represent a form of regulatory control for public service broadcasters and, in the EC's own words, are undertaken to explore whether new media or significant changes to existing services 'serve the democratic, social and cultural needs of the society, while duly taking into account its potential effects on trading conditions and competition' (EC 2001: 20). While these formal EC regulatory controls were introduced in 2009, in Danders and Moe's *Exporting the Public Value Test* (2012) scholars from across Europe observed that variations – of what are also legally known as ex-ante tests – have not developed uniformly: some countries have already established a mechanism to assess public value or market impact whereas others have had to hastily respond to increased EC pressure (cf. Moe 2010). A growing body of literature has begun tracing the adaptation of ex-ante tests around Europe and the comparative ways they are being implemented; the legal wrangling between national governments and the EC ruling; the threatened independence of public service broadcasters and the marketization of new media services; or the conceptualization of 'public value' and the use of evidence-based decision-making (cf. Moe 2010; Sjøvaag 2011; Danders & Moe 2012).

This chapter will enter into debates about public service value tests by exploring how editorial standards of impartiality and plurality in journalism can be assessed, measured and applied empirically to deliver 'public value'. While much academic literature in this area understandably focuses on the regulation of new media – this is, after all, where the EC rules pertain most prominently – my aim is to widen the discussion to existing services, most notably in broadcasting, and to specifically discuss the public value of news supplied by public- and market-driven journalism. Although this is not an area of public service media formally assessed by public value tests, it has been observed that this EC form of disciplining public service broadcasters could be extended in the future to evaluate the quality of content more generally (Freedman 2008), such as in the provision of news and current affairs.

Since market-driven media continue to expand across Europe, prompting further confrontations with public service broadcasters about their routine output, the chapter will argue that scholars need to consider ways in which to routinely assess, measure and apply 'public value' to news and current affairs programming in order to help shape how future evidence-based reports interpret the quality of journalism. This is not to make the case for routine public service tests of all publicly-funded news, but to proactively safeguard or enhance journalistic standards in the face of commercial competition and market-shaped regulation. As Freedman observes from a United Kingdom (UK) perspective:

> [It is] very likely that the proposed market impact assessments and public value tests will generate enormous amounts of data – the 'evidence-based' approach favoured by Ofcom [commercial regulator] – that are better suited to an understanding of broadcasting as a straightforward economic, rather than a complex social and cultural, practice. (Freedman 2008: 157)

The focus of this chapter is to identify where evidence-based studies can inform and shape the value of news beyond economic concerns to deliver journalism consistent with public service goals distinctive from the commercial market. It does so by first drawing on a collaborative study between the BBC Trust – the UK body that monitors all BBC content – and the Cardiff School of Journalism, Media and Cultural Studies, which was established to assess whether BBC journalism was abiding by its impartiality requirements in the reporting of the nations and regions – one of the public service broadcaster's key mission statements – and to compare a large output of coverage with its commercial rivals.

The second part of the chapter draws on a comprehensive review of over 200 empirical studies to compare and contrast the 'public value' of news on market-driven news and public service media (Cushion 2012a). In so doing, a normative framework was developed to evaluate the democratic quality of news in routine periods of time, during elections or wars, and on 24-hour news channels.[1] Since it has been claimed that media pluralism has been significantly enhanced over the last 20–30 years, the aim of this comprehensive review of empirical news studies was to compare journalism standards – including the application of impartiality – on different media systems to identify where 'public value' was, and was not, being fulfilled.

Interpreting impartiality in the reporting of the four nations in the UK and devolved politics

For many public service broadcasters, impartiality is central to their journalistic ethos (see Chapter 1). In most European countries, a regulatory framework exists that, in some form, polices goals broadly associated with ensuring news is fair, balanced, objective or impartial (Almiron, Capurro Robles & Santcovsky 2010). Impartiality is seen to represent 'public value' since it prevents outright bias or partisanship in the presentation of news and current affairs programming. But measuring how impartiality should operate in routine journalistic practice has proven difficult not just for scholars but practitioners too (as Chapter 10 outlines).

In the UK, the BBC Trust has carried out several reviews into BBC journalism, assessing how impartial its news is in the world of politics, science and business, and in how the four nations are covered and devolved politics reported. However, these were not the kind of formal public service value tests previously described. Public service value tests have been reserved for new media services, such as the introduction of an iPlayer or a high definition (HD) television channel in 2007 (both of which were approved subject to certain conditions being met). However, the impartiality reviews were mostly evidence-based commissioned reports into existing news and current services in new political, cultural and economic environments, such as coverage of the Arab Spring or the reporting of the nations in a post-devolution UK. The latter study was carried out by Justin Lewis and myself at Cardiff University,[2] and it is what this section will now focus on. It will be used as an instructive case study of how an empirically-grounded study in broadcasting can interpret the 'public value' of impartiality in UK-wide television news reporting.

Firstly, some context is needed. Since 1999, when new political institutions were established across Scotland, Wales and Northern Ireland, UK-wide media have struggled to reflect the new political powers that each nation now holds. Each new political institution holds different political powers (most notably in health and education). For journalists this can prove highly confusing when reporting the UK generally due to sometimes subtle policy differences that may exist between the nations. While Scotland, Wales and Northern Ireland have their own national and local media, each remain reliant on English-produced news, and continue to watch UK network news bulletins (Cushion, Lewis & Groves 2009b). There have therefore been fears about an 'information deficit' in the UK, since many citizens do not regularly tune into news that may inform them about the functions of each institution and what political powers they now hold.

As a result, the BBC Trust put out to tender a research project entitled 'The Four Nations' Impartiality Review'. Cardiff University won the bid for a proposal that developed a quantitative framework for exploring whether news was impartial, together with more qualitative measures in a large-scale empirical project. To explore whether the information provided about the four nations was even-handed and accurate, the quantitative analysis examined story length, the position of a story in the bulletin, the issue/topic explored and the sources used.[3] To assess the resources put into UK-wide coverage, the location of the report and whether the reporter was based in England, Northern Ireland, Scotland or Wales was examined. To interpret the accuracy and impartiality of devolved political coverage, more qualitative measures were developed.

While assessing both accuracy and impartiality might appear to be a straightforward quantitative task, it became a more qualitative judgement since it required an enormous amount of piloting and proactive research from coders, who had to explore whether an issue was devolved or not. To explore the accuracy of devolved politics, a greater level of analysis and discursive detail was required than with most forms of content analysis, which are often limited to measuring simple categories. Qualitative case studies were carried out to explore certain topics/issues in more depth, and to comparatively assess how each broadcaster reported the same topic/story. Therefore the aim of the study was to interpret impartiality using both quantitative and qualitative measures.

Two comprehensive content analyses of BBC and commercial television bulletins over eight weeks in October and November in 2007 and 2009 were carried out.[4] This included *BBC News at One, BBC News at Six, BBC News at Ten, BBC News* (BBC One Saturday and Sunday afternoons), and one hour per day of the BBC News Channel (5–6 p.m. Monday to Friday, 6–7 p.m. Saturday and Sunday), and, for the commercial channels, this included *Channel 4 News* (including Saturday and Sunday), *ITV News at Ten, ITV News* (Saturday and Sunday), and one hour per day of Sky News (5–6 p.m. Monday to Friday, 6–7 p.m. Saturday and Sunday). Overall, 4794 news items were examined in both studies. After the first study was completed, as part of a wider review into the reporting of the nations and devolved politics,[5] the BBC developed a set of evidence-based recommendations about improving the quality of coverage (cf. Cushion, Lewis & Ramsay 2012).

The follow-up study explored whether the BBC Trust's set of evidence-based recommendations had impacted on BBC coverage. But it also enabled a comparative assessment of commercial television news. After all, the report was in the public domain and many of the suggestions made by the BBC Trust after the first review applied equally, if not more so, to ITV, Channel 4 and Sky News. However, Ofcom – the commercial regulator – did not ask these broadcasters to address any of the issues or develop their own internal review. Thus, the BBC Trust's interventionist approach to enhancing journalism standards can be contrasted to Ofcom's more light-touch regulatory oversight of commercial television news (cf. Cushion, Lewis & Ramsay 2012).[6]

Both content analyses generated a large data set overall, and the findings have been discussed previously in different contexts (Lewis et al. 2008; Cushion, Lewis & Groves 2009a & 2009b; Cushion 2012b; Cushion, Lewis & Ramsay 2012). For the purposes of this chapter's focus on delivering public value, only the key findings will be drawn upon to interpret the impartiality of news coverage of the four nations and the reporting of devolved politics.

To provide a broad interpretation of the impartiality of UK-wide news reporting, the quantitative analysis measured both the geographical relevance of a story by nation (see Table 1) and reporter on location (if a journalist was reporting from a specific locale in the UK whether live or pre-packaged) (see Table 1.1).

Both tables indicate that BBC television news has enhanced its coverage of the nations beyond England. So, for example, BBC television news on Scotland, Wales and Northern Ireland increased (collectively) by 6.4%, compared with an increase of 2.7% across ITV, Channel 4 and Sky News (see Table 1). Likewise, reporters on location rose from 9.4% to 15.4% on the BBC compared to a fall from 6% to 3.5% on commercial television (see Table 1.1). The significance of these results should not be overblown, however: England remains the dominant nation reported. But there is a clear difference between the more commercial broadcasters and the UK's main public service broadcaster, the BBC, in *how far* the four nations are reported. Indeed, Sky News had no stories from Wales or Northern Ireland in 2009.

As previously acknowledged, interpreting the relevance of devolution to the nations beyond England can be complex, since many powers overlap with Westminster. In 2007, it was identified that this compromises the accuracy of devolved politics: polices were often reported as if they were UK-relevant when they only related to England. So, for example, a number of stories in the 2007 study were based on a speech by the then prime minster, Gordon Brown,

Table 1: Per cent of geographical relevance of story item (brackets change from 2007 to 2009)

	England	Northern Ireland	Scotland	Wales	Westminster	Total
BBC TV	60.3 (-8.6)	3.7 (+1.2)	6.7 (+3.4)	3.8 (+1.8)	25.5 (+2.2)	100 (522)
Commercial TV	67.5 (+4)	3.3 (+1.2)	4.1 (+1.2)	1.3 (+0.3)	23.9 (-6.6)	100 (394)

Table 1.1: Per cent of reporters on location in the four nations in 2007 and 2009

	England		Scotland		Wales		Northern Ireland	
	2007	**2009**	**2007**	**2009**	**2007**	**2009**	**2007**	**2009**
BBC News at One	91.5 (75/82)	86.0 (74/86)	3.7 (3/82)	4.7 (4/86)	3.7 (3/82)	4.7 (4/86)	1.2 (1/82)	4.7 (4/86)
BBC News at Six	88.8 (87/98)	84.5 (98/116)	4.1 (4/98)	6.9 (8/116)	4.1 (4/98)	6.0 (7/116)	3.1 (3/98)	2.6 (3/116)
BBC News at Ten	91.5 (43/47)	83.6 (61/73)	4.3 (2/47)	9.6 (7/73)	/	2.7 (2/73)	4.3 (2/47)	4.1 (2/73)
BBC News Channel	91.4 (85/93)	84.1 (90/107)	5.4 (5/93)	9.3 (10/107)	/	3.7 (4/107)	3.2 (3/93)	2.8 (3/107)
ITV News at Ten	95.2 (59/62)	92.2 (83/90)	1.6 (1/62)	3.3 (3/90)	1.6 (1/62)	3.3 (3/90)	1.6 (1/62)	1.1 (1/90)
Channel 4 News	96.2 (51/53)	98.7 (77/78)	3.8 (2/53)	/	/	1.3 (1/78)	/	/
Sky News	91.7 (77/84)	98.3 (113/115)	3.6 (3/84)	1.7 (2/115)	1.2 (1/84)	/	3.6 (3/84)	/
BBC Combined	**90.6 (290/320)**	**84.6 (323/382)**	**4.4 (14/320)**	**7.6 (29/382)**	**2.2 (7/320)**	**4.4 (17/382)**	**2.8 (9/320)**	**3.4 (13/382)**
Non-BBC Combined	**94.0 (187/199)**	**96.5 (273/283)**	**3.0 (6/199)**	**1.8 (5/283)**	**1.0 (2/199)**	**1.4 (4/283)**	**2.0 (4/199)**	**0.3 (1/283)**

about providing 'British Jobs for British Workers'. The aim was to improve the educational prospects of young people in order to ensure the government generated 'British jobs for British workers'. While it worked well as a sound bite, it potentially caused confusion as it was an educational announcement – an English policy – for young people in England only.

To ascertain whether stories were about a particular nation, in 2009 a new category was added to quantify whether a news story clearly stated it related to England only. We found that 65 per cent of BBC news items correctly identified when a story applied only to England, whereas commercial broadcasters only made this fact clear in 35 per cent of the relevant news items. Put a different way, many commercial Scottish, Welsh or Northern Irish television viewers may have been left with the impression what was happening in England actually applied UK-wide. So, for example, in a story about the review of police cautions which was only relevant to England and Wales, a *Channel 4 News* item began:

The way the police issue cautions and fixed-penalty notices is to be reviewed. The Justice Secretary, Jack Straw, said that the assessment would be carried out jointly with the Home Office. Up to 40,000 assaults are dealt with by a caution every year […]. (*Channel Four News* 9 November 2009)

At no point did *Channel 4 News* make viewers aware that the measures were not relevant to Northern Ireland or, indeed, Scotland, since criminal justice is devolved to the Scottish Parliament and the police do not use the cautions system.

While the BBC remained guilty of not always clearly pointing out whether stories related to England only, there were instances where the relevance of a policy was pointed out for all four nations. Indeed, in order to explain the powers each nation hold within a single story, the BBC increased the number of cross-national comparisons of policy differences across the four nations. In 2007, they supplied just eight, whereas in 2009 there were 39 comparisons. With the exception of Channel 4, the commercial broadcasters had no comparisons. And yet making policy comparisons between all four nations can enhance the UK-wide relevance of a story. So, for example, a number of BBC television news bulletins featured an education story about proposals in England to move to a more play-based infant curriculum:

Children do start school in the UK at a younger age than in many other countries, but the more important issue for the review is when the switch takes place from play-based learning, to a more formal, structured curriculum. In England and Scotland, the curriculum starts at five, whereas in Wales and Northern Ireland, the emphasis on learning through play continues right through, until children are seven. (*BBC News at Six* 16 October 2009)

By referencing the school policy in all four nations, this compare and contrast approach allows journalists to not just communicate information relevant UK-wide, it opens up a path to convey how education policies are pursued in different political institutions. By not making comparisons between the four nations, it would be understandable if viewers were led to believe that the English-policy decision referred to the whole of the UK. So, for example, Sky News did not put the review in a wider UK context:

Now, the Schools Minister has rejected proposals for children to start school a year later, at the age of six. The recommendation was made in the most comprehensive review of primary education for 40 years, but Vernon Coaker said the plans were 'counterproductive'. (Sky News 5–6pm bulletin, 16 October 2009)

Throughout this report, the words 'England' and 'the UK' were used interchangeably, which could mistakenly develop a connection between this English-only policy and its relevance to Wales, Scotland and Northern Ireland.

It should be stressed that this is just a brief flavour of the quantitative and qualitative headline findings of a far larger research project of the four nations' impartiality review (Lewis et al. 2008; Cushion, Lewis & Groves 2009b; Cushion, Lewis & Ramsay 2010; Cushion 2012b; Cushion, Lewis & Ramsay 2012). It would be difficult to argue that there has been a radical transformation of the BBC's coverage,[7] but there were some clear and, in some cases striking, improvements after the BBC's Trust recommendations. All of which have arguably enhanced the BBC's impartial treatment of the nations and accuracy in reporting devolved politics. With the exception of Channel 4, there was little evidence of any major readjustments of coverage on commercial television news.

Of course, measuring impartiality is not something that can always be easily agreed upon (see Chapter 4), as is the case with this study into the reporting of the nations and devolved politics. Moreover, as this book demonstrates, debates about impartiality in news coverage are complex and should not be simplified. On many issues and topics there is a lack of agreement about precise measures that define what impartiality constitutes and, more generally, whether it improves upon 'public value'. But the argument advanced in this section is that while measures interpreting impartiality in news can be empirically complex to develop, this should not discourage scholars from attempting to understand how evidence-based analysis can help or hinder the quality of journalism and deliver greater 'public value'. The next section broadens this discussion with a related project about measuring the public value of news on public and market-driven news media more generally.

From normative values to empirical judgements: identifying 'public value' in news produced by competing media systems

While broadcasting was once dominated by just public- or state-run organizations, in recent decades the media environment has changed dramatically with the rise of commercial competition. The marketization of media culture has prompted concerns that there is a crisis in public service media, since market-driven and public service broadcast models share different political, philosophical and economic aims in the supply and delivery of content (Cushion 2012a). In the production of news, for example, the shift towards more market-led journalism has generated considerable academic debate and anxiety about potentially diminishing the quality of information available in the public sphere for citizens to remain informed about, or attentive to, the burning issues of the day (McChesney 2000; Aalberg & Curran 2011).

Whereas publicly funded journalism is subject to robust regulatory requirements and safeguards, the dominant trend in many countries is that commercially-driven news is left to market forces or 'lighter touch' regulation. In doing so, there is an underlying assumption that a non-market-led system of journalism – supplied by either a state or public service broadcaster – provides news of more 'public value' than the commercial world of media. And yet, while many public service broadcasters share a broad philosophy to enhance an understanding of the world and contribute to informed citizenship, differences remain within and beyond many countries in their editorial aims and independence from the state, or in their funding models and regulatory structures. Like commercial broadcasters, public service broadcasters have had to remain competitive in order to ensure that they continue to attract large enough audiences to justify either state funding or expect citizens to pay for programming via a licence fee. But at a time when 'choice' and 'competition' are touted as market-driven solutions to enhancing media standards, the role and relevance of public service broadcasters has come under fire. Bardoel and d'Haenens, for example, have argued that 'PSBs [public service broadcasters] have to legitimize their existence, both in terms of positive and explicit political and cultural purposes' (2008: 351). Thus, in order to compare the quality of news on competing media systems, it is necessary to evidence how journalism could be understood as being distinctive and, importantly for this chapter, how 'public value' can be empirically measured in respect of delivering impartial news and media plurality.

To analyze the relative merits of journalism, loaded terms such as 'quality' news or news of 'public value' need to be understood in the context of debates about advancing informed or active citizenship. While the concept of plurality is often invoked to secure the supply of a diverse culture of news, it is often used to measure the amount of news outlets available to audiences rather than comparatively examining the diversity of news content produced. In Brian McNair's *Cultural Chaos* (2006), for example, it is suggested that twenty-first century news media offer an abundance of choice across many platforms, preventing any dominant ideology from emerging or any media bias from being meaningfully exerted. But there is not a great deal of empirical evidence to support what is being argued or observed.

The aim of a large research project developed in *The Democratic Value of News: Why Public Service Media Matter* (Cushion 2012a) was to question whether commercial choice had significantly enhanced the standards of journalism in recent decades by conducting a comprehensive review of empirical news studies examining public and market-driven news. Since journalism studies has rapidly expanded over the previous decade, with more publishers interested in book length endeavours, more dedicated journalism journals arriving on the scene and more established scholarly networks emerging (cf. Cushion 2012b), the intention of this project was to draw extensively on this rich supply of evidence.[8]

Moreover, the project aimed to assess whether the normative claims of public service broadcasting stand up to empirical scrutiny, such as supplying editorially diverse agendas or remaining impartial in sensitive political times (Curran 2003). Drawing on over 200 empirical news studies, four areas of journalism were examined on competing media systems. Firstly, routine agendas were examined to identify what news typically featured on competing media systems, such as the balance between local, national and international news stories. The public value of news was likely to be enhanced, it was argued, when more hard news[9] was supplied over soft news,[10] even if these were not always precise categories and could overlap. Secondly, the reporting of election campaigns was explored to assess the performance of news media at a critical democratic moment. News of 'public value' was interpreted as being election news containing policy information that citizens can use to make an informed decision about the relative merits of a political party, or a particular politician, if they decide to cast their vote on election day. Thirdly, the reporting of wars and conflicts were examined, another decisive moment for journalism when concerns about impartiality or independence are raised, as propaganda distorts the informational climate. The 'public value' of war reporting was interpreted by whether different media systems were able to remain objective, impartial and balanced at times when journalists could be susceptible to heightened political, social and cultural pressures and influences. Finally, dedicated news channels were evaluated to explore what information is conveyed in a fast-moving format, and whether journalistic ideals about objectivity, accuracy and analysis can be sustained in a 24/7 environment. In assessing the 'public value' of 24-hour news, what was of interest was not just what information is conveyed, but how it is crafted and communicated to audiences in a 24/7 format and environment. Since the empirical detail of every study drawn upon cannot be fully retold in length now (cf. Cushion 2012a), the broad thrust of evidence drawn upon will be summarized in this section.

In routine – what might be described as 'everyday' news output – the review of empirical news studies longitudinally traced shifting news agendas over recent decades and found an enhanced tabloid agenda across news media generally, displacing more serious news topics in politics and public affairs. Many scholars accounted for the rise in soft news by the privatization of state media and deregulation of the broadcast news industries triggered at different points in time cross-nationally. However, since deregulation has not had as direct an impact on public media, several studies have shown they had not been subjected to the same level of commercial pressure to report soft news or relegate international or local news.

In contemporary coverage, several nationally and internationally comparative studies found that public service television journalism broadly adopted a serious news agenda, supplying more local or international affairs, policy or analytical information, and containing less personalized coverage than commercial media. However, some studies found public service media tended to deliver a top-down view of the world, turning primarily to elites to explain what is happening in the world, as opposed to a wider constituency of actors that could add greater breath and depth to the interpretation of politics and public affairs. While the Internet could potentially enhance engagement of audiences or diversify news agendas, many of the comparative studies drawn upon suggested that they have not radically altered day-to-day journalistic norms or news values. Nonetheless, public service media have sought to experiment most with online news, encouraging users to follow external links beyond their own services. But, overall, the evidence amassed showed that viewers tuning into or surfing the websites of public and market-driven news will most likely find in day-to-day coverage public media reflected a more diverse and in-depth 'window on the world' than their commercial counterparts.

The next part of the analysis examined studies of news reporting during election campaigns, an important democratic moment when voters need information to make informed decisions at the ballot box. Longitudinal trends of election coverage showed that, in most countries, public service media tended to report more news over the campaign period than their commercial competitors. This was especially the case in the reporting of 'second order elections', with public service television news more committed to covering local, state or supranational elections. The most prominent theme in studies about media coverage of election campaigns was in how far different media systems had become 'Americanized', prioritizing game or strategy frames, whilst downsizing the time and space granted to understanding the differences between the polices of competing political parties. Despite longitudinal trends suggesting there were traces of Americanization on some public media outlets, for the most part these covered more policy-related stories than their commercial rivals at election time, with less emphasis on game-type coverage and the personalization of reporting.

But the analysis of election studies also established that public service media have had an impact on national journalistic cultures, acting as a buffer against the influence of commercial news values such as incorporating game or strategy frames into election coverage. It was found that in countries where a strong infrastructure of public media had remained in place, while commercial news outlets had not necessarily matched the volume of coverage available on publicly-funded sources, many of them had resisted adopting more explicit Americanized conventions in election reporting. Put another way, public media appear to be indirectly maintaining the volume of election stories and the amount of policy-related stories on commercial coverage during election campaigns.

In examining studies of war journalism, the focus of the analysis was reviewing empirical news studies that made sense of the events surrounding September 11, and the reporting of the most intense phase of the 2003 war in Iraq. The most striking differences were identified as being cross-national rather than between media systems. So, for example, the nature of Iraq war coverage was shaped most significantly by the geopolitical environment of individual nation states, their level of involvement in a war (militarily or diplomatically), along with their past and present relationship with the US. Western influence, however, was not as globally influential as the first Gulf War in the early 1990s. Studies showed Middle Eastern news channels, most notably Al Jazeera (a Qatari-financed and sponsored broadcaster), conveyed a more human interest perspective about the military conflict and the Iraqi casualties of war than western news organizations.

But it was on US television news where cross-national differences were the most striking. Systematic content analyses of US television news suggested that all the major broadcasters did not adequately scrutinize the government's response to September 11, the existence of WMD and the reasons why military action was taken in Iraq. Fox News, in particular, had an explicit pro-war bias, abandoning any conventional notion of balance or impartiality. If this could be explained by the presence of US soldiers leading the wars in Iraq and Afghanistan, UK troops were also involved in military action, but neither commercial nor public broadcasters indulged in similar explicit pro-war coverage. Indeed, the BBC heavily scrutinized the presence of WMD months after the war had begun, demonstrating how public media can operate independently from the state in times of war and conflict. But, overall, whereas previous areas of journalism had found public broadcast media was distinctive from commercial coverage in routine periods or at election time, it was harder to make this case cross-nationally during moments of war and conflict.

The final part of the analysis examined the rise of 24-hour news channels, and found that there were more commercial than public broadcasters operating around the world with the influence of CNN, over 30 years since it was launched, continuing to shape the genre's routine conventions today. The commercial dominance of CNN was challenged by public broadcasters over a decade later, with more channels offering a menu of scheduled programming and less continuous news reported at a frenetic pace. But it was argued that the arrival of Al Jazeera and other Middle Eastern news channels in the 1990s had most disrupted the influence of US/western journalism on 24-hour news culture. Funded by the Qatari government, Al Jazeera's ability to practise non-market journalism and operate with somewhat relative editorial freedom meant it can offer an alternative 'window on the world' from other international news channels.

On national and more localized news channels, longitudinal studies showed rolling news conventions tended to be shaped by live or breaking news stories. As more rolling news channels were launched in the 2000s, it was identified that many market-led conventions had challenged editorial guidelines, such as sacrificing breaking news first for accuracy or analysis, even on the public service broadcaster, the BBC News Channel. At the same time, since rolling news channels were launched in more lightly regulated environments than conventional broadcasters, channels such as Fox News and MSNBC in the US had been able to report more opinionated and partisan journalism. In countries where a stronger public media infrastructure existed, it was suggested that more formally imposed regulatory requirements had safeguarded editorial standards of 24-hour news journalism, including on commercial broadcasters. Nevertheless, even though public service news channels and more robust regulation can be seen to have restrained the import of a full blown Fox-style journalism to other regions around the world, the commercial conventions that first defined the 24-hour news genre, such as live or breaking news, continued to exert their influence on many commercial and public broadcasters.

While it was established that public service media were generally more likely to supply news of 'public value' than their market-driven competitors, they did not escape criticism either. Some longitudinal trends showed public service media adopting an increasingly soft news agenda, sharing some of the commercialized characteristics of election news journalism imported from the US, such as game or campaign strategy reporting, or increasing market-led conventions into routine 24-hour news coverage, such as hyping up breaking news stories or broadcasting live for sustained periods. In coverage of the war in Iraq, many studies found public service media were not sufficiently impartial, accepting western perspectives and failing to challenge the presence of WMD until after military action had commenced. All of which was interpreted as conventions and practices that were not consistent with news of 'public value'.

But despite public service news media not always being consistent with the production of news with 'public value', the comprehensive review of empirical news studies demonstrated that in most of the areas examined, they had more diverse agendas and higher editorial standards than market-driven media. In other words, despite all the commercial choice and competition in contemporary news culture, public service media remain editorially distinctive from market-driven news.

Shaping the future of news: why scholars should inform 'evidence-based' reviews in media policy-making

The chapter began by acknowledging how the increasingly competitive market-driven media environment had, in recent decades, prompted media regulators at a national and European level to intervene in territorial disputes about the services delivered by public service media. In doing so, public service value tests have – in different ways – been instituted in many countries to assess whether a new public service media service, or a significant change to an existing one, will adversely affect commercial trading or competition. At the same time, the test is designed to evaluate the democratic, social and cultural qualities a service will bring to public service media culture.

It is, in the latter respect, that this chapter sought to assess how public service tests could be used to enhance the editorial standards of journalism. While this falls outside of their current remit, it was suggested that this kind of approach could be applied as a future method of evaluating the quality of journalism on public and commercially driven news media. Indeed, some scholars have raised concerns about media regulators carrying out these assessments alone, and allowing economic priorities to override democratic, social and cultural values.

There has not been a considerable amount of attention paid to how scholars inform media debates or, more specifically, the standards of journalism. In the UK, media academics have sometimes had a hostile relationship with the news industry after producing critical reports about journalism coverage. Consider, for example, the dismissive reception to books by the Glasgow Media Group, such as *Bad News* or *More Bad News*, which criticized journalists for reproducing the views of the ruling elite (cf. Quinn 2007). In more recent years, it could be observed that journalists have been more receptive to media research, such as the Glasgow Media Group's latest book, *More Bad News From Israel* (Philo & Berry 2011). Likewise, relationships between practitioners and academics have grown stronger, with new collaborative journals – for example, the *Journal of Applied Journalism and Media Studies* – aiming to bridge the gap between academics and the news media industry. But there arguably remain greater research synergies that could be exploited between journalists and scholars to enhance the quality of journalism.

Freedman has explored the impact of media scholarship and concluded that policy-makers often see scholars as promoting interesting theoretical ideas, but many are seen as lacking the empirical credentials to generate compelling evidence about how journalism could be improved: 'Media policy-making in the UK is increasingly dominated by the presence of corporate actors, the articulation of corporate interests and depends on the mobilization of narrowly empirical, quantitative forms of research data' (Freedman 2006: 95–96). Moreover, academics are viewed as having a diminishing influence in media debates, and policy-makers have turned elsewhere for reliable evidence. In my view, this not only represents a missed opportunity, but also displays a curious paradox. Journalism studies as an academic discipline has expanded over the last decade or so, with dedicated journals such as *Journalism: Theory, Practice and Criticism, Journalism Studies* and *Journalism Practice*. All of which, according to the editors, are heavily oversubscribed, having to reject many more articles than they can accept (Harcup 2011). At the same time, over the last decade or so journalism studies has become a more globalized scholarly pursuit. Large scholarly networks such as ICA and ECREA have now established journalism divisions to encourage interdisciplinary post-national scholarship.

So journalism studies post-2000 has grown more globally diverse and popular. Thus, at a time when journalism studies has rapidly expanded, it seems somewhat paradoxical that the role of media scholars should be a diminishing force when they have so much to contribute to ongoing media policy-making debates. Of course, this is not to imply media scholars have all the solutions, nor even that all published academic research can be of practical use to the life of a working journalist or editor. But there does appear a lot of untapped potential to help shape the future of journalism and inform media policy debates. The two case studies drawn on in this chapter were instructive examples of how normative values of news could be empirically measured by media scholars (not, as feared, regulators) in order to interpret the quality of journalism. In so doing, the role public service media play in maintaining journalism standards and producing news of democratic value was emphasized.

This is not to imply that public service media are immune from criticism, nor that regulation alone is the solution to maintaining journalism standards. As media scholars have pointed out, there are many areas where BBC impartiality does not deliver fair or balanced perspectives – on the Middle East, for example, differences are less to do with media type, and more between western media and Middle East outlets such as Al Jazeera (Barkho 2010; Philo & Berry 2011; Thomas 2011). But at the same time there is a willingness – like with the BBC Trust's review of the four nations and devolved politics – to be reflective about impartiality within a public service framework and where robust regulatory obligations exist.

In my view, scholars have a critical role to play in evidencing narratives of exclusion and misrepresentation to help shape empirically-based interventions that can be a constructive force, enhancing rather than diminishing the quality of journalism and democratic culture. As the chapter began exploring, under both national and wider EC pressure, many countries appear to be turning to public service value tests to assess, measure and apply to proposed new media services. While one should remain sceptical of the market-driven ethos behind the institution of public service value tests, this should not inhibit collaborative efforts between media scholars and regulators to evaluate journalism or define what 'public value' constitutes. In upholding journalistic values such as impartiality or plurality, public value tests could be seen by media scholars as an opportunity to demonstrate the largely high editorial standards most public service media display compared to their market-driven competitors.

References

Aalberg, Toril and Curran, James (eds) (2011), *How Media Inform Democracy: A Comparative Approach*, London: Routledge.

Almiron, Núria, Capurro Robles, María and Santcovsky, Pablo (2010), 'The Regulation of Public Broadcasters´ News Coverage of Political Actors in Ten European Union Countries', *Comunicación y sociedad: Revista de la Facultad de Comunicación*, 23: 1, pp. 205–36.

Baker, Edwin C. (2002), *Media, Markets and Democracy*, Cambridge: Cambridge University Press.

Bardoel, Johannes and d'Haenens, Leen (2008), 'Reinventing Public Service Broadcasting in Europe: Prospects, Promises and Problems', *Media, Culture & Society*, 30: 3, pp. 337–55.

Barkho, Leon (2010), *News from the BBC, CNN, and Al-Jazeera: How the Three Boradcasters Cover the Middle East*, New York: Hampton Press.

Barnett, Steven, Seymour, Emily and Gaber, Ivor (2000), *From Callaghan to Kosovo: Changing Trends in British Television News 1975–1999*, Harrow: University of Westminster.

Curran, James (2003), *Media and Power*, London: Routledge.

Cushion, Stephen (2012a), *The Democratic Value of News: Why Public Service Media Matter*, Basingstoke: Palgrave.

—— (2012b), *Television Journalism*, London: Sage.

Cushion, Stephen, Lewis, Justin and Groves, Chris (2009a), 'Prioritizing hand-shaking over policy-making: A study of how the 2007 devolved elections was reported on BBC UK network coverage', *Cyfrwng: Media Wales Journal*, 6.

—— (2009b) 'Reflecting the four nations? An analysis of reporting devolution on UK network news media', *Journalism Studies*, 10: 5, pp. 1–17.

Cushion, Stephen, Lewis, Justin and Ramsay, Gordon Neil (2010), *Four Nations Impartiality Review Follow-up: An analysis of reporting devolution*, London: BBC Trust.

—— (2012), 'The impact of interventionist regulation in reshaping news agendas: A comparative analysis of public and commercially funded television journalism', *Journalism: Theory, Practice and Criticism*, 13: 7, pp. 831–49.

Danders, Karen and Moe, Hallvard (2012), *Exporting the Public Value Test: The Regulation of Public Broadcasters' New Media Services Across Europe*, Gothenburg: Nordicom.

Danders, Karen and Pauwels, Caroline (2010), 'What if Competition Policy Assists the Transfer from Public Service Broadcasting to Public Service Media? An analysis of EU State aid Control and its Relevance for Public Broadcasting', in Jostein Gripsrud and Hallvard Moe (eds), *The Digital Public Sphere: Challenges for Media Policy*, Gothenburg: Nordicom.

European Commission (2001), 'Communication from the Commission on the Application of State Aid Rules to Public Service Broadcasting', http://ec.europa.eu/competition/state_aid/legislation/broadcasting_communication_en.pdf. Accessed 3 March 2012.

Freedman, Des (2006), 'Do scholars matter? Some reasons for the declining influence of academics on the media policy-making process', *International Journal of Media and Cultural Politics*, 2: 1, pp. 92–97.

—— (2008), *The Politics of Media Policy*, Cambridge: Polity Press.

Harcup, Tony (2011), 'Research and Reflection: Supporting journalism educators in becoming scholars', *Journalism Practice*, 5: 2, pp. 161–76.

Iosifidis, Petros (ed.) (2010), *Reinventing Public Service Communication: European Broadcasters and Beyond*, London: Palgrave Macmillan.

Lowe, Gregory Ferrell (ed.) (2010), *The Public in Public Service Media*, Gothenburg: Nordicom.

Lowe, Gregory Ferell and Bardoel, Jo (eds) (2008), *From Public Service Broadcasting to Public Service Media*, Gothenburg: Nordicom.

Lowe, Gregory Ferrell and Jauert, Per (eds) (2005), *Cultural Dilemmas in Public Service Broadcasting*, Gothenburg: Nordicom.

Lewis, Justin, Cushion, Stephen, Groves, Chris, Bennett, Lucy, Reardon, Sally, Wilkins, Emma and Williams, Rebecca (eds) (2008), *Four Nations Impartiality Review: An analysis of reporting devolution*, London: BBC Trust.

McChesney, Robert (2000), *Rich Media, Poor Democracy: Communication Politics in Dubious Times*, Urbana and Chicago, IL: University of Illinois Press.

McNair, Brian (2006), *Cultural Chaos – Journalism, News and Power in a Globalised World*, London: Routledge.

Michalis, Maria (2010), 'Is the public interest under threat? Public service broadcasting, market failure and new technologies: the view from the European Union', *Interactions: Studies in Communication & Culture*, 1: 2, pp. 185–201.

Moe, Hallvard (2010), 'Governing Public Service Broadcasting: "Public Value Tests" in Different National Contexts', *Communication, Culture & Critique*, 3: 2, pp. 207–23.

Philo, Greg and Berry, Mike (2011), *More Bad News From Israel*, London: Pluto Press.

Quinn, Adrian (2007), 'Contrary to Claims, Cultures & Conventions: An Apologia for the Glasgow Media Group', *International Journal of Media & Cultural Politics*, 3: 1, pp. 5–24.

Sjøvaag, Helle (2011), 'Regulating Commercial Public Service Broadcasting: A Case Study of the Marketization of Norwegian Media Policy', *International Journal of Cultural Policy*, 18: 2, pp. 1–15.

Thomas, Lisa (2011), 'Reconstructions of "Reality?" The coverage of the Gaza withdrawal in the British media', *Journalism Studies*, 12: 4, pp. 522–38.

Trappel, Josef, Meir, Werner A., d'Haenens, Leen, Steemers, Jeanette and Thomass, Barbara (2011), *Media in Europe Today*, Bristol: Intellect.

Notes

1 While the book interpreted news with democratic value, the term 'democratic' applies equally to delivering 'public' value.

2 I would also like to acknowledge the assistance of Chris Groves, who was a research assistant on the 2007–08 project, and Gordon Neil Ramsay, who was a research assistant on the 2009–10 project.

3 The intercoder reliability scores remained high, nonetheless, between 90–100 per cent.

4 The study also sampled BBC radio and online news media, but these have been omitted for this chapter as the findings are presented comparatively with the commercial news bulletins.

5   The report we produced was part of a wider study the BBC Trust commissioned professor Anthony King (2008) to undertake which drew not just on our first content analysis study, but a large scale survey and his own anecdotal evidence about the reporting of devolution.

6   There are, of course, limitations to the methodological framework of the study. The evidence drawn upon is based entirely on the content analysis and cannot pass judgement on the managerial decision-making or the newsroom culture which may have influenced the nature of coverage. Without any audience aspect to the study, any alteration to the volume or editorial style of news cannot be assumed to have enhanced viewers' knowledge or understanding of devolution.

7   So, for example, devolution is not referenced in most news overall, let alone political news. And there remains a London-centric perspective in much of its coverage.

8   While the project aimed to be as globally ambitious as possible, most of the empirical studies are drawn from the US and UK, Western Europe, New Zealand and Australia. In other words, from advanced western democracies.

9   Hard news topics tend to include politics/economic policy, business/industry/finance, social affairs, legal, foreign relations/diplomacy, European Union issues, unrest/civil disobedience, war, Northern Ireland, health, education, employment/industrial relations, environment/ecology/planning, natural disasters, science/technology, transport, religion, culture/media/arts, moral/ethical issues and military/national security (cf. Barnett, Seymour & Gaber 2000).

10   Soft news topics tend to include crime, consumer, tragedy, weather, sport, royalty, showbiz/entertainment, human interest/animal, humour/quirky and expeditions/adventure (cf. Barnett, Seymour & Gaber 2000).

PART II

Applications

Chapter 3

PSYOPS or journalism? Norwegian information warfare in Afghanistan

Rune Ottosen

Through a case study of the Norwegian military's use of Psychological Operations (PSYOPS) in Afghanistan, this chapter examines the established NATO doctrine on PSYOPS and 'perception management' in the ISAF operation in Afghanistan. The chapter argues that Johan Galtung's model of war journalism and peace journalism can be an effective tool for the analysis of the differences over white and black PSYOPS within NATO. While the established NATO PSYOPS doctrine builds on the principle of white PSYOPS, US armed forces have, on several occasions, been known to use black PSYOPS. Galtung suggests that the sides abolish PSYOPS and disclose how their propaganda manipulates events and their social reality. He even calls for replacing the nomenclature with 'military information' to avoid the issue of white and black PSYOPS. Analyzing the Norwegian PSYOPS doctrine in Afghanistan through case studies of the ISAF forces' use of newspapers and radio broadcasts, the chapter argues that the forces introduce practices such as Miltary Information Support (MISO) to blur the differences between journalism and propaganda. MISO in this respect can be seen as a PSYOPS operation in itself.

Introduction[1]

Psychological operations (PSYOPS) are an integral part of modern warfare, operating on the borderline between the battlefield and civil society; they have the potential to cause ethical problems by blurring the difference between journalism and military operations, and represent a potential threat to journalistic impartiality. In a wider sense, this is also a part of the bigger picture of the role of journalism in the public sphere (see Chapter 9). As a member of NATO, Norway is committed to NATO's PSYOPS policy, but the Norwegian armed forces also have their own policies. In this chapter I shall discuss some of the ethical problems concerning the PSYOPS operations of the International Security Assistance Force (ISAF) forces in Afghanistan.[2] On the one hand, the Norwegian ISAF forces are bound by loyalty to NATO, but on the other hand they have a commitment to respect the integrity of the Norwegian media, and spokesmen for the Norwegian armed forces explicitly express respect for the impartiality of journalists (Ottosen 2008). My argument is that ISAF's PSYOPS policy in Afghanistan is in fact a challenge to such statements. With the help of

Johan Galtung's model of peace journalism (Galtung 2002), I hope to shed light on the dilemmas the ISAF forces face when they operate in the grey areas between the military system and civil society.

Historical background

In 1999, as a result of increased awareness of the importance of information warfare and psychology operations, the Norwegian Armed Forces (NAF) established the Psychological Defence Unit under the NAF's School of Intelligence and Security Services (Forsvarets skole i etterretnings- og sikkerhetstjeneste 2001: 6). One year prior to the establishment of the Psychological Defence Unit, the National Joint Headquarters issued a directive in which they expressed the need for a more active and conscious effort as far as PSYOPS is concerned (R. Ottosen 2009: 41). Here it was expressed clearly that a PSYOPS policy was part of Norway's obligation towards NATO: 'Norwegian troops, operating together with allied forces, must be able to support joint psychological operations' (Forsvarets overkommando 1998: 5). The responsibility of the NATO allies is formulated in NATO's 2007 PSYOPS doctrine which specifies that the allies are to 'provide, within their means and capability, resources and trained personnel to support NATO PSYOPS in operations and exercises' (NATO 2007c: 29).[3] This development shows how Norway gradually realized the requirement to implement PSYOPS in its military policies, and eventually in its strategies.

PSYOPS in the Balkans

NAF took part in NATO operations in the aftermath of ruinous civil war that tore apart the former Yugoslavia in the 1990s. As a part of the Norwegian participation in the SFOR forces in Bosnia and KFOR forces in Kosovo,[4] PSYOPS operations were systematically conducted in a number of fields such as 'weapons collection' and 'mine awareness'. This chapter dwells exclusively with the PSYOPS activities that are relevant to media and journalism.

Part of PSYOPS activity was establishing some form of contact between local media and foreign (international) journalists to garner domestic support and understanding for NATO's position. Even though the existence of PSYOPS in general was no secret, specific details of these activities, including the targeting of media, were classified information – the PSYOPS program was in part established to help build a positive image of the NATO forces. Aimed at the media, it was given the code name Lancelot, and the officers involved in it were not allowed to reveal that they were involved in PSYOPS operations.[5] In Bosnia, TV SFOR was set up to produce news and commercials for local media, and celebrities were recruited to talk favourably about the NATO forces. A radio station, Radio Mir, was started as a local propaganda tool. A magazine, *Mirko*, was distributed free of charge once a month to target youth between the ages of 13 and 18. With a circulation of 160,000, the magazine was distributed by SFOR soldiers. Another free magazine, *The Herald of Progress*, targeted young adults between 23 and 30, and had a circulation of 80,000. As part of the PSYOPS operation, cultural activities such as the film festival in Sarajevo were sponsored on condition that propaganda trailers for SFOR appeared before the Hollywood movies.[6]

As we shall see later, this short history serves as a backdrop for the study's research question: Do PSYOPS operations on the borderline between the military and civil society have the potential to harm the integrity and impartiality of journalism?

Peace journalism as a theoretical tool

In this study, I draw on Johan Galtung's model for peace journalism as a tool to analyze PSYOPS operations. The model was successfully used to unpack the practices and processes of Norwegian media's coverage of the Norwegian military presence in Afghanistan (R. Ottosen 2010). In short, Galtung's model of peace journalism builds on the dichotomy between what he calls 'war journalism' and a 'peace journalism' approach. The model includes four main points of contrast between the two approaches: war journalism is violence-oriented, propaganda-oriented, elite-oriented and victory-oriented. This is often linked to a dualistic method, a zero-sum game where the winner takes all (as in sports journalism). A potential consequence is that war journalism contributes to escalating conflicts by reproducing propaganda and promoting war and violent solutions to conflict (Galtung 2002).

Scholars have been in disagreement about the relevance and usefulness of Galtung's approach (Hackett 2006; Loyn 2007; Lynch 2007). Together with my Swedish colleague Stig A. Nohrstedt, I have suggested the use of critical discourse analysis (CDA) as a supplement to the peace journalism model (Nohrstedt & Ottosen 2008). A combination of Galtung's peace journalism model and CDA has the advantage of being able to include a historical framework for case studies (Wodak 1996; Nohrstedt 2009).

For the current study, I find Galtung's approach useful since the aim of military information operations is obviously to benefit other military activities in a 'win-oriented' manner. Galtung's model identifies power structures and sociological connections in a thought-provoking and complex way. There is scholarly thought into the practical consequences of Galtung's theory on Norwegian mainstream journalistic writing about Norway's military presence in Afghanistan (R. Ottosen 2010). One of the arguments I have used in defence of Galtung's model is that many of his critics who suggest traditional ideals, such as 'objectivity' (Loyn 2007; see Chapter 4) as an alternative to peace journalism, underestimate the power of propaganda and PSYOPS operations in the battlefield. There is empirical evidence from previous research that propaganda and PSYOPS operations influence the framing of stories. The author of the present study has used the toppling of the statute of Saddam Hussein (see below), and the framing of the coverage of the battle over Fallujah through enemy images of the al-Qaeda leader al Zarqavi, as examples of this (R. Ottosen 2009). The battle for hearts and minds thus starts before a reporter enters a war zone to cover any given conflict (Dimaggio 2009; R. Ottosen 2009).

Information warfare and PR

Information warfare must also be seen in the larger context of media-corporate relations (Dinan & Miller 2007). In recent decades, business communities and the state have both increasingly invested in public relations and spin doctors to influence the media agenda and, in a wider sense, the public discourse (ibid.). In his paper 'Political Public Relations' (2011), Guy Golan argues that an increasing number of news stories in the media have their origin in information subsidies from power circles in society. By introducing the notion of agenda-indexing, Golan argues that topics related to national security and financial issues are more vulnerable to PR campaigns than other issues because of their complexity and the lack of resources in the newsrooms to check facts and sources. This has grown worse after 2009 because of the cutbacks in staff owing to the financial crisis (McChesney & Pickard 2011). The mainstream media is thus more likely than ever to reflect the thinking of governments and the military-industrial complex in their coverage of war and security policy issues (Golan 2011).

In a study of the Canadian government's policy for PSYOPS in Afghanistan, Patricia Mazepa underlines the role of communication strategies developed by the government to mobilize civilian and military resources in support of the war effort in the so-called 'global war on terror' (GWT). Mazepa underlines that the role of the neo-liberal state should not be underestimated as a key factor in implementing a strategy for information warfare and 'selling' the war in Afghanistan to the public:

> Understanding the militarisation of communication therefore means identifying the state as the primary source of power in the coordination of communication across the spectrum of conflict. Whether the state's deployment of communication is called propaganda, psychological-operations, information-operations or public diplomacy, its function in liberal-democratic governments in Canada, the United Kingdom, and the United States continues to evolve. Particularly in the present era of 'the global war on terrorism', we might well ask how this militarisation is being reshaped and extended into government communication, currently under development in what is called the 'whole-of-government approach'. (Mazepa 2011: 3)

Smaller NATO members like Canada and Norway routinely pursue policies of their mightiest NATO partner – the US – in terms of the overall analysis of information warfare and PSYOPS. It is worth nothing that the Canadian governments' PSYOPS definition is almost identical as the one of Pentagon (Mazepa 2011: 8).

An interesting example in Mazepa's study is the Canadian military's effort to set up an international broadcasting station in Kingston, Ontario, run by the Canadian Department of National Defence (DND), and broadcast via satellite to Kandahar, Afghanistan. It employed young Pashto-speaking Canadians, and developed a broadcasting profile combining commercial music with content (Mazepa 2011: 7).

NATO's PSYOPS policy

Information strategies are increasingly becoming an integral part of modern warfare. In the *Information Operations Roadmap* charter, Donald H. Rumsfeld, the former US Defence Secretary, states that information is currently 'critical to military success and will only become more so in the foreseeable future' (American Department of Defence 2003: 3). An implication of this awareness is that substantial resources are invested in 'non-kinetic' measures aimed at influencing the hearts and minds of the people. The American 2009 budget for research on the development of psychological operations was $15.5 million (United States Special Operations Command 2009: 255), and NATO has acknowledged that the Alliance should learn from the US' emphasis on PSYOPS (Collins 2003). What are the consequences of this development for the NAF's policy in this area? This is a question little debated in Norway. In the Norwegian media, there is limited awareness and knowledge about what PSYOPS entails, and few questions are asked about the extent to which Norway is involved in these kinds of operations (R. Ottosen 2009).

Official PSYOPS policy is documented in Allied Joint Doctrine for Psychological Operations (AJP-3.10.1(A)). The use of media is a priority: 'A wide range of media may be employed in a protracted PSYOPS effort, including radio, TV and film' (NATO PSYOPS 2007a10: 66). The distinction between, white, black and grey PSYOPS is underlined:

a. White. An accurately acknowledged source. The actual sponsor correctly advertises production or sponsorship.
b. Grey. An unacknowledged source. It is not clear which individual, organisation or government is claiming production or sponsorship responsibility.
c. Black. Falsely advertised source. The product or activity was actually produced by a different individual, organisation or government than that claimed. (NATO PSYOPS 2010: 99)

In plain words, white and black PSYOPS are the difference between whether the propaganda emanating from its practice is based on true or on false information. There is no secret that there are different schools of thought within NATO on this issue. While the US has a tradition of using black propaganda on some occasions, Norwegian policy is to only use white PSYOPS. During the administration of George W. Bush, the 'Office of Strategic Influence' was established and authorized to use black propaganda in the international battle for hearts and minds. When the *New York Times* leaked the story about the existence of the office in January 2004, it was formally closed down. However, in a speech a few months later, Donald Rumsfeld, then Defence Secretary, made clear that 'the black operation' would continue through other channels (R. Ottosen 2009). The *Los Angeles Times* claimed in a news story that the responsibilities for these operations were transferred to Central Command (ibid.). The disagreement between the US and other NATO members on policy regarding white and black propaganda is expressed in the NATO document quoted above. Even though white and black PSYOPS are not explicitly mentioned in the document, they are referred to indirectly (NATO PSYOPS 2007a: 2).

Definitions

The Norwegian PSYOPS definition is similar to that of the US and Canada cited above: 'Psychological operations (PSYOPS) are defined as planned operations in times of peace, emergency, armed conflict and war directed at hostile, friendly and/or neutral targets to influence attitudes, emotions and behavior to achieve political and military aims' (Forsvarets overkommando 2000: 77). NAF thus define psychological operations as a mean of controlling the cognition and behaviour of its recipients – who are usually the civilians living in the area where military operations are being carried out. Scholars and governments abbreviate the term 'psychological operations' in slightly different ways. The US government has it as PSYOP, dropping the final 'S'. However, both abbreviations – PSYOP and PSYOPS – are the same in meaning as they stand for psychological operations (Paul 2008:57). In this chapter I use 'PSYOPS', as do the Norwegian government and military.

According to NATO's 'Allied Joint Doctrine for Psychological Operations' (2007), PSYOPS have three basic aims: '(a) Weaken the will of the adversary or potentially adversary target audiences; (b) Reinforce the commitment of friendly target audiences; (c) Gain the support and cooperation of uncommitted or undecided audiences' (NATO 2007c: 18).

Within NATO, the main target of PSYOPS operations is often the foreign audience on the ground where a conflict or war is taking place. But the operations also have consequences for home audiences. The US army has used local television stations as training posts for some of its psychological operations personnel. The information on the blog site *The Upshot* (2009) reveals that since at least 2001, both WRAL (a CBS affiliate in Raleigh, NC) and WTOC (a CBS affiliate in Savannah, GA) have regularly hosted soldiers on active duty from the army's Fourth Psychological Operations Group as part of the army's 'Training With Industry' program.

Taylor cites PSYOPS operations during the Iraq war in 2003 to drive his message home. He emphasizes that 'the battle for hearts and minds was [...] also directed at world opinion' (Taylor 2003: 11). He finds that the three main aims for PSYOPS mentioned above are carried out as an integral part of military operations. According to Paul (2008), PSYOPS is a part of military strategies, and the core provider of information under the umbrella of Information Operations (INFO OPS). INFO OPS can be defined as '[t]he integrated employment of the core capabilities of electronic warfare, computer network operations, psychological operations, military deception, and operations security' (Paul 2008: 163).

This differentiation applies to NATO's structure as well. NATO does not see INFO OPS as a separate area of warfare, but as a coordinating and synchronizing unit of several military capacities. NATO's INFO OPS include the core capacities of psychological operations, military deception, operation security, electronic warfare and computer network warfare (Bøe-Hansen 2009: 25–26). According to NATO, PSYOPS are a 'key contributor of INFO OPS activity' (NATO 2007a: 23). Technical differentiations like these, though useful, fall short of shedding light on the importance of how PSYOPS is defined in the military organization in order to assess its importance in the overall military strategies: 'Another term often used in the context of media and war is "propaganda" which can be defined as "…the deliberate and systematic attempt to shape perceptions, manipulate cognitions, and direct behavior to achieve a response that furthers the desired intent of the propagandist"' (Jowett 1993: 75).

From PSYOPS to Miso?

In July 2010, the Pentagon decided to replace PSYOPS with the more 'euphemistic' and 'modern' Military Information Support (MISO). In a statement to the Associated Press, the US Special Operations Command spokesman, Ken McGraw, said that the new name would more accurately reflect the unit's job of producing leaflets, radio broadcasts and loudspeaker messages to influence enemy soldiers and civilians: 'One of the catalysts for the transition is foreign and domestic sensitivities to the term "psychological operations" that often lead to a misunderstanding of the mission' (Associated Press 2010). The change was apparently driven from the top, by Pentagon policy-makers working for the former Defence Secretary Robert Gates. It was stated that PSYOPS reflected unease with the Cold War echoes of the old terminology, and the implication that the work involved subterfuge.

The change, however, left some current practitioners of psychological operations frustrated. 'With a name like MISO,' one wrote, 'you might as well join the supply command.' A blogger, expressing frustration, said:

Yeah, well, some of us joined Psychological Operations because it sounded awesome for its name alone. Today, we fall under people who get to dictate and control what we do without knowing fully what our capabilities are. To now have the name changed from PSYOP to MISO is a slap in the face. (*Small Wars Journal* 2010)

Norwegian PSYOPS

NAF define PSYOPS as '[p]lanned operations in times of peace, emergency, armed conflict and war directed at hostile, friendly and/or neutral targets to influence attitudes, emotions and behaviour to achieve political and military aims' (Forsvarets overkommando 2000: 77).

In a 2007 joint doctrine, Norway's National Joint Headquarter discussed some of the requirements for carrying out PSYOPS, including competence in psychology, sociology, anthropology, linguistics, graphic design, printing and publishing (National Joint Headquarters 2007: 137). While the definition embraces the use of offensive PSYOPS, the NAF are conscious of distinguishing between white, grey and black propaganda; whether this is also NATO policy can be discussed. A 2003 statement from the chief of PSYOPS at NATO's supreme headquarters, Lieutenant Colonel Steven Collins, doubts whether NATO's PSYOPS policy is restricted to white PSYOPS. In his speech, Collins in fact brags about American employment of black PSYOPS in Operation Iraqi Freedom, and provides the example of Radio Tikrit, officially run by loyal Iraqis but in reality managed by American forces. After an initial 'friendly' period, it became increasingly critical of Saddam Hussein. After talking about the 'successful' American PSYOPS, Collins concludes: 'Incorporating lessons learned from "*Iraqi Freedom*" into the ongoing restructuring of the NATO military organization offers a unique opportunity to strengthen NATO perception-management capabilities [...]' (Collins 2003).

One cannot be certain from the above that NATO has changed its official policy towards the use of black PSYOPS, but in the 2007 PSYOPS doctrine NATO continues to emphasize that all PSYOPS missions must be based on 'true information' (NATO 2007c: 21–22, as quoted in P. Ottosen 2010). This document provides the founding guidelines for Norwegian PSYOPS policies and strategies.[7] But it is worth noting that there seem to have been some discrepancies between the official policies regarding black and grey PSYOPS and possible strategies discussed in classified documents. Six months after Collins' speech in 2003, Norwegian media started questioning the development of the Norwegian PSYOPS policies; the reason was a classified document on the development of the Norwegian military, which was referred to as a 'general document' in a report published later and called 'Forsvarssjefens militærfaglige utredning 2003 – Militære informasjonsoperasjoner'. The most controversial section of this document was deleted from the part of official report that was made public, but the Norwegian newspaper *Klassekampen* gained access to one of the classified documents written by the Ministry of Defence, and wrote about it in its two-page story headlined 'Planlegger info-krig i skjul'/'Planning covert info-war'. Quoting the classified report, *Klassekampen* writes: 'In principle, all aspects of information operations can be executed or handled as a part of all types of operations' (Leer-Salvesen 2003). One cannot necessarily conclude that this includes the use of black PSYOPS, but in the quote, the Norwegian Ministry of Defence does emphasize that *all* aspects of operations regarding information can be employed. In addition, the official report defines the use of PSYOPS capacities in Norway as: 'The capacities must be able to support a broadest possible spectrum of operations, nationally as well as internationally' (Forsvarssjefen 2003: 4).

Norwegian PSYOPS in Afghanistan came to a halt by the end of 2009 when Norwegian PSYOPS soldiers were withdrawn following a government's decision to slash funding by 100 million Norwegian crowns ($18 million). The soldiers returned to Norway by the end of December 2009.[8] However, because the withdrawal is indefinite and caused by a financial cutback, there is little reason to believe that the withdrawal signals a change in the NAF's policy or strategies towards PSYOPS.

Responsibility and emphasis[9]

The Norwegian Chief of Defence (Forsvarssjefen) points to some uncertainty in both Europe and in the US with regard to the degree of political control over information operations (Forsvarssjefen 2003: 2). However, the same report is clear about which body is charged with administering the policy of Norwegian information operations: 'The Ministry of Defence is responsible for the staff and policy of military information operations' (2003:4). One can deduce from this that the Norwegian policy towards information operations, and thus also towards PSYOPS, is the responsibility of the head of the Ministry of Defence, meaning that Norwegian PSYOPS policy is defined at the highest level in the Norwegian government.

Having observed how PSYOPS have been developed and included in Norwegian military strategy, it is interesting to see the importance ascribed to these strategies by the NAF. Although it is not new to claim that information is gaining importance in modern warfare, it is important to understand *how* significant the NAF consider the role of information and PSYOPS to be. The 2007 Doctrine for Joint Operations leaves little doubt about this: 'In its last chapter, battle is decided in the cognitive domain' (Norwegian Armed Forces 2008: 70). This means that, according to the NAF, one needs to win the minds of the people to win the war. PSYOPS are an important contributor to the battle of the mind, and consequently should be implemented in military strategies to provide a successful outcome.

PSYOPS and the media

Captain Ola Bøe-Hansen, in an article in *Forsvarets Forum* (NAF's independent magazine) provides examples of how Norwegian troops have contributed to PSYOPS in Afghanistan (2007). According to Bøe-Hansen, the troops have, inter alia, been involved in the ISAF-produced newspaper, *Sada-e Azadi* ('Voice of Freedom') and a radio station with the same name (Bøe-Hansen 2007). The newspaper is the largest in Afghanistan, and the radio station broadcasts 24 hours a day.

In an interview in *Forsvarets Forum*, the editor of *Sada-e Azadi*, Dirk Christiansen, said that PSYOPS messages dominate the newspaper, but that regular news is also included. He also says that 'the magic of selling your message in this way is that the readers do not understand that it is PSYOPS. It has an effect as long as the public don't know about it' (Nygaard 2006). The former PSYOPS officer Lieutenant Colonel Svein Holtan was, in 2006, one of the executives of the international ISAF force in Kabul. Bøe-Hansen says that the role ISAF's media is not intended to serve as a watchdog, like normal media. It is to inform the Afghani population about ISAF's work, since NATO troops are there at the request of the Afghani government (Bøe-Hansen 2007). Bøe-Hansen's descriptions of the purpose of these operations correspond to statements given by the chief of psychological operations at the Norwegian camp in Maymaneh in Afghanistan, Knut Bjørn Andersen, in 2006. In an interview with *Dagsavisen*, Andersen says that the troops hand out radios so that the civilians can listen to *Sada-e Azadi*. In addition, they meet with local religious and political leaders. Asked whether these operations were meant to deceive the population, Andersen said: 'Yes, that can be a part of it'. He then mentions that such practices do go beyond 'normal marketing' (Hammer 2006).

Statements like these illustrate some of the problematic aspects of using media and PSYOPS in military operations. The intent behind the PSYOPS messages is seldom announced. It can therefore be difficult to separate between messages from normal media and those from PSYOPS media. The role of media in PSYOPS is explained in NATO's PSYOPS doctrine:

> Media for PSYOPS use are the approved means, technical or non-technical, which establish any kind of communication with a target audience. They can be used to supplement or replace direct interpersonal communication in cases where the audience is inaccessible, unreceptive or simply too large to be approached exclusively by interpersonal methods. (NATO 2007c: 65)

The doctrine also outlines the benefits of using radio broadcasting in PSYOPS. It describes radio stations as 'exceptionally well suited to the dissemination of PSYOPS products'. Among the benefits are its range, timeliness and 'speed that is rivalled only by TV' (NATO 2007c: 72).

PSYOPS in the Afghanistan strategy

PSYOPS operation was an integral part of the attacks on Afghanistan in October 2001. Air force planes dropped hundreds of thousands of leaflets over Afghanistan (Waller 2001). The leaflets, printed on flimsy, dollar-sized pieces of paper, were made by the Army's Fourth Psychological Operations Group based at Fort Bragg, NC. The leaflets had a fairly simple message – they showed an American soldier shaking hands with an Afghan in front of a mountain range. The message, 'The Partnership of Nations is here to Help', was in two languages: Dari on one side and Pashtu on the other.

A second set of leaflets amounts to a programming guide for radio PSYOPS. Printed on the guide were the times and frequencies when Afghans could tune in to receive radio broadcasts from Commando Solo. Commando Solo is a US Air Force special operations EC-130 plane flying near the Afghan border. A $70 million converted cargo aircraft, flown by the Pennsylvania Air National Guard, Commando Solo is an airborne RadioShack. The hardware allows the plane's eleven-member crew to jam a country's broadcasts, and to substitute, on any frequency, radio and TV messages intended to confuse, deceive or inform. The CIA supplied portable radios, dropped from the air or trucked into Afghanistan. Commando Solo's message was simple: 'We are here to take measures against terrorists who have rooted themselves in your country,' one broadcast began: 'It is not you, the honourable people of Afghanistan, who are targeted, but those who oppress you, seek to bend you to their will, and make you their slaves' (quoted from Waller 2001).

Norway versus US?

I will now turn to a discussion of the nature of American PSYOPS, and then compare Norwegian and American PSYOPS policies and strategies. The discussion will situate Norwegian PSYOPS within a comparative, international perspective.

The American 'Doctrine for Joint Psychological Operations' states that 'PSYOP are a vital part of the broad range of US diplomatic, informational, military, and economic activities' (Joint Chiefs of Staff 2003: ix). Hence, the Americans place great emphasis on PSYOPS as a part of their military strategies. And, as mentioned in the introduction, they invest large resources in developing PSYOPS strategies. Another relevant perspective is the use of black PSYOPS. In his discussion on American PSYOPS, Paul states that 'grey and black are in the PSYOP toolbox too' (Paul 2008: 65). He then presents what the US sees as advantages of employing black PSYOPS, among them the ability to make a target audience believe that the message originates from within their own country. This leads to increased credibility and the possibility of 'planting' dissident messages, lessening moral objections and the likelihood of real dissidents (2008: 66).

Examples of American PSYOPS

There are several examples of American black PSYOPS, especially with regard to Iraq war in 2003, code-named Operation Iraqi Freedom. Taylor argues that PSYOPS 'enjoyed an unusually high profile' during the war (Taylor 2003: 1). We have already mentioned the example of Radio Tikrit, an operation also discussed by Taylor. Another example from the 2003 Iraq war is the fall of the Saddam statue. On 9 April 2003, American forces took control of Baghdad. It was important to the Americans to show the world that the Iraqis welcomed them with open arms, and to produce this image, the American PSYOPS unit orchestrated the fall of the Saddam statue on Firdos Square (R. Ottosen 2009: 174–80). Images from this event were sent around the world, and have, in the aftermath, become the symbol of the defeat of Saddam Hussein and America's victory. Former President George W. Bush described it as a historical moment (2009: 174). But were the images of massive crowds of celebrating Iraqis, and a fallen statue, true images? Not entirely. The fact is that it was American troops who had torn down the statue, and the event was directed with a firm American hand. First an American soldier draped Saddam's head with an American flag. That interfered with the image the PSYOPS unit tried to create (that this was an Iraqi celebration), so the flag was soon replaced with an Iraqi flag. Then, there were actually rather few Iraqis in the streets that night. The 'crowds' reported were in fact merely 100 to 200 civilians according to an official report from the American PSYOPS unit (2009: 176). But the picture shot on the scene was taken from an angle which gave the impression that the square was packed. In addition, there is debate about whether those civilians were there voluntarily, or if they were a so-called 'rent-a-crowd' (ibid.). A lengthy article in *The New Yorker* went through the whole story behind the affair of the statue, and concluded that it was not planned in advance as a PSYOPS operation, but that the PSYOPS personnel arrived on the scene after the toppling had started, seized the opportunity when it occurred, and used it as a PSYOPS operation (Maas 2011). Based on the facts of the event, one can argue that this was a black PSYOPS. First, the source is misrepresented because the American PSYOPS unit tried to present it as an Iraqi-led celebration. Second, the information was false; the image of a couple of hundred Iraqis was manipulated, staged and managed for the world and the audiences to believe that Iraqis en masse were celebrating the overthrow of Saddam Hussein.

A third example of American PSYOPS is from Afghanistan. The operation was revealed by the Australian journalist Stephen Dupont, who was embedded with the 173rd Airborne Brigade of the US Army on 1 October 2005. The footage broadcast on the Australian TV channel SBS showed a US Army PSYOPS unit burning the bodies of two Taliban soldiers, and messages mocking villagers in Gonbaz situated near the former Taliban stronghold of Kandahar (Knight 2005). According to Dupont, the PSYOPS soldiers burned the bodies for reasons of hygiene, but used the incident to frighten the local population by giving the impression that they did it to desecrate the Taliban soldiers. Dupont was given a translation of the messages afterwards, and according to him, the soldiers announced: 'Taliban, you are all cowardly dogs. You allowed your fighters to be laid down facing the West and left behind to be burned' (ibid.). According to Islamic tradition, Muslims should not be cremated. Dupont told SBS that: 'They deliberately wanted to incite that much anger from the Taliban so the Taliban could attack them [...] that's the only way they can find them' (ibid.). This is not black PSYOPS because the source was true. But the message was false because, according to the American soldiers, they burned the bodies for reasons of hygiene, but gave the Taliban the impression that they did it to spite and threaten them. Even though this operation does not perfectly fit the definition of grey PSYOPS, it is somewhere between black and white, and I therefore argue that grey is the most appropriate label.

Norwegian PSYOPS in a comparative perspective

The US perspective is also interesting for an assessment of the direction Norwegian PSYOPS might take in the future. The US is in charge of Operation Enduring Freedom, in which PSYOPS units are free to employ the kind of information practices and operations they deem necessary and, as the discussion above makes clear, even if they involved black PSYOPS. At the same time, the US is engaged in the NATO-led International Security Assistance Force (ISAF). When these two forces operate in Afghanistan together, it is important to see the influence they exert on each other's strategies. This is how NATO envisages the relationship between the two organs: 'ISAF and Operation Enduring Freedom (OEF), the ongoing US-led military operation in Afghanistan, continue to have separate mandates and missions' (NATO 2007a). The quote leaves no doubt about the links between the two. Therefore, it is relevant to highlight this relationship because of the possible consequences it may have for the development of a more extreme Norwegian PSYOPS in the future, including both grey and black operations. In addition, the overlapping operations pose a problem for the Afghanis, as one cannot expect that they will be able to separate black from white PSYOPS (R. Ottosen 2009: 43). Again, this can create confusion and mistrust among the civilians.

ISAF's PSYOPS operation in the media: *Sada-e Azadi* magazine as case study

Sada-e Azadi has been published monthly in Dari, Pashto and English by ISAF in Afghanistan, and distributed by ISAF soldiers. It is also available online.[10] NATO/ISAF, as mentioned earlier in the article, also run a radio station with the same name.

Obviously NATO/ISAF have a need to provide information about their activities, but the point, as outlined in this chapter's research question, raises ethical dilemmas when military personnel are involved in propaganda activities in a format similar to journalism. Another ethical issue is whether PSYOPS operations looking like journalism can cause problems for real media and journalists in a future democratic society in Afghanistan. How can the people of Afghanistan respect the integrity of journalism when they experience the self-proclaimed defenders of democracy (like the ISAF forces) blurring the distinction between real, impartial journalism and propaganda?

Case study: *Sada-e Azadi* (issue 215)

Below, I will undertake a content analysis of issue 215 of *Sada-e Azadi* magazine (see the Appendix for a full overview). The magazine is published in two versions – one for the north and one for the other parts of the country (I will concentrate on the latter). The magazine was published in August 2010, one month before the parliamentary elections in Afghanistan, and the entire back page of the north edition features a photo of a drawing of a man casting his vote, with another man smiling and pointing a finger at the readers so as to urge them to vote.

On the front page there is an ISAF logo and the chief editor is identified as Major KC Busch. Despite this obvious military connection, the *Sada-e Azadi* magazine appears to be a newspaper with a mixture of information, political stories, religion, foreign news, culture and entertainment.

On the front page of the north issue there is a feature story on the fruit market entitled 'Summer: Fruit season'. Among other stories there is an informative article about Ramadan, the Muslim month of fasting. This Ramadan story is framed as propaganda:

> The Afghan government appreciates this month, and has declared the first day of this month a holiday. ISAF will also respect Ramadan time and all Afghan employers will be allowed to follow the special rules of Ramadan without restrictions. Furthermore, the personnel of ISAF are instructed to act in a respectful way concerning the important period of time. (*Sada-e Azadi* 2011: 3)

Using a critical discourse analytical approach, the combination of 'every day stories' on growing vegetables and a propagandistic story about the coming election creates connotations to the promise of a democratic future if the ISAF-supported Karzai is elected.

The propagandistic style is even more evident in the front page of the Kabul edition. One report is from the international Kabul conference on 20 July with the title, 'Karzai: Afghans will lead security by 2014'. Much of the article is quotes from the president and references to President Karzai's speech: 'President Karzai also addressed anti-corruption issues, pledging to strengthen the rule of law and government agencies that enforce it'. Nowhere in the article (or elsewhere in the magazine) is there mention of the harsh criticism from international media over the inability of Karzai to deal with security and corruption.

An article about the coming elections, under the title 'Parliamentary elections ready to be held Sept 18', provides detailed information about the elections, which is mostly framed in an optimistic fashion, despite the fact that after the presidential election of 2009, many observers warned against hold such elections in the future so long as allegations of fraud and corruption are not tackled properly. The United Nations, the US and election observation missions, including one representing the European Union, had asked the Afghani government to refrain from further elections until it had written a new election law and created a list of registered voters. No such criticism was reflected in the coverage by *Sada-e Azadi*. Such propagandistic and optimistic framing was in sharp contrast to the critical story that the *New York Times* published a few weeks following the elections:

> 'The president has lost his confidence in the capability of either the coalition or his own government to protect this country,' Mr Saleh said in an interview at his home. 'President Karzai has never announced that NATO will lose, but the way that he does not proudly own the campaign shows that he doesn't trust it is working.' People close to the president say he began to lose confidence in the Americans last summer, after national elections in which independent monitors determined that nearly one million ballots had been stolen on Mr Karzai's behalf. (Elkins 2010)

In another article in the Kabul edition, there is praise of the United States' financial aid: 'Farmers who need a little cash to get their next growing season started can now get help from the Afghan government, thanks to a $100 million grant from the United States'. *Sada-e Azadi* magazine also contains useful information on the illness 'typhus', educational stories and agricultural research, but the framing is propagandistic in favour of NATO/ISAF activities.

Conclusion: *Sada-e Azadi* magazine in light of Johan Galtung's model

The content of *Sada-e Azadi* magazine reflects the official view of NATO/ISAF, and lacks a critical journalistic perspective. The content has many similarities with the 'war journalism' in Galtung's model outlined above. It is a clear voice 'for us' (NATO/ISAF) and sees 'them' (the Taliban) as the only problem and source of violence. Peace journalism, according to Galtung, should give 'voices to all parties' (Galtung 2002). In his book *Drømmekrigen*, Anders Sømme Hammer, who covered Afghanistan as a journalist, provides evidence that NATO and Norwegian soldiers killed civilians in their hunt for the Taliban (Hammer 2010). To expose such stories one has to have a critical approach, to 'expose untruths' on all sides. In *Sada-e Azadi* magazine there is not one single comment critical of the Afghanistan president or the government. Not even a single word is mentioned of the need for negotiation or talks with the Taliban, while many journalists and independent media seem to believe a military victory for NATO/ISAF is impossible. This lack of focus on peace-makers is another indication in Galtung's model of war journalism. It is no surprise to find that *Sada-e Azadi* magazine, as a part of a PSYOPS operation, has all the signs of propaganda-oriented war journalism. The problem is that the thousands of people who receive this publication are not told that they are being subjected to PSYOPS when reading it. Through NATO/ISAF propaganda, the civilian population is promised a future democracy. A free press is an integral part of a democratic society. When a free press is replaced with MISO, we are left wondering whether any role is left to play for critical discourse in a civil society. And, most importantly, how can the people of Afghanistan gain confidence to the notion of impartial journalism when they are introduced to a perverted form of war journalism in the guise of a journalistic product?

References

American Department of Defense (2003), *Information Operations Roadmap*, 30 October.

Associated Press (2010), 'Psychological Operations are now Military Information Support Operations', *Army Times*, 3 July, http://www.armytimes.com/news/2010/07/ap_psy_ops_070210/. Accessed 10 July 2010.

Bøe-Hansen, O. (2007), 'En etisk utfordring?' (An ethical challenge), *Forsvarets Forum*, 30 April, http://www.fofo.no/En+etisk+utfordring%3F.b7C_wZrS3E.ips. Accessed 19 December 2011.

—— (2009), *Kampen om den uimotståelige historien (A battle for the irreristable history)*, Oslo: Norwegian Armed Forces, School of Staff.Collins, Steven (2003), 'Mind games', *NATO* website, 1 April, http://www.nato.int/cps/en/natolive/opinions_20499.htm?selectedLocale=en. Accessed 22 August 2010.

Cox, L. V. (1997), *Planning for Psychological Operations – A Proposal*, Montgomery AL: Air Command and Staff College (US).

Dimaggio, A. (2009), *When Media Goes to War: Hegemonic Discourse, Public Opinion, and the Limits of Dissent*, New York: Monthly Review Press.

Dinan, W. and Miller, D. (2007), *Thinker, Faker, Spinner, Spy: Corporate PR and the Assault on Democarcy*, London: Pluto Press.

Elkins, D. (2010), 'Karzai Is Said to Doubt West Can Defeat Taliban', *New York Times*, 12 June, p. A1.

Forsvarets overkommando (Head of Command Norwegian Defence Forces) (1998), *Forsvarssjefens direktiv 402-1 for psykologisk forsvar The Chief of defence´s directive)*, FO/O, 9 January.

—— (2000), *Forsvarets Fellesoperative Doktrine (The Norwegian Armed Forces Common Operative Doctrine)*. Doctrine, February 2000.

—— (2003), *Doctrine for Joint Psychological Operations (Joint Publication 3–53)*. Doctrine, September 5, 2003.

Forsvarssjefen (2003) (Chief of staff Norwegian Armed Forcerces), Forsvarets retning for Forsvarets framtidige utvikling (The direction of the future for Norwegian Armed Forces). Forsvaret.

National Joint Headquarters (2007), *Forsvarets Fellesoperative Doktrine. (The Norwegian Armed Forces Common Doctrine)* June 2007.

Forsvarets skole i etterretnings- og sikkerhetstjeneste (Norwegian Armed Forces School for Intelligence and Security) (2001), 'Psykologiske virkemidler i fred, krise og krig' (Psychological measures during peace, crisis and war), 24 October.

Forsvarssjefen (Chief of staff Norwegian Armed Forces) (2003), *Forsvarssjefens militærfaglige utredning - Militære informasjonsoperasjoner*, Sluttrapport (The Norwegian Armed Forces Military Study – Military information Operation. End-report).

Galtung, J. (2002), 'Peace Journalism – A Challenge', in Wilhelm Kempf and Heikki Loustarinen (eds), *Journalism and the New World Order, vol. 2: Studying the War and the Media*, Gothenburg: Nordicom.

Garbo, G. (2009), 'Selling Wars', in Birgit Brock-Utne and Gunnar Garbo (eds), *Language and Power: The Implications of Language for Peace and Development*, Dar es Salam: Mkuki na Nyota Publishers.

Gifford, C. (2006), *Espionage & Disinformation: The Unseen World*, Oxford: Heinemann.

Gjems-Onstad, E. (1994), *Psykologisk krigføring i Norge under anden verdenskrig 1940–45, (Psychological Operatons in Norway during the Second World War)*Oslo: ISTAR.

Golan, G. (2011), 'Political Public Relations and News Management', *International Communications Association*, Boston, MA, 26–30 July.

Hackett, R. A. (2006), 'Is peace journalism possible? Three frameworks for assessing structure and agency in news media', *Conflict & Communication*, 5: 2, http://www.cco.regener-online. de/2006_2/pdf/hackett.pdf. Accessed 15 January 2010.

Hammer, A. S. (2006), 'Smil og gaver skal sikre NATO-støtte' (Smile and gifts shall secure NATO-support), *Dagsavisen*, 28 September.

——— (2010), *Drømmekrigen (The Dream War)*, Oslo: Aschehoug forlag.

Joint Chiefs of Staff (2003), *Doctrine for Joint Psychological Operations (Joint Publication 3–53)*, 5 September.

Jowett, G. S. (1993), 'Toward a Propaganda Analysis of the Gulf War', in Bradley S. Greenberg and Walter Gantz (eds), *Desert Storm and the Mass Media*, New Jersey: Hampton Press.

Kaye, D. (1995), 'Are There Limits to Military Alliance? Presidential Power to Place American Troops Under Non-American Commanders', *Transnational Law & Contemporary Problems*, 5, pp. 400–47.

Knight, S. (2005), 'US Army Accused of Taliban Burning', *Times Online*, 20 October, http://www.timesonline.co.uk/tol/news/world/article580594.ece. Accessed 13 November 2009.

Leer-Salvesen, T. (2003), 'Planlegger info-krig i skjul' (Clandestine planning of information warfare), *Klassekampen*, 3 October.

Loyn D. (2007), 'Good journalism or peace journalism', *Conflict & Communication*, 6: 2, http://www.cco.regener-online.de/. Accessed 19 April 2010.

Lynch, J. (2007), 'Peace journalism and its discontents', *Conflict & Communication*, 6: 2, http://www.cco.regener-online.de/. Accessed 19 April 2010.

Maas, P. (2011), 'The Toppling: How the media inflated a minor moment in a long war', *The New Yorker*, 10 January.

Mazepa, P. (2011), 'Militarizing Communication? From Psychological Operations to the Whole of Government Approach, Canadian Examples', *'Mediating War and Technology'* An International Communication Association, Pre-Conference Organized by the Communication History Interest Group of the ICA, 26 May, ICA: Boston, MA.

McChesney, R. W. and Picard, W. (2011), *Will the last reporter please turn out the lights: The Collapse of journalism and what can be done to fix it*, New York: The New Press.

McChrystal, Stanley A. (2009), 'COMISAF's Initial Assesment', *Report*, 30 (August).

NATO (2007a), *Revised operational plan for NATO's expanded mission in Afghanistan*, 18 May.

NATO, July 4, 2007b. (http://www.nato.int/issues/afghanistan_stage3/index.html). Accessed 18 October 2010.

NATO (2007c), *Allied Joint Doctrine for Psychological Operations AJP-3.10.1(A)*, 22 October.

Nohrstedt, S. A. (2009), 'New War Journalism: Trends and Challenges', *Nordicom review*, 1, pp. 95–112.

Nohrstedt S. A. and Ottosen, R., (2008), 'Brothers in arms or peace? The media images of Swedish and Norwegian defence and military policy', *Conflict & Communication*, 7: 2, http://www.cco.regener-online.de/. Accessed 20 July 2010.

Norwegian Armed Forces (2008), *De norske avdelingene i Afghanistan*, (The Norwegian units in Afghanistan) http://www.mil.no/fol/afg/start/styrken/. Accessed 3 November 2010.

Norges Offentlige Utredninger (2007), *Et styrket forsvar (A strengthend defence force)* , NOU 2007:15, Oslo: Grafisk AS.

United States Special Operations Command (2009), *Fiscal Year 2010 Budget Estimates*, May, USSOCOM.

Nygaard, K. (2006), 'Propagandasoldatene' (The propaganda soldier), *Forsvarets Forum*, 20 November, http://www.fofo.no/Propagandasoldatene.b7C_wZjGXh.ips. Accessed 20 March 2010.

Ottosen, R. (2009), *VG, Saddam og vi*, (VG, Saddam and us) Kristiansand: IJ/Høyskoleforlaget.

—— (2010), 'The War in Afghanistan and peace journalism in practice', *Media, War & Conflict*, 3: 3, pp. 178–261.

Ottosen, P. (2010), 'PSYOPS and Norwegian Armed Forces', unpublished working paper.

Paul, C. (2008), *Information Operations: Doctrine and practice. A reference handbook*, Westport: Praeger Security International.

Scott, P. D. (2010), *American War Machine: Deep Politics, the CIA, Global Drug Connection and the Road to Afghanistan*, New York: Rowman & Littlefield.

Small Wars Journal (2010), 'MISO: Is it Soup Yet?', *Small Wars Journal*, 23 June, http://smallwarsjournal.com/blog/2010/06/miso-is-it-soup-yet/. Accessed 22 June 2011.

Taylor, P. (2003), *Psychological Operations in Operation Iraqi Freedom 2003*, Leeds: University of Leeds.

The Upshot (2009), 'Army embeds active-duty PSYOPS soldiers at local TV stations', *The Upshot*, http://randysright.wordpress.com/2010/10/03/alert-army-embeds-active-duty-psyops-soldiers-at-local-tv-stations-including-wral-in-nc/. Accessed 21 October 2011.

Waller, D. (2001), 'Opening Up the Psyops War', *Time*, 16 October.

Wodak, R. (1996), *Disorders of Discourse*, London: Longman.

Appendix

Full content of *Sada-e Azadi* magazine (no. 215) (2011)
Karzai: Afghans will lead security by 2014 (p. 1)
Planting made easier: programme gets loans for farmers (p. 2)
Insight (information about the banning of trade and use of ammonium nitrate (p. 2)
Parliamentary elections ready to be held Sept 18 (p. 3)
Kabul conference (p. 4)
Historic deal to boost exports (p. 4)
International news: A big date in Cambodian history (p. 5)
Impressions: Readers' children (p. 6) (pictures of children sent in by readers)
The merchant and the broken ship (p.7) (humour)
Public health message Typhus (p. 8)
Poetry page (p. 9)
Ask Baba Jan – *Sada-e Azadi*'s advice page (p. 10)
Star Profile: Laughter and joy (p. 11) (celebrity page)
Information: how to behave at road block/check point (p. 12)

Full content of *Sada-e Azadi* magazine North edition (no. 215) (2011)
Summer: Fruit season (p. 1–2)
The holy month of Ramadan (p. 3)

Saffron: Afghan red gold (p. 4)
A farm for agricultural research (p. 5)
A strong Afghan woman: Shukria Asil (p. 6)
Whatever harms a human being is Haran (p. 7)
Helicopter support (p.7)

Notes

1 An earlier version of this paper was presented to IAMCR in Istanbul, 12–17 July 2011. Many thanks to my research assistant, Peder Ottosen, for valuable help with research, interviews and analysis.
2 NATO is in Afghanistan as a part of the Bonn Agreement of 5 December 2001. On 20 December 2001, the UN Security Council approved the first resolution authorizing the International Security Assistance Force (ISAF).
3 The author is responsible for all translations from Norwegian to English.
4 The SFOR (Stabilization Force) replaced the IFOR force from 20 December 1996. The KFOR (Kosovo Force) was established in June 1999.
5 Information provided by former PSYOPS officer who spoke on condition of anonymity
6 The source for these facts is a Power Point presentation by the Norwegian Armed Forces to instruct PSYOPS personnel made available to the author.
7 Interview on telephone with Lieutenant Colonel Geir H. Karlsen, 18 November 2009.
8 Interview on telephone with Eli Therese Schjenken, 1 December 2009.
9 The sections on this page are substantially based on P. Ottosen (2010).
10 http://sada-e-zadi.net/Joomla/index.php/en/media.

Chapter 4

A strategic ritual for all?

Morten Skovsgaard

M ost debates on journalism revolve around objectivity. Whether they deal with politically slanted news, stereotyping or negativity bias, the underlying normative standard is objectivity. The norm is central in nearly any account of the journalistic profession (cf. Deuze 2005; Tumber & Prentoulis 2005), and has been called the defining norm of modern journalism (Patterson 1998: 28) and the key legitimating professional ethics of liberal journalism (McNair 1998: 65). In these accounts of journalism, objectivity stands as a common beacon for a unified profession. The argument is based on the notion of journalism as a public service, and the ideal that journalists should provide audiences with the information they need to be free and self-governing (cf. Kovach & Rosenstiel 2001). In this sense, objectivity is closely connected to the central role of journalism in a well-functioning democracy.

However, the norm might not be as uniform as these accounts suggest. People turn to journalism for different reasons, and journalists also provide people with entertainment, relaxation and amusement with no higher democratic purpose. This challenges a one-size-fits-all idea of professional ideals in journalism; or, put another way, different types of journalists may very well assign different significance to the objectivity norm. In fact, studies have shown differences between journalists across countries and with different role perceptions (Donsbach & Klett 1993; Skovsgaard et al. 2012a).

Tuchman describes objectivity as a strategic ritual that stands as a bulwark between journalists and their critics, and that when attacked journalists 'invoke their objectivity almost the way a Mediterranean peasant might wear a clove of garlic around his neck to ward off evil spirits' (1972: 660). In this manner, McQuail believes that objectivity serves an important function for journalists, since media audiences in general 'appear to understand the principle of objective performance well enough, and its practice helps to increase public credence and trust both in the information and also in the opinions which the media offer' (2005: 201).

If the objectivity norm serves to create trustworthiness and to shield journalists from critique, the 'strategic ritual' may not be equally important to all journalists. The dominant position of objectivity in journalism emerged after the decline of the partisan press, and is thus also closely linked to impartiality, which will be discussed later in this chapter (cf. Chalaby 1998; Kaplan 2006). Consequently, debates about biased journalism are often focused on political bias in news (cf. D'Alessio & Allen 2000; Lee 2008; Hopmann, van Aelst & Legnante 2012). Based on this, I argue that journalists covering topics, which are often politicized (hard news), emphasize objectivity more than journalists covering less politicized topics such as entertainment, culture and sports (soft news). I also argue that they are more inclined to believe that objectivity creates trustworthiness for their product than journalists covering less politicized topics.

The chapter draws on a large-scale representative survey of Danish journalists, which included a number of questions on objectivity. In Denmark, the press was generally separated from political parties through the first part of the twentieth century, and journalism was professionalized. In the process, the objectivity norm emerged and grew strong, and it still receives strong support from Danish journalists (Skovsgaard et al. 2012a). In this sense, journalists in Denmark are quite similar to journalists in other western countries. Donsbach and Klett (1993) show that the objectivity norm in general appears to be important among journalists across countries belonging to the three different types of media systems described by Hallin and Mancini (2004). This makes Denmark a suitable case to examine whether journalists who produce different types of journalism show different support for the objectivity norm. It also means that the results of this study are relevant beyond the Danish borders. Especially, it can be expected that the results provide general insights into the objectivity norm in western-type democracies where objectivity plays a central role in journalism.

The chapter proceeds as follows: first, objectivity as a journalistic norm is presented and two aspects of objectivity are outlined; next, the argument is made that journalists working with hard news and soft news respectively assign different significance to the two aspects of objectivity in their work; then the survey of the population of Danish journalists (N=2008) is described, and subsequently, the results are presented and discussed.

Objectivity and impartiality in journalism

As the press in most countries gradually separated from the political parties and journalism professionalized, the objectivity norm became 'the defining norm of modern journalism' (Patterson 1998). As opposed to the time of the partisan press when news was openly slanted, the news should now command its legitimacy not from being slanted or biased, but rather from independent factual accounts of the world as it is (Chalaby 1998). This also implies that facts and opinion can be separated, and that news can be reported exclusively by means of facts.

Just as positivism was heavily challenged within the philosophy of science throughout the twentieth century, the same happened to the notion of objectivity in journalism, which fed on the same notion of value-free accounts of an independently existing reality. The objectivity norm has been criticized for being unrealistic and impossible to realize, since news is a construction of reality rather than a description of reality (cf. Tuchman 1978; Merrill 1984; Poerkson 2008).

It is the general understanding that a one-to-one representation of reality is not possible, and the inevitable consequence is that objectivity needs to be defined in terms other than as a depiction of the world as it is. Because the objectivity norm emerged along with the decline of the partisan press, it has come to be tightly connected to impartiality. An important quality of the objectivity norm is that journalists aim to give accounts of reality from a detached and impartial standpoint rather than a distinct political or ideological standpoint (cf. Chalaby 1998).

To some, this means that objectivity and impartiality can be used interchangeably, while others contend that concepts like factuality, relevance and completeness should be included under the umbrella of objectivity along with impartiality (cf. Westerståhl 1983; Chalaby 1998; Vos 2012). As such, impartiality is seen as a necessary, but insufficient, condition for objectivity.

In this chapter, objectivity is understood as an umbrella concept containing impartiality – the same as in Westerståhl's model of objectivity. In any case, impartiality and neutrality are important components in most journalists' professional ideals, and have also been at the centre of some critique of the objectivity norm both from within and from outside the profession.

Critics contend that the impartial standpoint leads to a detachment of journalists. They criticize the detachment for being undesirable, since it leads to disinterested journalism which does not engage citizens in important democratic debates (cf. Merritt 1995; Glasser 1999; Voakes 1999). Despite the challenges, debates and the ongoing controversy, objectivity has to a large degree held its ground. It is an important element of journalists' professional ideology (e.g. Deuze 2005; Tumber & Prentoulis 2005). Debates are often based on the assumption of objectivity as a yardstick for 'correct' journalism, and journalists show substantial support for the norm, even if some claim that it is at odds with other professional ideals such as the watchdog role and the role of mobilizing public debate in democracy (Skovsgaard et al. 2012a). With the objectivity norm in hand, journalists claim to give valid and true descriptions and explanations of the world (Donsbach & Klett 1993). As McNair puts it: 'Journalism is presented to its audience as a truthful discourse about the real world and it must command legitimacy on these terms or it is without value in the cultural marketplace' (1998: 65). Thus, despite the debate and the criticism, adhering to an objectivity norm is a means of achieving trustworthiness both for journalists themselves and for their journalistic products (McQuail 2005: 201).

Objectivity as attitude and method

Journalists do not have blind faith in their ability to represent reality on a one-to-one basis. On the contrary, they reject such a naïve notion of objectivity (Mindich 1998; Skovsgaard et al. 2012b). Fierce debates within the scientific community show that objectivity is a complex concept – both in theory and practice. However complex it is to handle, newsmen are 'men of action' (Tuchman 1972), who must make immediate decisions on validity, reliability and 'truth', and who do not have time for reflexive epistemological examination. She concludes that journalists must have some working notion of objectivity. This means that they must operationalize the norm to be able to handle it in their daily practice.

Though several scholars have embarked on dissecting the ambiguous concept to clarify how journalists operationalize objectivity, there is widespread agreement that no easy definition of objectivity presents itself (cf. Westerståhl 1983; Chalaby 1998; McNair 1998). However, there are two main ways that journalists operationalize objectivity. One is through a certain attitude of neutrality, which means that journalists should not be connected to any special interests, but rather be detached and disinterested. A second is through a particular form of media practice or journalistic methods (McQuail 2005: 200; Hackett 2008).

First, the attitude of detachment and neutrality serves to convince audiences that journalists maintain impartiality, have no ulterior motive and provide no service to a third party (Hackett 2008; for a discussion of a similar impartiality in the judicial system, see Chapter 1). This means that in many countries, and at many news organizations, it is not *comme-il-faut* to be members of political parties or express political views in public (Reese 1990).

An interesting example occurred in Denmark when former Social Democratic minister Lotte Bundsgaard decided to retire from politics to study journalism. She terminated her long-term membership of the Social Democrats. Her only comment was that as a journalist she should not flaunt her membership of an organization. The head of the journalism education at the University of Southern Denmark at the time, Troels Mylenberg, said, 'She shows that she wants to be a journalist neck and crop, and that she takes her new profession so seriously that she will go to great lengths to avoid potential conflicts of interests' (Andersen 2008).

A similar point has been made in connection with journalists who return to positions as news journalists or editors after stints as political communication advisers. The editor-in-chief of the Danish newspaper *Jyllands-Posten*, Jørn Mikkelsen, says, 'It is a severely slippery slope. Without blinking an eye you dismiss important and precious principles. Of course it has a cost in terms of credibility and integrity [...]' (Malacinski 2010). This shows that the concern is not that these journalists cannot do their jobs in an acceptable manner, but rather that they have compromised their neutrality and independence in the view of the audience. Therefore, one important way to operationalize the objectivity norm is by signalling impartiality and neutrality.

Second, Schudson (2001) points out that objectivity is at once a moral ideal and a set of reporting and editing practices. The reporting practices function as tools that constitute practical ways of dealing with the objectivity claim in the journalistic production process.

As the world cannot be described one-to-one, journalists need standards to convince their audience that they give an accurate account of the world. One tool is based on the idea that facts can be separated from opinion and the news is based on facts verified with reference to authoritative sources (McNair 1998; Schudson 2001; Harcup 2009). Jean Chalaby (1998) calls journalism a fact-based discourse, and the media usually support this by making clear distinctions between commentary or opinion pieces and news items. But the idea of separating facts from opinion is also evident in the individual news story. Views or opinions are assigned to named (or in special cases anonymous) sources, and marked by quotation marks so that it is clear that they are not the journalist's (Tuchman 1972). Verifying facts by attributing them to sources is an important part of claiming objectivity (cf. Meyer 1987: 50–51; McQuail 2005; Harcup 2009: 90–91).

But as facts do not speak for themselves, and not all 'facts' can be verified, another important tool for journalists to meet objectivity standards is to generate balance in news reports (cf. Westerståhl 1983; McQuail 2005). This means that conflicting views or possibilities are presented in a news story (cf. Tuchman 1972; Meyer 1987; Harcup 2009), and that 'the views of legitimate spokespersons of the conflicting sides' are presented 'with roughly equivalent attention' (Entman 1989: 30; see Chapter 10 for a critical discussion of this point). Political bias is often measured as imbalance in the proportion of coverage that political actors get (Hopmann, Van Aelst & Legnante 2012), the implicit or explicit premise being that balance is a normative standard that should be met. This is a practical tool for implementing neutrality, and thus objectivity, in the daily journalistic practice. Surveys do indeed confirm substantial support for balance as a norm among journalists, who find it important to include the conflicting perspectives in a dispute (Tsfati, Meyers & Peri 2006; Skovsgaard et al. 2012a). This notion that 'we have presented all sides of the story without choosing sides' logic is also what Tuchman sees as a defence mechanism against accusations of bias (1972). In sum, journalists see objectivity as a means to achieve trustworthiness, and they operationalize it both as an attitude and a reporting tool, which is based on factuality and balance in the journalistic products.

Uniform objectivity?

When objectivity is called the defining norm of modern journalism (Patterson 1998: 28) and the key legitimating professional ethics of liberal journalism (McNair 1998: 65), it leaves an impression that objectivity is a uniform journalistic norm shared and worshipped across the board (Cook 1998). However, accounts of the professional ideology of journalists point out that journalists' professional ideals are not carved in stone, but vary among journalists and over time (Deuze 2005). Empirical studies show that journalists' support for, and understanding of, the objectivity norm vary across countries (Donsbach & Klett 1993) and among journalists with different role perceptions (Skovsgaard et al. 2012a).

To understand how support for the norm might vary, it is important to understand that objectivity developed as an antidote to the political parallelism between parties and newspapers when the partisan press dominated the media scene in the nineteenth and early twentieth centuries (Hallin & Mancini 2004). As the newspapers became increasingly detached from the political parties, the objectivity norm steadily became the beacon of the emerging journalistic profession in response to the former dependence on political criteria for writing journalistic stories (cf. Chalaby 1998; Kaplan 2006). Although the increased detachment of the press and the political parties has not occurred at the same pace in all democratic countries, and in some less than in others, it has been a general development witnessed by most western democracies (cf. Hallin & Mancini 2004).

Thus, the objectivity norm is originally connected to the coverage of politics, and has been seen as a way for the press to gain new credibility after its separation from political parties (Chalaby 1998; Kaplan 2006). This also implies that all journalists might not, to the same extent, need this bulwark against critics or the credibility flowing from the adherence to objectivity. Obviously, journalism is diverse and some news is more connected to the political sphere than other news; not all journalists convey information of paramount importance to the well-being of democracy. Journalism is also produced and consumed as entertainment and relaxation, such as when journalists write about fashion, sports, music or gossip about celebrities. Journalists producing this kind of content are less likely to be exposed to criticism for being biased or partial.

The debates on bias in journalism usually revolve around whether distinct parties, politicians or political ideas are given preferential treatment to others in the news (cf. D'Alessio & Allen 2000; Lee 2008; Hopmann, Van Aelst & Legnante 2012). In one recent example from Denmark, journalists were criticized for one-sided and biased coverage of a proposal to tax motorists entering or leaving Copenhagen in order to reduce traffic and congestion in the capital (Meilstrup 2012).

This type of criticism is regularly levelled at journalists, and therefore journalists who cover this kind of topics, which are often politicized, have a clearer incentive to utilize objectivity as a strategic ritual to shield themselves from attacks. In light of this argument, it can be expected that these journalists are more inclined to believe that objectivity bestows trustworthiness on their output than journalists covering less politicized topics, such as entertainment, culture and sports. It would also mean that journalists covering politics, or topics that are often politicized, are more inclined to endorse a strict attitude of neutrality, and to support an operationalization of objectivity through the reporting of facts and balancing of accounts than is the case for other journalists.

To thoroughly explore whether these expectations hold true, it is important to highlight two distinctions: first, a distinction between journalists covering hard news and soft news; and second, a distinction between journalists who consider themselves to be news journalists and those who do not. These two distinctions put the expectations to a harder test, since hard news journalists cover politicized topics more often than soft news journalists, and since news journalists can be expected to cover politicized topics more often than non-news journalists. If the expectations are found to be true both for hard versus soft news journalists and news versus non-news journalists, the result buttresses the consistency of the argument above.

Methods

Data collection

The analysis draws on a large-scale survey of Danish journalists. The survey was conducted in cooperation with the Danish Union of Journalists (Dansk Journalistforbund). Members working with editorial journalism (excluding, for instance, journalists working in PR and unemployed journalists) were extracted from the union's member records by choosing relevant media categories, e.g. magazines, daily newspapers, radio/TV and the web. The union estimates that more than 90 per cent of this type of journalist in Denmark is a member, and the membership records provided the opportunity to reach almost the entire population.

An invitation was circulated to all these journalists by e-mail. They received a link to the questionnaire, which was to be filled out on a website. Journalists were assumed to use e-mail and the Internet as tools in their daily work, so a web-based survey should not affect the response rate negatively.

The questionnaire was sent via e-mail to 5519 potential respondents. Of these, 327 turned out not to belong to the population and 664 e-mails were not delivered correctly and thus never reached the intended respondent. Of the 5519 potential respondents, 2008 filled in the questionnaire resulting in a response rate of 44.3 per cent of the total population – a sound result compared to similar surveys in other countries (Weaver & Willnat 2012).

The union had information on variables such as gender, age, place of residence and media type. This made it possible to compare respondents and non-respondents. The analysis shows that the two groups are largely similar. The proportion of women is a bit larger among the respondents than among the non-respondents. However, in the sample women are overrepresented only by three percentage points in comparison to the population (for more information and details about the survey, see Skovsgaard 2010).

Variables

To distinguish between news journalists and non-news journalists, respondents were asked: 'Would you say that you work with news journalism?' They were allowed to answer either 'yes', 'no' or 'don't know'. The variable was recoded into a dummy by adding the mere 39 respondents who answered 'don't know' to the 'no' category (N = 2005, news journalists = 70.8%; non-news journalists = 29.2%).

The dummy for hard news/soft news journalists was constructed drawing on a battery of questions concerning which issues they cover in their work. On a seven point scale from 0 ('not at all') to 6 ('exclusively'), they were asked to state how much they covered these different topics: national politics, local politics, foreign affairs, business, crime, culture, entertainment, sports, 'life style'.

The dummy variable was then created by including the journalists who scored above the midpoint of the scale on national politics, local politics, foreign affairs or business in the hard news category. The journalists scoring above the midpoint of the scale on culture, entertainment, sports and 'life style' were included in the soft news category. The rest of the respondents were considered missing values, thus ending up with a dummy (N = 1569, hard news journalists = 50.7%, soft news journalists = 49.3%). There is an ongoing debate on the definition of hard news versus soft news, and as Reinemann et al. (2012) point out, there is no uniform definition available in the literature. The concept has been defined by means of several dimensions, including topic, news focus and news style, etc. Topic is the most frequently recurring dimension utilized to define both news types, and since this study does not look at content, but rather journalists and their ideals, it seems justified to define the distinction between hard news and soft news in terms of topic (for a similar operationalization, see Curran et al. 2009).

Findings

Journalists show substantial support for the objectivity norm when asked (cf. Donsbach & Klett 1993; Skovsgaard et al. 2012a). This general support is explored further in Table 1.

Table 1 shows three things. First, journalists generally 'admit' that making choices in the production of journalism means that the product cannot be objective. Presented with the statement 'Selection in journalistic work means that journalistic products can never be objective', 77.8% of the respondents answered 'agree to some extent', and more than half 'agree' or 'very much agree'. On a scale ranging from 0 to 6 indicating the level of agreement with the statement, the mean score is 4.31. Second, despite the constraints of selection on their work, journalists still believe objectivity is attainable when they produce journalism. Presented with the statement 'Journalistic methods can ensure a high degree of objectivity', 85.7% of the respondents answered 'agree to some extent', and six in ten 'agree' or 'very much agree'. The mean score for the level of agreement with the statement is 4.52. Third, it shows that journalists generally believe that pursuing objectivity gives their products trustworthiness. Presented with the statement 'Striving for objectivity means that citizens can trust the journalistic product', 81.6% 'agree to some extent', and more than six in ten either 'very much agree' or 'agree'. The mean score for agreement is 4.46.

The results show that journalists generally support the objectivity norm and believe that it generates trustworthiness, though they also have reservations in terms of the possibility of achieving a high degree of objectivity. This only tells us what journalists think of the objectivity norm and not how they handle it. The question is addressed in Table 2, where questions related to the way they deal with objectivity as a notion in their daily work were raised. For instance, the respondents were asked to indicate how much they agreed or disagreed with different notions of objectivity as practice. The results in the factor analysis clearly show two dimensions.[1]

One dimension has to do with applying certain methods in the journalistic production. It is measured through the statements: 'Good journalism represents all sides in a dispute

Table 1: Mean scores on statements about objectivity

	Mean*	SD	% who agrees or very much agrees**	N
Selection in journalistic work means that journalistic products can never be objective	4.31	1.53	53.0	1839
Journalistic methods can ensure a high degree of objectivity	4.52	1.13	60.8	1840
Striving for objectivity means that citizens can trust the journalistic product	4.46	1.21	60.6	1838

* On a seven-point scale ranging from 0 ('very much') disagree to 6 ('very much agree')
** The two highest answering categories

Table 2: Factor analysis of objectivity items

	Component 1*	Component 2**
Good journalism represents all sides in a dispute fairly		.773
Good journalism requires equally thorough questioning of all sides of a dispute		.830
Good journalism goes beyond the statements of the disputing sides in a dispute and gets to the concrete facts in the dispute		.767
Journalists should abstain from being members of political parties	.857	
Journalists should abstain from expressing political beliefs in public	.822	
Journalists should abstain from being members of associations which they cover	.737	

Varimax rotated
* Eigenvalue: 2.39
** Eigenvalue: 1.50

fairly'; 'Good journalism requires equally thorough questioning of all sides of a dispute'; and 'Good journalism goes beyond the statements of the conflicting sides in a dispute and gets to the concrete facts in the dispute'. This is combined into a scale (alpha = .72) that taps the extent to which journalists operationalize objectivity by means of journalistic methods.

The other dimension has to do with the attitude of neutrality and detachment. It is measured by the statements: 'Journalists should abstain from being members of political parties'; 'Journalists should abstain from expressing political beliefs in public'; and 'Journalists should abstain from being members of associations which they cover'. This is combined into a scale that taps the extent to which journalists operationalize objectivity through an attitude of neutrality (alpha = .74).

This means that two indexes can be created by adding up answers on the three variables respectively and dividing them by three. Respondents answered on a seven point scale ranging from 0 ('very much disagree') to 6 ('very much agree'). The index scores thus indicate how much a respondent supports the two distinct operationalizations of objectivity, which makes it possible to compare support for the two.

The results show that journalists support both ways of operationalizing objectivity, but they also show that journalists clearly support the journalistic methods as a way of acquiring objectivity more than they support neutrality and detachment as attitudes (see Table 3). On a scale from 0 ('minimum support') to 6 ('maximum support'), the mean score for journalistic methods is 5.2, whereas the mean score for the attitude of neutrality and detachment is 4.0 (see Table 3). Furthermore, the standard deviation is substantially lower for the journalistic methods than for the attitude of neutrality and detachment, which means that support for the methods is much more unified than support for the attitude. Though journalists in

Table 3:   Mean scores on means for operationalizing objectivity

	Mean*	SD	N
Objectivity through journalistic methods	5.20**	.85	1832
Objectivity through an attitude of neutrality and detachment	3.98**	1.51	1853

*On a seven-point scale ranging from 0 ('minimum support') to 6 ('maximum support')
** The difference between the mean scores is statistically significant at the .001 level

general find it somewhat important to take off the cape of subjectivity by abstaining from public political statements and membership of parties or associations, they are much more inclined to show unified support for distinct journalistic practices to ensure objectivity. This supports the results in Table 1 indicating that journalists believe that journalistic methods can ensure a high degree of objectivity and that objectivity creates trustworthiness.

The next step is to study whether the objectivity norm receives different levels of support from different types of journalists. To achieve this aim, the support for objectivity through methods and through attitudes, as well as to which extent objectivity creates trustworthiness, are compared between hard news journalists and soft news journalists respectively, and news journalists and non-news journalists respectively.

The results in Table 4 show that there generally are statistically significant differences between the different groups. As expected, hard news journalists perceive the objectivity norm as a source of trustworthiness to a higher extent than soft news journalists. They also show more support for the attitude of neutrality and detachment. Both results are statistically significant. This indicates that signalling a neutral and objective standpoint to create trustworthiness is important to the journalists who are most likely to end up in the line of fire from critics. Hard news journalists only show slightly more support for objectivity through journalistic methods than soft news journalists. The difference is not statistically

Table 4:   Comparison of the support for distinct operationalizations of objectivity and the trustworthiness through objectivity for different groups of journalists

	Objectivity through journalistic methods[1]	Objectivity through attitude of neutrality[1]	Trustworthiness through objectivity[2]	Lowest N
Hard news journalists	5.23	4.10***	4.60***	732
Soft news journalists	5.18	3.84***	4.34***	697
News journalists	5.24**	4.12***	4.56***	1299
Non-news journalists	5.10**	3.65***	4.23***	531

1) Mean scores on a scale ranging from 0 ('minimum support') to 6 ('maximum support')
2) Mean score on a scale ranging from 0 ('minimum agreement') to 6 ('maximum agreement')
** Statistically significant at the .01 level
*** Statistically significant at the .001 level

significant, indicating that different types of journalists do agree that objectivity should be obtained through journalistic methods.

When it comes to news journalists compared to non-news journalists, the results are as expected – all statistically significant. This means that news journalists more than non-news journalists believe that the objectivity norm creates trustworthiness for the journalistic product, and they support the journalistic method s for obtaining objectivity and the attitude of neutrality and detachment more than non-news journalists.

To control that the substantial differences between hard news and soft news journalists, as well as between news and non-news journalists, are not caused by other factors, regression analyses are presented in Tables 5 and 6. Here the gender and the experience of the journalists,

Table 5: The effect of 'hard news' journalists vs. 'soft news' journalists on the perception of objectivity – OLS regressions unstandardized coefficients

	Objectivity through journalistic methods[1]	Objectivity through attitude of neutrality[1]	Trustworthiness through objectivity[2]
Constant	3.525***	.2798***	3.136***
Gender (Male=1)	–.118**	–.128	0.051
Journalistic experience (in years)	.002	–.004	.003
Role perceptions:			
Passive mirror	.196***	.278***	.213***
Watchdog	.440***	.408***	.354***
Public forum	.093*	–.105*	.024
Public mobilizer	.000	–.017	–.011
Type of organization (ref. radio)			
Daily newspaper	.137	.332	–.070
Tabloid newspaper	–.216	.054	–.512*
Television	.025	.160	–.066
Web	.113	–.070	.116
Freelance	.027	–.340	–.374**
Other	.085	–.178	–.262
Hard news journalists (ref. soft news journalists)	–.012	.212**	.201**
Adjusted R^2	.132	.066	.065
N	1373	1360	1364

1) Mean scores on a scale ranging from 0 ('minimum support') to 6 ('maximum support')
2) Mean score on a scale ranging from 0 ('minimum agreement') to 6 ('maximum agreement')
* Statistically significant at the .05 level
** Statistically significant at the .01 level
*** Statistically significant at the .001 level

Table 6: The effect of 'news' journalists vs. 'non news'-journalists on the perception of objectivity – OLS regressions unstandardized coefficients

	Objectivity through journalistic methods[1]	Objectivity through attitude of neutrality[1]	Trustworthiness through objectivity[2]
Constant	3.389***	.2798***	3.043***
Gender (Male=1)	–.167***	–.125	0.031
Journalistic experience (in years)	.003**	–.001	.003
Role perceptions:			
Passive mirror	.175***	.280***	.224***
Watchdog	.453***	.384***	.396***
Public forum	.114***	–.147*	.008
Public mobilizer	–.016	–.045	–.027
Type of organization (ref. radio)			
Daily newspaper	.113	.258	–.100
Tabloid newspaper	–.295*	.053	–.711***
Television	.079	.127	–.065
Web	.099	–.162	.010
Freelance	.063	–.336*	–.304*
Other	.125	–.220	–.298*
News journalists (ref. non-news journalists)	.153***	.257**	.234***
Adjusted R^2	.149	.070	.073
N	1760	1743	1745

1) Mean scores on a scale ranging from 0 ('minimum support') to 6 ('maximum support')
2) Mean score on a scale ranging from 0 ('minimum agreement') to 6 ('maximum agreement')
* Statistically significant at the .05 level
** Statistically significant at the .01 level
*** Statistically significant at the .001 level

as well as the type of news organization, are entered as control variables. Journalists' role perceptions have been shown to influence their perception and implementation of the objectivity norm (Skovsgaard et al. 2012a), and these are included as controls as well to see if the distinctions between hard news and soft news journalists, as well as between news and non-news journalists, have an independent effect.

The regression analyses show that the results are statistically significant after controlling for these other factors. This supports the argument that different types of journalists perceive and handle objectivity differently.

Discussion

Objectivity is continuously disputed – be it the failure of journalists to live up to the ideal (cf. D'Alessio & Allen 2000), the impossibility of meeting the standards set by the ideal (cf. Merrill 1984; Poerkson 2008), or the undesirability of the ideal (cf. Glasser 1984; Stoker 1995). By studying the objectivity norm by means of a large-scale survey, this chapter adds to the understanding of how journalists themselves think about the objectivity norm and how they handle it in their daily practice. It shows that journalists are not in denial about the impossibility of describing the world on a one-to-one basis and the difficulties of handling the objectivity norm that follows from that (see Chapter 10 for a discussion of these difficulties). In this sense, it might be argued that critics who claim that journalists are entirely naïve in their approach to the objectivity norm are erecting a straw man for an easy tear-down. However, the results also show that journalists in general do believe that a high degree of objectivity can be obtained through journalistic methods, and that journalists believe that aiming to be objective creates trustworthiness for the journalistic product. This tells a story of a somewhat ambiguous relationship with the objectivity norm that in any case remains a treasured ideal of the journalistic profession.

The results also demonstrate two ways that journalists handle the objectivity norm in their daily practice. One is to maintain an attitude of neutrality; the other to follow certain journalistic methods that secure accounts that are balanced and contains facts verified by sources, with the latter receiving substantially more support. This indicates a belief in joint methods to obtain objectivity, which is not far removed from the ideal of the adherence to scientific methods to ensure objectivity, which Walter Lippmann introduces as an ideal in his book *Liberty and the News* (1920).

The results also show that there are significant differences between distinct groups of journalists. The ones who more often work with politicized topics support the objectivity norm more, and believe more in its utility in terms of creating trustworthiness, than journalists who never or rarely deal with these topics. This finding is very much in line with a recent study from Reich (2012), who finds that journalists on the political beat apply higher standards in their work than other journalists by including, for instance, more sources and doing more cross-checking.

Interestingly though, the results also show that the differences between the distinct groups of journalists are higher when it comes to the attitude of neutrality and detachment than when it comes to the journalistic methods. This makes sense considering that journalists covering the most politicized topics are more prone to accusations of political bias and slant. This way, the signal of a neutral attitude becomes a shield or a strategic ritual in the face of accusations of partiality and bias.

But is it enough? And can the objectivity norm hold its ground in a changing media environment. In the American context, the argument has been made that a partisan selectivity among the news audience is on the rise, paving the way for polarization (Bennett & Iyengar 2008). The argument goes that the media try to meet the audiences' wishes and demands for news that reinforces their pre-existing attitudes and beliefs. This would in turn mean a decline in the utility of the objectivity norm. But even the media which are ostensibly biased and partisan like Fox News and MSNBC trumpet a claim to objectivity. For instance, Fox News, often accused of conservative bias, uses the slogan 'Fair & Balanced'.

In Denmark also, claims based on the demand/supply logic have been made that the partisan press is reappearing (Hjarvard 2007). However, it has also been argued that media systems with strong electronic public service media, such as Finland and Denmark, lead to smaller gaps in political knowledge between the most and the least politically interested than is the case in the US (Iyengar et al. 2010). It might be that media systems with strong public service media are able to circumvent the demand/supply logic, which in Bennett and Iyengar's argument leads to polarization, and the inevitable question of the value of the information coming from the news in such a system. Ironically, it might be journalists in these European media systems with strong public service media who are able to maintain the objectivity norm, while journalists in the market-driven media system in the US will have a harder time doing so. Ironic because the US has been considered home of the objectivity norm, while political parallelism was much stronger for a longer time in Europe.

Objectivity could be at a crossroad right now. On the one hand, since it is the main way for journalists to distinguish themselves from others who disseminate information to a mass audience, it can be argued that it will become increasingly important in the coming years. The Internet has provided potential access to mass audiences for anyone who can afford a computer and a modem. The amount of information available and the number of sources are immense, and in this cacophony of information, trustworthy information is needed more than ever; it might be that the objectivity norm is the way to create this trustworthiness.

On the other hand, people might turn to the sources which give them what they want, thus rendering the objectivity norm superfluous. If the news should be reported from a distinct perspective to cater to the need of the consumers who constitute the target group, the supply and demand logic will take over and eliminate, or at least change the nature of, the objectivity norm as we know it.

This study shows that apparently it has not come to that yet, or at least the professional ideals of journalists do not reflect that. The study is a step on the way to a more nuanced understanding of the objectivity norm, since few large N-studies explicitly deal exhaustively with the objectivity norm (see Donsbach & Klett 1993 for an exception). Of course, it has its limitations. The data is limited to one country. But despite cross-country differences, the objectivity norm has been shown to receive substantial support from journalists across different western democracies (ibid.).

Thus, the general conclusion is that although there are differences in the support for the objectivity norm and its distinct operationalization, there is also substantial support for the norm more or less across the board. Thus, objectivity is to a large extent a strategic ritual for all, but also with the important qualification that it is so more to some than to others. The question remains whether it will stay that way.

References

Andersen, Vagn Erik (2008), 'Lotte Bundsgaard forlader Socialdemokraterne'/ 'Lotte Bundsgaard leaves the Social Democrats', *Fyens Stiftstidende*, 9 April, p. 1.

Bennett, Lance and Iyengar, Shanto (2008), 'A New Era of Minimal Effects: The Shifting Foundations of Political Communication', *Journal of Communication*, 58: 4, pp. 707–31.

Chalaby, Jean (1998), *The Invention of Journalism*, New York: St. Martin's Press.

Cook, Timothy E. (1998), *Governing With The News*, Chicago, IL: The University of Chicago Press.

Curran, James, Iyengar, Shanto, Lund, Anker Brink and Salovaara-Moring, Inka (2009), 'Media system, public knowledge and democracy: A comparative study', *European Journal of Communication*, 24: 1, pp. 5–26.

D'Alessio, Dave and Allen, Mike (2000), 'Media Bias in Presidential Elections: A Meta-Analysis', *Journal of Communication*, 50: 4, pp. 133–56.

Deuze, Mark (2005), 'What is journalism? Professional identity and ideology reconsidered', *Journalism*, 6: 4, pp. 442–64.

Donsbach, Wolfgang and Klett, Bettina (1993), 'Subjective objectivity – how journalists in four countries define a key term of their profession', *International Communication Gazette*, 51: 1, pp. 53–83.

Entman, Robert (1989), *Democracy Without Citizens: Media and the decay of American politics*, New York: Oxford University Press.

Glasser, Theodore. L. (1984), 'Objectivity precludes responsibility', *The Quill*, 72: 2, pp. 13–16.

——— (1999), 'The Idea of Public Journalism', in Theodore L. Glasser (ed.), *The Idea of Public Journalism*, New York: The Guilford Press, pp. 3–18.

Hackett, Robert A. (2008), 'Objectivity in Reporting', in Wolfgang Donsbach (ed.), *The International Encyclopedia of Communication*, Blackwell Publishing. Blackwell Reference Online. Accessed 22 March 2012.

Hallin, Daniel and Mancini, Paolo (2004), *Comparing Media Systems: Three Models of Media and Politics*, Cambridge: Cambridge University Press.

Harcup, Tony (2009), *Journalism: Principles and Practice*, London: Sage.

Hjarvard, Stig (2007), 'Den politiske presse. En analyse af danske avisers politiske orientering'/ 'The Political Press: An Analysis of Political Parallelism in Danish Newspapers', *Journalistica*, 5, pp. 27–53.

Hopmann, David, van Aelst, Peter and Legnante Guido (2012), 'Political Balance in the News: A Review of Concepts, Operationalizations and Key Findings', *Journalism*, 13: 2, pp. 240–57.

Iyengar, Shanto, Curran, James, Lund, Anker Brink, Salovaara-Moring, Inka, Hahn, Kyu S. and Coen, Sharon (2010), 'Cross-National versus Individual-Level Differences in Political Information: A Media Systems Perspective', *Journal of Elections, Public Opinions & Parties*, 20: 3, pp. 291–309.

Kaplan, Richard L. (2006), 'The News About New Institutionalism: Journalism's Ethic of Objectivity and Its Political Origins', *Political Communication*, 23: 2, pp. 173–85.

Kovach, Bill and Rosenstiel, Tom (2001), *The Elements of Journalism: What News People Should Know and the Public Should Expect*, New York: Three Rivers Press.

Lee, Tien-Tsung (2008), 'Bias in the News', in Wolfgang Donsbach (ed.), *The International Encyclopedia of Communication*, Blackwell Publishing. Blackwell Reference Online. 22 March 2012.

Lippmann, Walter (1920), *Liberty and the News*, New York: Harcourt, Brace & Howe.

Malacinski, Leny (2010), 'Spindoktorer giver hovedpine'/ 'Spin doctors provide a headache', *Jyllands-Posten*, 11 November, p. 15.

McNair, Brian (1998), *The Sociology of Journalism*, London: Arnold.

McQuail, Denis (2005), *Mass Communication Theory*, 5th edition, London: Sage.

Meilstrup, Per (2012), 'Betalingsringen III: Pressen og den falske vagthund'/ 'Payment Ring III: The Press and the Fake Watchdog', *Mandag Morgen*, 10 February, https://www.mm.dk/blog/betalingsringen-iii-pressen-og-den-falske-vagthund. Accessed 26 March 2012.

Merrill, John C (1984), 'Journalistic Objectivity is *not* Possible', in John C. Merrill and Everette E. Dennis (eds), *Basic Issues in Mass Communication: A debate*, New York: Macmillan, pp. 104–10.

Merritt, Davis (1995), *Public Journalism and Public Life: Why telling the news is not enough*, Hillsdale, NJ: Lawrence Erlbaum.

Meyer, Philip (1987), *Ethical Journalism*, New York: Longman.

Mindich, David T. Z. (1998), *Just the Facts: How 'Objectivity' Came to Define American Journalism*, New York: New York University Press.

Patterson, Thomas E. (1998), 'The Political Roles of the Journalist', in Doris Graber, Denis McQuail and Pippa Norris (eds), *The Politics of News The News of Politics*, Washington DC: CQ Press, pp. 17–32.

Poerkson, Bernhard (2008), 'The Ideal and the Myth of Objectivity: Provocations of constructivist journalism research', *Journalism Studies*, 9: 2, pp. 295–304.

Reese, Stephen (1990), 'Understanding the global journalist: a hierarchy-of-influences approach', *Journalism Studies*, 2: 2, pp. 173–87.

Reich, Zvi (2012), 'Different Practices, Similar Logic: Comparing News Reporting across Political, Financial, and Territorial Beats', *International Journal of Press/Politics*, 17: 1, pp. 76–99.

Reinemann, Carsten, Stanyer, James, Scherr, Sebastian and Legnante, Guido (2012), 'Hard and soft news: A review of concepts, operationalizations and key findings', *Journalism*, 13: 2, pp. 221–39.

Schudson, Michael (2001), 'The objectivity norm in American journalism', *Journalism*, 2: 2, pp. 149–71.

Skovsgaard, Morten (2010), *The Danish Journalist*, Ph.D. dissertation, Odense: Centre for Journalism, University of Southern Denmark.

Skovsgaard, Morten, Albæk, Erik , Bro, Peter and de Vreese, Claes (2012a), 'A Reality Check: How Journalists' Role Perceptions Impact Their Implementation of the Objectivity Norm', *Journalism*, 14: 1, pp. 22–42.

——— (2012b), 'Media Professionals or Organizational Marionettes? Professional Values and Constraints of Danish Journalists', in David Weaver and Lars Willnat (eds), *The Global Journalist in the 21st century*, New York: Routledge, pp. 155–70.

Stoker, Kevin (1995), 'Existential Objectivity: Freeing Journalists to be Ethical', *Journal of Mass Media Ethics*, 10:1, pp. 5–22.

Tsfati, Yariv, Meyers, Oren and Peri, Yoram (2006), 'What is good journalism? Comparing Israeli public and journalists' perspectives', *Journalism*, 7: 2, pp. 152–73.

Tuchman, Gaye (1972), 'Objectivity as Strategic Ritual: An Examination of Newsmen's Notions of Objectivity', *The American Journal of Sociology*, 77: 4, pp. 660–79.

———— (1978), *Making News: a study in the construction of reality*, New York: The Free Press.

Tumber, Howard and Prentoulis, Marina (2005), 'Journalism and the Making of a Profession', in Hugo de Burgh (ed.), *Making Journalists*, London: Routledge, pp. 58–74.

Voakes, Paul S. (1999), 'Civic Duties: Newspaper journalists' views on public journalism', *Journalism & Mass Communication Quarterly*, 76: 4, pp. 756–74.

Vos, Tim P. (2012), '"Homo journalisticus": Journalism education's role in articulating the objectivity norm', *Journalism*, 13: 4, pp. 435–49.

Weaver, David and Willnat, Lars (eds) (2012), *The Global Journalist in the 21st century*, New York: Routledge.

Westerståhl, Jörgen (1983), 'Objective News Reporting: General premises', *Communication Research*, 10: 3, pp. 403–24.

Note

1   The factor analysis was run on the different subgroups of journalists, and the two dimensions were remarkably consistent for hard news journalists and soft news journalists, as well as for news journalists and non-news journalists. The factor analysis was also run to include more items. The same two dimensions with the same items loading high came out. This shows that they are highly consistent.

Chapter 5

Web hate in social and mainstream media: 'Why Anders Behring Breivik is (not) a hero'

Eva Kingsepp

The article examines the relations between mainstream news media and alternative grassroots discourse, focusing on the mass murders in Oslo in July 2011 and the controversial Swedish chat room Flashback.org. Flashback is known as a place where one can rapidly find detailed (more or less correct) information about recent events and the people involved in them. It is also an open forum where all kinds of topics are being discussed, often including expressions of values and ideas that are considered offensive and/or 'politically incorrect'. In Sweden following the Oslo events, a media debate about hate speech in the commentaries on news media websites and in social media began, in which it has been argued that the latter provides fertile grounds for hate speech, and consequently also hateful actions.

The study shows that several of the texts in mainstream press were heavily biased and extremely negative towards social media, especially Flashback. References were frequently being made to one of the most controversial threads, 'Varför Anders Behring Breivik är en hjälte'/'Why Anders Behring Breivik is a hero', although the actual contents of it were either neglected or heavily distorted. This resulted in a discourse in which almost all the characteristics of moral media panics identified by Cohen (1972) are present. The article concludes with a discussion on possible explanations.

Introduction

This chapter investigates relations between mainstream news media and alternative grassroots discourse in social media[1] within the context of the debate in Sweden on web hate in the aftermath of the deadly attacks in Oslo on 22 July 2011. It has been argued that the attacks have fuelled hate speech in Internet chat rooms, creeping into, or at least influencing, the discourse on the commentary fields on mainstream news media websites. As a result, several Swedish newspapers decided on different strategies to stall web hate-related discourse through measures like denial of access to anonymous comments and vetting any material prior to publications, among others. Two major themes have characterized the debate on web hate in Sweden: (1) how can mainstream news media sites best handle web hate in commentary fields; and (2) what is the role of social media concerning right-wing Islamophobic extremism. Talking about controversial web chat rooms in Sweden, one discussion forum often pops up, namely Flashback Forum (www.flashback.org). Swedish Internet users know Flashback as both a site where all kinds of topics can be discussed, including expressions of values and ideas that are considered offensive and/or 'politically incorrect', and as a place where one can rapidly find detailed (more or less accurate) information about recent events, often long before it is published in mainstream media. The crowdsourcing activities of 'Flashbackers' have even gained official recognition by being awarded a new journalistic prize by SR, the Swedish public radio, which is usually conferred in recognition of boosting the relations between traditional journalism and social media.[2] The forum has around 2 million weekly visitors, of which non-college graduate males aged between 18 and 34 are over-represented.[3]

The data for this study is drawn from two main sources: the first comprises articles from Swedish mainstream press on the Oslo attacks and the perpetrator Anders Behring Breivik, and in which Flashback is mentioned; the second includes the discourse of the forum itself, especially the thread that seems to have put more fuel on fire – 'Varför Anders Behring Breivik är en hjälte'/'Why Anders Behring Breivik is a hero' (Flashback 2011d). The material thus represents two seemingly opposing discourse strands, a dual perspective that offers opportunities for examining important questions about impartiality, involving accuracy, balance, context, distance, open-mindedness and, not least, self-awareness and ethics. In the longer term this has implications for mainstream media's role in a rapidly changing society (cf. Chapter 2). Impartiality belongs, of course, to the basic components of news production in a democratic state. The ideal image of news and other factual genres representing an unbiased reality is crucial for the audience, and when the perceived genre conventions seem to be violated – for example through an overtly non-neutral or explicitly partisan presentation – this may result not only in criticism, but also in disillusion with the media system and society on the whole (Westerståhl 1972; Hill 2007; see also Chapter 4).

This chapter will be dealing with the discursive relation between the established media system and grassroots social media, here represented by Flashback Forum. The binary quality of this relation – already visible in the concepts mainstream/grassroots – contributes to shaping the audience's attitude to, as well as the reception of, mainstream news media content, which in turn gives rise to questions concerning power relations and democracy in contemporary society (cf. Chapter 4). The aim is more to offer food for thought than to provide answers. As the material shows, several of the mainstream press texts express hostility towards social media, which although veiled in anti-racist and anti-fascist rhetoric, can also be interpreted as – perhaps unconsciously – being rooted in professional self-interest. What hints can the data give us about the power relations between 'old' and new media, established journalists and the audience? What implications might this have for issues about the free exchange of thoughts on the web, and/or for democracy in a broader perspective?

Knowledge communities, epistemophilia and moral panics

Audience-media relation is an issue that media theorist Henry Jenkins (2006a & 2006b) has been exploring in several of his works. He describes how in the last decades not only media technology has converged, but also the conditions for production, as well as consumption of the content. The traditionally clearly-defined roles of media producers versus audience have changed as access to digital media technology and the Internet has opened up the possibilities for the audience to themselves become independent producers and distributors of media material. Jenkins is especially interested in the rise of alternative, web-based knowledge communities, where people gather to collect, share and discuss information about their common topic of interest. These groups are self-organized through

> [...] voluntary, temporary, and tactical affiliations, defined through common intellectual enterprises and emotional investments. Members may shift from one community to another as their interests and needs change, and they may belong to more than one community at the same time. Yet, they are held together through the mutual production and reciprocal exchange of knowledge. (Jenkins 2006b: 137)

Jenkins borrows the idea of collective intelligence, a 'deterritorialization' of knowledge enabled through the ability of the web to facilitate rapid many-to-many communication, from French philosopher Pierre Lévy. He fruitfully adapts Lévy's thoughts to online fan culture as well as to grassroots activism, noticing the common important factor of what Nancy Baym calls the 'socioemotional': fans 'are motivated by epistemaphilia – not simply a pleasure in knowing but a pleasure in exchanging knowledge' (Jenkins 2006b: 139). They 'see the exchange of speculations and evaluations of soaps as a means of "comparing, refining, and negotiating understandings of their socioemotional environment"' (ibid.). Such models taken from popular culture can, according to Jenkins, provide us with a prototype for what a mature, fully-realized knowledge culture would look like (Jenkins 2006a: 250). In socio-emotionally driven knowledge communities 'people with very different politics and ethics interact', resulting in disputes that

> [...] often foreground those conflicting assumptions, forcing people to reflect more deeply on their choices. What was once taken for granted must now be articulated. What emerges might be called a moral economy of information: that is, a sense of mutual obligations and shared expectations about what constitutes good citizenship within a knowledge community. (Jenkins 2006a: 255)

Jenkins sees the expansion of the potentials for participation, made possible by the increasing flow between grassroots and mainstream (broadcast) media, as an opportunity for cultural diversity (2006a 257–59). However, he also notices that this evolution is not applauded by all, as powerful interests within mainstream media corporations are striving to maintain their traditional positions and stay in control:

> That is why it is so important to fight against the corporate copyright regime, to argue against censorship and moral panic that would pathologize these emerging forms of participation, to publicize the best practices of these online communities, to expand

access and participation to groups that are otherwise being left behind, and to promote forms of media literacy education that help all children to develop the skills needed to become full participants in their culture. (Jenkins 2006a: 248)

Jenkins might be criticized for being optimistic, and perhaps even naïve, but I think his arguments are valid and definitely worth taking into consideration. The grassroots perspective is also important in Stanley Cohen's (2002) theory on media moral panics, which is relevant to include in the present analysis, as some of the press texts in the Swedish debate obviously carry certain traits associated with this type of discourse. As Cohen notices, '[t]he objects of normal moral panics are rather predictable; so too are the discursive formulae used to represent them' (2002: vii). Such panics are prone to occur when something new and seemingly dangerous enters society; however, this something can also be a new version of traditional evils. It is something that is either damaging in itself or a warning sign of a much deeper condition, and it is simultaneously transparent and opaque: anyone can see what is happening, but 'accredited experts must explain the perils hidden behind the superficially harmless' (2002: viii). As Cohen notices, 'the most enduring of suitable enemies' are young, working-class, violent males, in later years – at least in Britain – increasingly highlighting racial identities and barriers (ibid.).

In his study of moral panic and the discursive construction of deviant groups as 'folk devils' in Great Britain in the 1960s, Cohen divides the opinion and attitude themes discovered into three ideal-typical categories that are also highly relevant for the present study: the emotional and intellectual standpoint from which the deviance is evaluated (orientation); the nature of the deviants (images); and opinions about the causes of the behaviour (causation). In the first category we find analogies of disaster, caused either by nature or humans: earthquake, forest fire, marauding army, etc. There is also the theme that Cohen calls 'Prophecy of Doom' – that deviance will recur and is likely to get worse; and 'It's Not Only This' – that deviance is in fact part of a whole spectrum of intertwined social problems (2002: 49–52). The category 'Images' contains labels using emotive symbols, like hooligans and thugs, providing a further chain of perceived stable attributes such as irresponsibility, arrogance, lack of respect for authority, etc. Another theme of interest to the present analysis is what Cohen calls 'Hot-blooded Youth or Lunatic Fringe', describing the two contradictory opinions on how representative the mods and rockers were to young people in Britain as a whole. Here he makes an important observation: 'Moral panics depend on the generation of diffuse normative concerns, while the successful creation of folk devils rests on their stereotypical portrayal as atypical actors against a background that is overtypical' (2002: 61). Finally, among the themes dealing with 'Causation' are 'A Sign Of The Times' and 'It's Like A Disease' – speaking for themselves – and 'Cabalism', in which the behaviour (despite its largely spontaneous and situational character) is seen as well planned 'as part of some sort of conspirational plot' (2002: 62–63).

As we will see from the mainstream media material, it might at first glance be tempting to adapt the concept moral panic to the discourse. However, while all of the above is applicable, there are also certain flaws that lead on to a more interesting discussion. First and foremost, the examined discourse about web hate is not only confined to mainstream media, but is simultaneously taking place in the very same forum that is being pointed out as the 'site of deviance'. As we shall see, there are in fact also several similarities between the arguments in the two discourse strands. This raises questions about structural relations and issues of power. In the words of media theorist Nick Couldry:

> It would be a mistake […] to deny that there are very powerful forces in most contemporary societies that encourage a conformity of cultural judgement and, therefore, to some extent, of cultural experience; what the Australian theorist John Frow […] has called 'regimes of value'. […] This directly leads on to important political issues about the unequal opportunities which people have either to participate in or to be represented by cultural production. (Couldry 2000: 50)

However, it would also be a mistake to believe that individuals' relations to their highly structural environment can be characterized as simple, as they are in fact full of contradictions that are themselves 'crucial to understanding wider issues of inequalities' (Couldry 2000: 50). Although the individual perspective is not in focus in this study, it is nevertheless important to keep in mind that we are here dealing with a more or less obvious construction of the Flashbackers as Others, and/or potentially dangerous deviants in the mainstream media texts, which is – albeit in a less coherent way – actually mirrored in the Flashback material. While the background issue here is about online promotion of racial violence, thus a very serious problem, it is important to examine the cultural structures behind the discourse, as well as the process it represents, in an unbiased way.

Although the concept of hate speech is not in itself the topic here, it is nevertheless relevant to consider what it is and how it functions, as this is connected to issues of power. As mainstream media, according to their own myth, not only provide us with all that is needed for knowing about the world but also setting the rules for societal conduct, they are thereby largely taking on the state's role in the defining of what is appropriate and what is not. Accordingly, media's responsibility for defining the Other, as well as the consequences, is central for any discussion dealing with this topic (Couldry 2003; Silverstone 2007).

Material and methodology

The material consists of two main groups of texts, all collected from the mainstream media and Flashback Forum. The main bulk of the mainstream media sample consists of 17 texts from Retriever's digital archives (26 July – 12 September 2011; search 'Breivik AND Flashback'). I found these after initially having been inspired by three articles from the Swedish debate on web hate, in which the connections between Breivik and alternative websites are highlighted (Werner 2011).[4] The Flashback material consists of pages from two threads about the Utøya mass murders, with the main focus on the one frequently mentioned in the mainstream sample, 'Why Anders Behring Breivik is a hero' (Flashback 2011d). Here I have studied the first 38 pages out of 380, comprising 456 posts from 225 participants,[5] and together with the 17 texts from Retriever, these constitute the main material of the analysis. The second thread is the one in which the events at Utøya are being discussed as they unfold, 'Tråden om skotten på Utøya'/'The thread about the Utøya shootings' (Flashback 2011c). It is included for two main reasons: it not only provides an interesting insight into Flashback crowdsourcing – which is, as we will see, acknowledged in one of the mainstream texts – but also shows how the discussion about the identity of the offender and the motives behind the attacks evolves, changes and is being challenged along with the assembling and evaluation of new leads. Focus has been on the first seven hours and 43 minutes (18:13, 22 July – 01:56, 23 July), which is the time it took for the participants to finally disclose Breivik's full identity, including photograph, home address and whereabouts on the web.

I rely on critical discourse analysis (CDA) as a tool to unravel issues of power relations and ideology. CDA has a critical view of social reality in which language is used to uphold, create and recreate certain meanings and values (Fairclough 1995; Wodak & Meyer 2001; Jäger 2004). It should be noted, however, that as this is a limited case study, only a few of the aspects ideally covered in an analysis of this kind are to be tackled.

Mainstream press

The 17 texts from the Swedish press all mention, either explicitly or implicitly, the word Flashback (from now on abbreviated to FB) in connection to the terror attacks in Norway. The articles come from print newspapers, local and regional as well as national dailies, and can be roughly categorized into three main groups – FB-negative (9), FB-positive (2), and FB-neutral (6) – according to the way the forum is being referred to, considering choice of words, tropes and context. I will first briefly refer to one of the two positive texts, then show how the negative discourse evolves, largely based on an article that itself is, interestingly enough, rather neutral.

Lerums Tidning (a minor, local newspaper) published on 27 July what is the most positive among all the texts in relation to FB. It is a column by Peter Pierrou in which he describes how the FB-users were way ahead of traditional media in reporting about, among other things, the Norwegian ethnicity of the offender. He compares this with *Sydsvenska dagbladet*'s decision on that very same night Friday (23–24 July) to focus on possible Islamic groups being behind the act: 'Their subscribers could basically throw away their paper on Saturday morning' (Pierrou 2011). Nonetheless, Pierrou writes, there is also people on FB with their ideological origins 'in the same brown mould as Breivik', and one has 'to be willing to wade through the dirt' in order to 'sift out' the 'grains of gold' (ibid.). Pierrou concludes: 'It can go wrong when a news editorial office tries to filter information and adjust it to as many as possible. Sometimes *it is* good to be able to find out about things yourself – and the internet has revolutionized that possibility' (ibid.). A similar view is expressed in the other FB-positive text in the main sample, by media scholars Jonas Andersson and Pelle Snickars (2011), and also supported by Werner (2011) and Olsson (2011) in two of the supplementary texts.

However, this is largely overshadowed by an entirely different type of discourse. On 28 July, *DN* carries a long and basically neutral piece by Ola Larsmo. This oft-quoted article in several ways sets the standard for the following discourse, in which the authors place paramount significance on the role of discursive practices in creating social reality. In his article, Larsmo discusses the power of language to create scapegoats and pave the way for violence and, as in the Norwegian case, even mass murder. Towards the end of the text, Larsmo briefly mentions the existence of the FB 'Hero' thread, after having urged people who have developed the habit of using verbal constructions used in immigration-hostile discourse to reflect upon what they are doing: 'But I don't think that will happen, not as long as there is a thread on Flashback called Why Behring Breivik is a hero (about 1200 posts), and not as long as representatives for the Sweden Democrats once again are trying to make excuses for the mass murder with multiculturalism' (Larsmo 2011).[6] In the mainstream sample, this is the first article that draws attention to the 'Hero' thread by noting its existence. Notably, although Larsmo does not say anything about the actual contents, several of the following mainstream texts will be referring to the 'Hero' thread as an example of the extremist and anti-humanist character of alternative web forums on the whole.

Two days later, on 29 July, FB-negative discourse – which is not only negative to FB but also to social media in general – becomes the dominant mode of expression in the sample. The FB-negative discourse does not differ significantly from the FB-neutral in its basic ideological or ethical content, which can be summarized as a condemnation of racism, violence and hate, and a call for serious ethical consideration concerning linguistic behaviour on the web. The main difference lies in the use of highly charged words used in connection to references to social media. These are given explicitly negative connotations by relating them to expressions like 'right-wing extremism', 'xenophobia', 'racism', 'Islamophobia', 'sexism', 'violence', 'hate', 'mass murder' (and 'mass murderer'), 'crude discussion' and 'terrorism', 'bin Laden' as well as the 'Sweden Democrats'. The FB-negative texts describe a state of affairs bordering on Cohen's (2002) notion of moral panic. Not only is there a 'Twitter *mob*' (Lagercrantz 2011); the deviants are also 'extremely dangerous' (Kärrman & Örstadius 2011) and even represent 'dark forces' (*Värmlands Folkblad* 2011). They are found 'in the sticky muck on the internet' (*Folket* 2011), '*spreading out from the dark corners of the web*, from forums like Flashback, blogs, Facebook and Youtube and land in our everyday life until we hardly react anymore' (Nitz 2011). The Sweden Democrats are 'taking over' established web sites like Flashback (Bergman 2011),[7] and 'the country's racists littered the hashtag #swpol on Twitter with their *hate* against Muslims. They are nesting daily on Flashback' (Wennberg 2011). The metaphor of a rapidly spreading multitude, of disease or flood, with references to nature, animals and/or insects, is also common in other contexts where an overwhelming threat to the society and the existing order is envisaged (cf. Cohen 2002).[8] Two texts use the word 'mould' as a metaphor for the environment in which extremist ideas get nourished and grow in a gigantic way, perhaps like thistles or other detestable weeds infesting the otherwise 'well-kept garden' of today's Sweden (Pierrou 2011; Ring 2011). The threat, discursively described in non-human and nature-related, is further highlighted by the lack of means for identification: these 'hateful' people (apart from a few exceptions, like Breivik, bin Laden or the SD politician Kent Ekeroth) are anonymous and, consequently, faceless (Wennberg 2011).

There are two basic themes in the texts, the first being that of warning, implying that the threat of evil comes from the web as this is a place where extremists gather in closed 'rooms' to share their harmful thoughts before disseminating them to others, thereby infesting ordinary mainstream media whether print or electronic. This is the theme that carries linguistic and rhetorical elements associated with moral panic. The second theme focuses on action, the solving of a specific problem: what can we do about hateful speech, xenophobia and Islamophobia in the commentary sections of newspaper websites? It is not difficult to discover traces of both themes in one outlet, with some authors highlighting, or at least supporting, the importance of dialogue and respectful communication as a way to handle the situation (cf. Bjurström 2011; Larsmo 2011; Nitz 2011; Novak 2011; Olsson 2011; Werner 2011), while others seem to promote the idea that the haters are not interested in dialogue; they are only interested in spreading their hate (cf. Wennberg 2011; Thente 2011).

Interestingly, some of the texts can be interpreted as symbolically positioning the participation of 'ordinary people' in the open, non-moderated discourse on the web as a threat to the established order; not only of good manners and high publicist standards, but of Swedish society on the whole. While it is wrong to exaggerate such discursive tendency, there are traces in the sample of what Andrew Ross noticed in his 1989 book about the dialectical relationship between intellectuals and popular culture, where the former's 'traditional business is to define what is popular and what is legitimate, [...] supervise the passports, the temporary visas, the cultural identities, the threatening "alien" elements, and the deportation orders, and who occasionally make their own adventurist forays across the border' (1989: 5). Although Ross's study is more than 20 years old, it is nevertheless fascinating to find what looks like parallels to the present case. In this material, the categories of cultural power are clearly visible with the traditional hierarchies intact: mainstream media is both in its own eyes and those on the alternative side, the main legitimate source for producing knowledge about our world. However, there are also signs of what Ross describes as 'popular complaint about the antidemocratic use of expert knowledge [...] a complaint that is felt, like all effects of power, across the body, in structures of feelings that draw upon hostility, resentment, and insubordination, as well as deference, consent, and respect' (1989: 231). This double articulation is visible in the discourse of Flashback, as the following section demonstrates.

Flashback texts

The thread 'Why Anders Behring Breivik is a hero' was started at 20:30 on 23 July by a user called TRAADGARDSVALSEN (abbreviated TS).[9] In a lengthy post he basically argues that Breivik's victims on Utøya were not innocent youth, but socialists caring more about immigrants from Africa and south-west Asia than ethnic Norwegians, thereby putting the future of Scandinavian culture at risk. TS's initial post is followed by seven critical responses. The first supporter, with user name 360, turns up after an hour. After having cited TS in full length, 360 posts a short message which is hard to translate properly due to its extremely poor Swedish.[10] Basically, he says Breivik is a hero opposing multiculturalism (360 23 July 2011: 21:28). The next immediate post by user Liberion declares: 'A hero doesn't sacrifice innocent children. Had he turned against politicians, journalists and other "responsible" people in the society the question about heroic deed might of course have turned into a matter of discussion' (Liberion 23 July 2011: 21:33). User Ola Schubert writes: 'Whether TS is a troll or not, I don't doubt for a second that Flashback has a large overrepresentation of Breivik lunatics, albeit of different right and left extremist shades' (Ola Schubert 23 July 2011: 21:41). As defined in another crowdsourcing context, Wikipedia, 'troll' is an Internet slang expression for 'someone who posts inflammatory, extraneous, or off-topic messages in an online community, such as an online discussion forum, chat room, or blog, with the primary intent of provoking readers into an emotional response or of otherwise disrupting normal on-topic discussion' (Wikipedia 2011b). The troll subtheme, as seen in Ola Schubert's post, shows a critical awareness about the nature not only of this forum but web forums in general, an observation in accordance with recent audience studies on news and factual television (Hill 2007).

The conversation continues during the night and in the early morning hours.[11] The 456 posts can be divided into three main categories: ABB-positive, ABB-negative, and ABB-neutral. (It should be noted that this does not say anything about the views of the individual writers: what is of interest here is the mode of expression in the different posts.) The posts in the ABB-positive category, group A (48 posts, 26 different users), all hail Breivik's deeds and express a negative attitude towards immigrants and/or Islam/Muslims. Here, TS himself is by far the most active, providing almost a quarter of all the posts. The ABB-negative category is by far the largest, with 269 posts, and can be divided into two opposing groups based on attitudes to immigration. Group B (75 posts) fiercely condemns both TS and Breivik, but expresses views that are sceptical or negative to immigration and/or Islam, and/or racist, xenophobic, etc., while the posts in the anti-racist group C (194 posts) are not only extremely negative towards both TS and Breivik, but often also toward racists and Islamophobes. It should be noted that I have gathered all kinds of supportive comments in group A, which means that this includes both users that seemingly share these views and others who probably only find pleasure in posting something shocking.[12] The users in groups B and C, on the other hand, all seem to be serious. Besides the main theme 'pro or against Breivik' there are subthemes that repeatedly turn up, like immigration, racism, democracy, political views and ethics.

There is also a subtheme regarding chat rooms like FB, which can be described as the grassroots counterpart to the mainstream media actors above. It includes 37 FB-critical comments that are usually part of other posts (most of them – 26 – belonging to the anti-racist group C) and express one, or more, of the following statements: (1) FB is a place with lots of madmen; (2) places like FB can have negative effects on people; (3) someone/we FB members must put a stop to hateful speech. The criticism is mainly aimed either at FB or – more often – some of its members. Several posts express their worries about Breivik and his likes being very similar to people writing on FB. The analysis reveals obvious parallels to mainstream press discourse, with one category waving the warning flag and one suggesting action. It is sometimes unclear if the problem can be solved internally or if external interference is required: 'I'm like certain others here afraid that forums like flashback have given birth to madmen like Anders. People with knowledge in the humanities and so on must intervene and change this dangerous direction' (berlinlondon 24 July 2011: 00:21). Other posts highlight the theme of self-criticism and self-reflection:

> [A]ll of us FB members who have been critizising [sic] Islam or immigration policy from a liberal, right-wing, atheist or feminist perspective should scrutinise ourselves. Maybe we have made an impression of adding to the debate so that TS, Breivik and others have been given the idea that they have support from some kind of underground 'Flashback-spirit', against the 'pk-media elite', which is an illusion. It's time to stop allowing hateful messages to set the agenda. (Valsharessa 24 July 2011: 00:42)

'Pk-media elite' is an expression that is frequently used on Flashback and other alternative chat rooms, by right- and left-wingers alike, designating mainstream media being governed by a dominant elite group basically silencing any opposition to what is considered politically correct. This view is important especially for understanding Flashback's reputation, not least self-image, as a forum for free speech.

Flashbackers versus 'pk media' and the pleasures of detective work

The construction of FB as distinctly Other is an important part of the forum's self-proclaimed identity, which becomes evident when Flashbackers compare their views with those of 'dominant society' as represented by mainstream media. The most common expression I have found in such cases is 'pk media', while there are also occasional depreciatory references especially to the tabloid press. It is obvious that many of the Flashbackers consider themselves part of a thinking community in Lévy's and Jenkins' terms, and that this community is an alternative in that it is not adhering to the dominant regimes of value in society. However, there are obvious correspondences between the value systems in mainstream media and FB. First, there are formal ethical rules of conduct on FB – including bans on hate speech – whose violation leads to both upset verbal assaults from other members, and formal punishment from the forum administrators, ranging from warnings to suspension. Nevertheless, there is also a crucial difference concerning the definition of hate speech: here it seems to be the form of the utterance, not the content, which is decisive. Secondly, it is apparent that journalistic ideals of, for example, open-mindedness, objectivity, transparency and truth are not only reflected in the FB value system, but are also being held in high esteem. Members frequently request sourcing the information. One frequent question in the posts, 'Källa på det?'/'Your source, please?', in some cases seems to have evolved into a way of insulting the previous commentator for lack of credibility, insinuating that he/she is intellectually inferior.[13]

The provision and evaluation of sources is especially manifest in the thread that evolved shortly after the Utøya killings took place. The thread starts with a citation of the headline from the web page of Norwegian newspaper *Verdens Gang*, and the posts that follow link their content to mainstream media sources, such as *VG Nett*, the Norwegian national TV web channel,[14] Scandinavian newspaper websites[15] and – without links – Swedish national television, the BBC and Sky News. Alternative web sources also occur, albeit sparsely, like a link to Utøya on Google Maps (Zarathustra01 22 July 2011: 18:17) and a tweet 'From a guy at the camp' (BodenSwe 22 July 2011: 18:23). The circulation of information between different kinds of sources becomes especially visible in one post containing a citation from *VG Nett*, in which they cite the Facebook log of a person present at Utøya (KaffeBlatte 22 July 2011: 18:26). Parallel to the sharing of new information, the members express their feelings of horror and dismay, and also begin a discussion about the possible circumstances, as well as the background and identity, of the offender. It is worth noting that sourcing is sometimes initially received with scepticism: 'I hate the idea of linking to Aftonbladet, but what the hell… [followed by link]' (Evocation 22 July 2011: 18:21).[16] This becomes more evident later on, as the writers begin to search for the information themselves using all kinds of possible web-based sources. These include mainstream media as well as for example to imageshack. us, Wikipedia, www.globaljihad.net, www.axt.org.uk, the Oslo phonebook, Facebook, anti-Islamic blog *Gates of Vienna*, and the member pages of online game *World of Warcraft*, just to name a few.

The themes on the 'Utøya' thread are partly similar to those of the 'Hero' thread (immigration, racism, ethics), but it is in this case more interesting to trace the following categories: (1) information sharing; (2) expression of feelings, most often related to the events but in some cases reactions to previous posts; (3) discussion related to the events, including the offender; and (4) discussion related to the events in a wider societal and political context, most notably issues on immigration and immigration policy. The last category is the one where racist, xenophobic, anti-Muslim and anti-Islamic views are most frequently being expressed, but also questioned or explicitly attacked. So, although there are similarities with the 'Hero' thread in terms of racist/antiracist rhetorics, the 'Utøya' thread is different in its basic character. It is rather to be seen as an evolving online, real-time detective story based on factual events, in which the emotional investment above all lies in the detecting of clues, gathering of information, discussion and knowledge-building.

Some reflections

In light of the discussion above, a few ideas emerge. A majority of the posts in the infamous 'Hero' thread – 59% – are in fact distinctly Breivik-negative, regardless of otherwise expressing racist (28%) or anti-racist (72%) views. Another 27% of the posts express no opinion concerning Breivik or his deeds. This leaves us with 14% of Breivik-positive posts, of which a substantial part (23%) is provided by the thread-starter himself. This renders the argumentation of some of the press texts rather problematic, especially as a quick glance at the first pages of the 'Hero' thread does provide a clear hint about the contents.

The analysis shows that the same basic themes are present in both the mainstream media texts and on Flashback, emphasizing a message like the following: 'what has happened in Norway is horrifying, extremists are spreading their hate on the web, and something must be done about it.' The differences that do exist appear on two levels. The first is based on Swedish society's well established value-system, where democracy, equal rights and the right to free speech and opinions are woven together with the equally high-held ideals of news reporting. To regard FB in terms of a knowledge community, largely powered by epistemophilia and the same kind of socio-emotional energy as in the online fan culture, offers several clues for understanding the social reality of the case under study. This material suggests that the Flashbackers view the forum as a place where one gets to learn things about the world, outside the formal settings of mainstream media. Nevertheless, mainstream media, as well as mainstream knowledge cultures in general, are also present: as sources, in the form of references, and not the least as a model for how to gather knowledge that is correct, unbiased, etc. Hence the constant emphasis on sources not only brings new pieces of possible information, but may also reveal something about the contributors world view and ideological background. The interesting thing here is that most of the Flashbackers seem to agree on a moral obligation of listening to opposing views. The presence of extremists on the forum is accepted by the other members, although extremist opinions can count on being contested.

It is interesting that more than half of the press texts create and forward the idea of FB as homogenous and extremist, while the FB samples provide evidence for the opposite. Taken together, the traits of moral panic in the mainstream press include almost all of the characteristics identified by Cohen: for instance, analogies of disaster and disease; the likelihood of things getting worse; the case is part of a whole spectrum of social problems; highly emotive symbols used for characterizing the people active on FB (extremists, terrorists, neo-Nazis, etc.); a sign of the times (new media technology); and not the least, part of 'some sort of conspirational plot' (Cohen 2002: 63). Certainly there are important factors in journalists' working conditions that have to be taken into account when pondering on possible reasons behind this kind of highly emotional rhetoric: time pressure, a commercial media logic that promotes sensationalistic texts, etc. Although all press texts in the sample explicitly share the same basic concerns about web hate and its consequences, it is hard to avoid the impression that some of them could be interpreted as promoting shallow, prejudiced and negative conclusions about people on FB as the deviant Other. The 'Otherization' is, however, in this case performed by mainstream news media, thus a respectable and legitimate operation. This highlights another dimension of the power structures in contemporary media discourse.[17]

When comparing the press texts with the FB threads we see that they mirror each other in more than one way, including the alarm about web hate. In parts of the press, the threat, as in conventional moral panics, comes from the *outside*; it is something new and threatening to 'all of us normal citizens', for whom the established media act as gatekeepers, guardians of cultural values and protectors of law and order. For the FB members, the threat is *within*; it is even part of the whole idea of the community as such, which both makes it more difficult and – at least potentially – easier to cope with: difficult, because the 'haters' are allowed to speak on the same premises as all the others as long as they respect the common rules of ethical conduct. But it can also be easier, as people with opposing views are actually meeting each other in these kinds of open forums, providing important first steps for communication.

Another main difference has to do with the attempt to challenge power structures and, not least, the professional self-view of journalists. The FB 'Utøya' thread shows a considerable degree of veneration of traditional journalist ideals as well as respect for mainstream news media. This suggests that an analysis of the relations between Flashbackers and established journalists has to take the basic common values into account: it is the media landscape and forms for communication that have changed, not really the consensus regarding journalistic value systems. However, the change brought about by new media, together with what has been described as a crisis for journalism in the present institutional order, suggests that mainstream media – and thereby the established journalist collective – are to some extent losing their previously uncontested position in society, thereby also their authority as intellectuals. Yvonne Andersson notices in her research on civil disobedience in Swedish press that mainstream media journalists are often disobedient in their own self-view, the intellectual scrutinizers who can oppose the might of established power (Andersson 2009: 25–29). As this analysis has shown, this identity is being symbolically challenged from the grassroots level, and not by other intellectuals, like an opposing avant-garde (cf. Ross 1989), but by relatively young, uneducated males gathering on the web. It is again very tempting to draw parallels to the moral panic concept as '[w]orking-class yobs are the most enduring of suitable enemies' (Cohen 2002: viii). The traits of moral panic in the press texts could on the one hand be interpreted as an unconscious reaction to this traditional threat in a new costume. However, the highly emotional, and sometimes even aggressive, vocabulary among some of the established journalists might also be a sign of a hardening mode of expression in the media more generally. This is a question well worth pondering upon.

References

Alexa.com (2011), 'Flashback,org Site Info', http://www.alexa.com/siteinfo/flashback.org. Accessed 21 October 2011.

Andersson, Jonas and Snickars, Pelle (2011), 'Övervakning leder inte framåt', *Svenska Dagbladet*, 6 August.

Andersson, Yvonne (2009), *Mellan lag och moral: Civil olydnad och militanta veganer i fyra svenska dagstidningar åren omkring millennieskiftet*, Ph.D. thesis, Stockholm: Stockholm University, JMK.

Bengtsdotter, Ulrica (2011), 'Årets Medieorm 2011: Flashbackgrävarna som avslöjade Terje Hellesøs bildfusk', *Sverige Radio*, 16 November, http://sverigesradio.se/sida/artikel.aspx?programid=3938&artikel=4804948. Accessed 10 November 2011.

Bergdahl, Gunnar (2011), 'Orden och morden', *Landskrona Posten*, 30 July.

Bergman, Fredrik (2011), 'Gullandet med SD', *Smålandsposten*, 17 August.

Bergmark, Staffan (2011), 'Utøya förändrar det offentliga samtalet', *Västerbottens-Kuriren*, 12 September.

Bjurström, Anna (2011), 'Radikalisering sker i slutna rum. När extrema åsikter får möta dagens ljus spricker de snabbt', *Oskarshamns-Tidningen*, 3 August.

Cohen, Stanley (2002), *Folk Devils and Moral Panics: The Creation of Mods and Rockers*, 3rd edition, London & New York: Routledge. First published 1972.

Couldry, Nick (2000), *Inside Culture: Re-imagining the Method of Cultural Studies*, London, Thousand Oaks, CA & New Delhi: Sage.

——— (2003), *Media Rituals: A critical approach*, London & New York: Routledge.

Douglas, Mary (1997), *Renhet och fara: En analys av begreppen orenande och tabu/Purity and danger: An Analysis of Concepts of Pollution and Taboo*, Nora, Sweden: Nya Doxa. First published 1966.

Egonsson, Dan (2007), *Om det politiskt korrekta*, Nora, Sweden: Nya Doxa.

Dagens Nyheter (2011), 'Breiviks åsikter återfinns på sajter i Sverige', *Dagens Nyheter*, 27 July.

Fairclough, Norman (1995), *Media Discourse*, London: Arnold.

Flashback (2011a), http://www.flashback.se/. Accessed 10 November 2011.

Flashback (2011b), 'Rules of conduct', https://www.flashback.org/regler. Accessed 10 November 2011.

Flashback (2011c), 'Tråden om skotten på Utøya'/'The thread about the Utøya shootings', *Flashback*, 22 July, https://www.flashback.org/t1605847. Accessed 10 November 2011.

Flashback (2011d), 'Varför Anders Behring Breivik är en hjälte'/'Why Anders Behring Breivik is a hero', *Flashback*, 22 July, https://www.flashback.org/t1606749. Accessed 10 November 2011.

Flashback (2011e), '"Källa på det tack". Attitydproblem på FB?'/'"Your source, please" Attitude problems on FB?', *Flashback*, 18 October, https://www.flashback.org/t1688464. Accessed 10 November 2011.

Folket (2011), 'Dagens The Haters är alltid anonyma', *Folket*, 29 July.

Hill, Annette (2007), *Restyling Factual TV: Audiences and news, documentary and reality genres*, London & New York: Routledge.

Jenkins, Henry (2006a), *Convergence Culture: Where Old and New Media Collide*, New York & London: New York University Press.

——— (2006b), *Fans, Bloggers and Gamers: Exploring Participatory Culture*, New York & London: New York University Press.

Jäger, Siegfried (2004), *Kritische Diskursanalyse: Eine Einführung*, 4th edition, Münster: UNRAST-Verlag.

Karlsson, Karl-Johan (2011), 'Veckan när medierna sa nej till näthatet', *Expressen*, 4 September.

Kärrman, Jens and Örstadius, Kristoffer (2011), 'Här hämtar extremister näring', *Dagens Nyheter*, 30 July.

Lagercrantz, Leo (2011), 'Twittermobb', *Kvällsposten*, 29 July.

Larsmo, Ola (2011), 'Så kan språket bana väg för massmord', *Dagens Nyheter*, 28 July.

Nitz, Catarina (2011), 'Att uppfatta samtidens ton', *Katrineholms-Kuriren*, 30 July.

Olsson, Anders R. (2011), 'Även det stötande förtjänar skydd', *Svenska Dagbladet*, 7 September.

Pierrou, Peter (2011), '…på internet', *Lerums Tidning*, 28 July.

Ring, Lars (2011), 'Det sjuder av uppläst hat', *Svenska Dagbladet*, 31 August.

Ross, Andrew (1989), *No Respect: Intellectuals & Popular Culture*, New York & London: Routledge.

Silverstone, Roger (2007), *Media and Morality: On the rise of the Mediapolis*, Cambridge, UK & Malden, MA: Polity Press.

Sveningsson, Malin, Lövheim, Mia and Bergquist, Magnus (2003), *Att fånga Nätet: Kvalitativa metoder för Internetforskning*, Lund: Studentlitteratur.

Thente, Jonas (2011), 'Ett monster föddes ur hatet på internet', *Dagens Nyheter*, 30 July.

TT (2011), '(norge-terrorinternet4: Hat och rädsla på nätet)', 26 July, 13:38.

Värmlands Folkblad (2011), 'SAXAT FRÅN ANDRA LEDARSIDOR', *Värmlands Folkblad*, 28 July.

Wennberg, Jenny (2011), 'Om orden', *Örnsköldsviks Allehanda*, 8 August.

Werner, Jack (2011), 'Breiviks mardröm: kärleken som föddes på internet', *nyheter24.se*, 1 August, http://nyheter24.se/blogg/jack-werner/2011/08/01/breiviks-mardrom-karleken-som-foddes-pa-internet/. Accessed 21 November 2011.

Westerståhl, Jörgen (1972), *Objektiv nyhetsförmedling*, Stockholm: Akademiförlaget.

Wikipedia (2011a), 'Flashback', http://sv.wikipedia.org/wiki/Flashback_%28forum%29. Accessed 10 November 2011.

——— (2011b) 'Troll', http://en.wikipedia.org/wiki/Troll_%28Internet%29. Accessed 10 November 2011.

Wodak, Ruth and Meyer, Michael (eds) (2001), *Methods of Critical Discourse Analysis*, London, Thousand Oaks, CA & New Delhi: Sage.

Notes

1 The distinction between grassroots/alternative and mainstream media is borrowed from Henry Jenkins, who uses the terms in his discussion on participatory culture (2006a & 2006b).

2 The prize, 'Årets Medieorm'/'Media Snake of the Year' was awarded to Flashback for its exposure of a wildlife photographer who had faked one of his much acclaimed pictures (Bengtsdotter 2011).

3   Flashback Forum was created in 2000 as a part of the alternative news site Flashback.se, and is owned by Flashback Media Group AB. For legal reasons it has been run by a separate company situated outside Sweden since 2003, called Flashback International Inc, which since 2010 has been based in the United States. Although the forum highlights freedom of opinion and of speech, the discussions are subject to moderation and have to follow certain regulations including rules of conduct (see Alexa.com 2011; Flashback 2011a, 2011b; Wikipedia 2011a). In this article 'Flashback' refers to the forum, not the news site.

4   Werner's work is a response to a highly critical article by Thente (2011). The third text is a reflection on web hate as connected to the freedom of speech (Olsson 2011). *Dagens Nyheter (DN)* and *Svenska Dagbladet (SvD)* are Sweden's two biggest daily quality newspapers.

5   Time span 20:30, 23 July – 23:57, 24 July.

6   Sverigedemokraterna (SD), the Sweden Democrats, is a right-wing party known for a highly negative attitude towards 'multiculturalism'.

7   Notably, here Flashback is an 'established' site; this text is one of the six neutral ones in the sample.

8   A classic study is of course Mary Douglas's *Purity and Danger* (1966).

9   I have chosen to mention the web aliases of participants in the thread, although this is also subject to ethical consideration about anonymity. As Sveningson et al. write (referring to Donath 1999), web aliases should be considered as a form of 'pseudonymity', not anonymity, as the users actually want to be recognized on the web by other users in the community (Sveningson, Lövheim & Bergqvist 2003: 182). However, in this article I regard traditional media and Flashback in the same way regarding the names of the authors, as the latter is well established as a public forum open for everyone to read. This is also visible in the thread, for example when users say that they hope SÄPO, the Swedish Security Service, place certain users under surveillance.

10 For someone who is not a native English speaker it is very problematic to make adequate translations from a Swedish often full of slang and jargon, or misspelt, as in several of the Flashback posts. I have tried to handle this as far as possible.

11 TS's eleven posts are found on pages 1, 11 (twice), 12, 21, 24 (twice), 28 (twice), 31 and 33. The only other participant from the first evening who returns in the morning is TS's supporter 360.

12 I have only examined the notes in groups A and F closely, as I find these most relevant for the present study. Of the 26 users in group A, six have made more than one comment of the A kind, which makes it possible that the number of 'shockers' is rather high. This might say more about the nature of Flashback as a chat room than the actual ideological views of the users.

13 The frequent request for sources has even led to a thread on attitude problems on FB; see Flashback (2011e).

14 www.nrk.no

15 www.sydsvenskan.se, www.aftonbladet.se, www.aftenposten.no and ekstrabladet.dk.

16 The evening tabloid *Aftonbladet* is Sweden's largest daily newspaper.

17 Cf. Chapter 7 in this volume on the constitutive role media discourse plays in defining reality and the social roles and relations within it.

Chapter 6

Connecting the DOT: A protocol for the practice and perception of journalism[1]

Miles Maguire

Journalists have long resisted the idea of a standardized approach to news-gathering, but it may be time for them to reconsider whether they can do without an accepted methodology or protocol for their work. One such methodology can be identified by acknowledging that nearly all news reports are based on a narrow set of activities: reviewing documents, making observations and talking to human sources. Using textual analysis of prize-winning articles, and of articles that played a problematic role in the preparations for the 2003 invasion of Iraq, this essay demonstrates how these three techniques achieve the best results when they are applied in an iterative fashion to authenticate facts and eliminate unsupportable allegations. The concept of an accepted protocol addresses multiple concerns of recent scholarship, including definitional issues pertaining to professional status and standards for the evaluation of journalistic practice.

The journalism profession has long resisted the idea of a standardized approach to its central function, namely the gathering of news. This attitude is reflected not only in the absence of universally-accepted practices, but also in pronouncements emanating from the kind of influential bodies that might be in a position to establish and enforce adherence to a manual of practice. In 2002, the Associated Press, which 'considers itself to be the backbone of the world's information system' (Associated Press 2012), published a *Reporting Handbook* as a guide to the craft, but warned in the introduction about the difficulty of developing a set of all-purpose principles or techniques: 'Reporters make up their own rules as they go along, depending on their own strengths – and weaknesses' (Schwartz 2002: 3). Even in the United Kingdom, which boasts a National Council for the Training of Journalists that offers preliminary and advanced certificates in reporting, the importance of on the job, as opposed to conceptual, training is emphasized. In the introduction to *Essential Reporting: The NCTJ Guide for Trainee Journalists*, the authors note that the text 'cannot possibly deal in depth with everything a trainee reporter needs to know' because there 'is no substitute for practical experience' (Smith & Butcher 2007: 1).

Shapiro cites 'journalism's historically feisty culture' (2010: 145) in explaining why the field lacks commonly accepted standards. Deuze argues that the challenge of developing a consensus about what constitutes accepted theories and methods in the fields is so problematic that it is more productive to view journalism as an 'occupational ideology' (2005: 443) rather than a set of practices and procedures. But as news organizations fight to maintain their sense of purpose and privilege in a media-saturated world, it may be time for the journalism profession to reconsider whether it can do without an accepted methodology for news-gathering, or at least a finite set of alternative methodologies appropriate to one set of circumstances or another.

In this chapter I will define a possible methodology, and discuss each of its individual elements. I will then demonstrate how the use of this methodology underpins some of the best examples of modern reporting, and show how it can be applied to evaluating published articles in a way that would dispel some of the mystery of the craft, and give ordinary readers, or at least reasonably astute ones, a basis for assessing the value and validity of a reporter's work. I will also apply this concept to some of the definitional issues that currently bedevil the field of journalism, while also dealing with possible objections to using a standardized approach.

For lack of a better term, and at the risk of appearing glib, the methodology I am advancing might be called 'connecting the DOT'. The phrase refers to the three ways in which reporters gather information: by analyzing documents (D); making observations (O); and talking to sources (T). But it's really the first word in the phrase, 'connecting', that is most significant. It is meant to underscore a way of approaching the news that is based on a mindful comparison of facts and purported facts as a way of getting closer to a true account of events. Rather than pretending to be a mere conveyor of information, a reporter who is connecting with the news in this way is using a kind of scientific method based on testing and retesting hypotheses and suppositions with the evidence that is provided through documents, observations and talk.

Press performance and perceptions

The timing for the adoption of an explicit and assessable news methodology is right. A 2009 survey showed that only 29 per cent of Americans believe that news organizations usually get the facts straight, the lowest level in two decades of polling (Pew 2009) and a reflection of doubts about journalistic credibility and impartiality. As Shapiro notes, it has become 'increasingly difficult to distinguish between journalism and other, related, forms of expression, such as blogs, "based on a true story" fiction, artistic photography, reality TV and propaganda' (2010: 144). More significant than the drop in public perceptions about journalism, and not unrelated, is the still largely unaddressed issue of press performance. 'The News Is Broken' was the headline on a *Washington Post* column the day after a group of pranksters tricked a couple of cable news outlets and a major wire service into reporting that the US Chamber of Commerce had changed its position on climate change (Milbank 2009: A2). Just the day before the phony Chamber stunt, the sheriff of Larimer County, CO, had announced that criminal charges were likely against the parents of 'Balloon Boy', a 6-year-old who captured the attention of major segments of the news media the week before when it was reported, falsely, that he might be trapped in a homemade helium balloon that was soaring over the suburbs of Denver (Elliott 2009: A3).

Such incidents reflect a relatively harmless kind of gullibility that may be traced largely to the intense desire of journalists to be ahead of the competition when it comes to breaking news. If the issue at hand is minor, then journalistic foolishness can be dismissed as simply that – journalistic foolishness. Far more serious problems arise when the stories are more significant than a press conference or an idea for a reality television show. A conceit among western journalists is that they form an indispensable pillar of democratic society: 'When democracy falters, journalism falters, and when journalism goes awry, democracy goes awry' (Carey 2001: 19). Perhaps no clearer example of journalism and democracy going awry can be found than the coverage of Iraq's military arsenal, including its non-existent weapons of mass destruction, in the months leading up to the invasion of that country by a coalition of forces led by the United States on 20 March 2003.

In the aftermath, journalists at two newspapers that help set the American political agenda acknowledged flaws in reporting by their publications. At the *New York Times* the editors said that after reviewing their coverage of the case for war they had found 'problematic articles' based on reporting that was 'not as rigorous as it should have been' (*New York Times* 2004: A10). But rather than point the finger at individual reporters, the *Times* said the problem was 'more complicated' (ibid.), citing insufficient skepticism and too much competitive zeal for scoops. The *Washington Post* reviewed its performance in a news article written by its long-time media critic based on interviews with reporters and editors at the paper. The *Post*'s executive editor dismissed some of the criticism, but also accepted blame for putting too much emphasis on covering the preparations for war without paying enough attention, either in reporting or in story play within the paper, to those who questioned the wisdom of war. Another factor that several editors cited was the difficulty of assessing the reporting done on a notoriously difficult subject, the semi-secret world of international intelligence (Kurtz 2004).

These kinds of post-calamity self-analyses are not new: *USA Today* did something similar after star reporter Jack Kelley was caught in a web of deceptions (Morrison 2004), and the *Times* also engaged in a public review of missteps in the Jayson Blair case (Barry et al. 2003). The problem that remains, however, is that absent a way of judging the credibility of a given report at the time of publication and based on observable characteristics of a news report, consumers and users of news remain vulnerable to future breakdowns and continuing doubts about impartiality. The approach proposed here would allow journalists, media scholars and individual readers to make a contemporaneous assessment about the credibility of a news report, and by doing so, begin to enforce a system of standards; standards that might provide new ways of evaluating such critical issues as accuracy, fairness, balance, context, objectivity and rigor.

Journalism's claim to exceptionalism

One of the arguments against a common methodology is that journalism is a special case. It would be hard to argue with the contentions that individual journalists develop idiosyncratic methods based on their own inbred skills and the situations they encounter, and that news events exhibit such huge variations across so many different dimensions that there is no substitute for on-the-job experience. But the truth is that the same can be said for many other professions. For a lawyer, doesn't each case present its own specific facts and circumstances to be dealt with? Doesn't a surgeon seek practical experience in the operating room to develop the necessary skills? In other words, the claim that journalism practice can't be codified or taught is one that cannot be justified on grounds of exceptionalism. As shown in Chapter 1, the media would do well to refer to other disciplines when analyzing their own standards and performance.

Some journalists have proposed that the profession's problems with credibility can be solved with increased transparency: the 'lack of openness about our tradecraft – this non-transparency – is really the mother of most of the press's troubles' (Schanberg 2005: 22). But even if journalism were to overcome what Schanberg called the 'reluctance to explain how reporters go about putting together a news story', what would be revealed? Scholars who have conducted ethnographic studies of reporting have come to the conclusion that 'reporting anything beyond the simplest event calls upon knowledge and methods that are not easily analyzed and taught' because journalism has 'an irreducible element of art' (Ettema & Glasser 1998: 22).

This assertion of irreducibility has gone largely unchallenged, even though all reporting is ultimately based on a narrow set of activities that are performed, to varying degrees, in just about every assignment. A reporter's pursuit of authoritative facts is based on three specific tasks: 'acts of observation, analysis of documents and interviewing' (Adam 2006: 357). Whether consciously or not, the best reporters use these three tools in an act of triangulation that allows them to cross-check and authenticate facts, to reduce or eliminate unsupportable allegations, and to lead them to a deeper level of insight and understanding.

Adam's three reporting tools do in fact represent an accepted methodology, although clearly they are not acknowledged as such. The journalism profession has much to gain from recognizing that this standard methodology, or protocol, has long been in place and provides a conceptual framework for the teaching and practice of journalism, and for the evaluation of the works of journalism, i.e. individual news accounts, or competing or complementary accounts.

The evolution of reporting practice

One reason why journalists may not consciously think about using documents, observation and talk as a unified methodology is the way that the practice of reporting has evolved. Schudson describes how reporting before the civil war was largely a matter of 'stenography, observations and sketches' (2003: 81). In the second half of the nineteenth century, a second technique was added: interviewing, which helped to identify 'journalism as a distinct occupation' (ibid.). Just as interviewing was not widely accepted as a legitimate journalistic tool initially, the profession took some time to overcome its concerns about documents.

MacDougall's seminal textbook, *Interpretative Reporting*, places far greater weight on cultivating human sources than on consulting documents, and even warns about the dangers posed by relying on careless writing often found in a police blotter (1938: 393). But the central role of documentary analysis, as opposed to the mere reprinting of official notices, was well established by the end of World War II, and exemplified in the Pulitzer Prize for national reporting that James Reston won for his coverage of the Dumbarton Oaks conference. Reston's key scoop explained the negotiating positions of the major world powers as they discussed the formation of what would become the United Nations. Reston explains in his memoirs that this story came about because his source, who was Chinese, 'opened up a big briefcase and handed me the whole prize, neatly translated into English' (1991: 134).

The elements of DOT have been used before, both by journalism scholars and practitioners, to differentiate journalism from other kinds of writing and to assess the credibility of written reports. In a discussion of the genre known as literary journalism, Connery, for example, describes the 'traditional means of news gathering or reporting' as 'including interviews, document review and observation' (1992: 15). In a critique of the coverage of the Tiger Woods sex scandal, Farhi (2010) complained that many publications had put aside the use of documents, observation and talk, which he described as 'the methods that journalists are supposed to employ to separate fact from speculation and substance from gossip'. It would appear, then, that the DOT methodology is a kind of second-nature approach to the news for journalists, but one that does not get much conscious attention. My conception of DOT as a methodology goes a step further, showing how the three tools are most successful when used dynamically; not as individual reporting techniques, but as part of a unified approach that seeks out contradictions and makes plain the places where fact-gathering has come up short. In this way, the DOT methodology can demonstrate and reinforce a journalist's commitment to impartiality as it would bring into relief the way that a story has been pursued using balanced sourcing, and then presented with a neutral point of view.

Each element of DOT represents its own epistemology, with intrinsic strengths and weaknesses. Documents, assuming that they are based on the work of fair-minded and disinterested researchers, reflect an accumulation of knowledge, but they provide no guarantee of accuracy, and may embody hidden or unconscious bias. Information gained through first-hand experience has the benefits of immediacy and authenticity, but it is also limited, in no small part because of its specificity of perspective. Talk with human sources can lead to colourful details and unexpected insights, but verbal communication is fraught with the possibility of misunderstanding and omission. Before considering the three information-gathering techniques in a unified way, one might find it useful to look at how they can operate independently. Such an examination also helps to explain why the three elements of DOT are rarely viewed as a holistic methodology. In truth, these reporting tools require different underlying skills and would appeal to different personality types.

The difficulty of documents

Documents, for example, can be dull, hard to get and hard to understand. For those three reasons, some professional journalists shun the idea of using documents in their research. They think that documents are just too time-consuming and require too much work. But many of the most accomplished journalists, including those with a string of gaudy prizes to their names, have made documents central to the way they work. At the same time, it must be acknowledged that documents are not always reliable and may not even be true, as former CBS News anchor Dan Rather learned to his great chagrin (Hagen 2012).

Documents come in many forms, everything from incident reports filed by police officers to e-mail messages, classified reports, audits, photographs, databases, books and newspaper articles. A good definition of a document comes from Gaines, a Pulitzer Prize-winning reporter for the *Chicago Tribune* who went on to become a journalism professor at the University of Illinois: 'A document is information that is preserved' (2007: 24). Using this broad definition, we can see that documents do not have to be on paper or even in a traditional medium.

There are at least three reasons why documents deserve so much attention. For starters, documents are authoritative. As Williams has noted, 'Documents are often the best evidence – far better than prejudiced recollections or oral accounts – of what happened' (1978: 37). The second key argument in favour of using documents is that they stick to their story. What's written on the page doesn't shift over time, in contrast to what human sources say, or even what a reporter remembers from observations.

A third reason to emphasize documents is that at least some of them will form a very effective deterrent against libel suits. A document can bolster a reporter's claim that what was published was true, which is an absolute defence against libel accusations under US law (Pember & Calvert 2010). In addition, official police arrest records or transcripts of court testimony are considered by the American legal system to be privileged, meaning that they can be quoted, as long as they are quoted accurately, in news stories. Even if the information in these privileged documents turns out to be false, it cannot be used as the basis of a libel claim. While many of the most commonly used documents can provide journalists with this peace of mind, it's important to remember that it does not apply to all kinds of documents, particularly private correspondence that turns out to be a forgery.

First-hand observations

Unlike documents, which at least in theory provide the same information to all comers, observations are highly individualistic and depend on a range of factors, including vantage point and the skill of the observer. For a reporter, the act of observation serves at least two purposes. First of all, the reporter wants to gain as complete an understanding of a story or situation as possible; and secondly, the reporter is gathering details that can be incorporated into an article. In the end, these two goals come together as the reporter seeks to strengthen the credibility of a finished account by demonstrating an authoritative understanding buttressed with compelling visual images.

It is certainly true that many stories, particularly breaking stories, have to be reported by phone. For many routine stories, the investment of time in making observations about well-known locations or sources cannot really be justified. But far too often reporters skip over the crucial step of first-hand inspection.

For readers, an article lacking observational details should be a signal that the reporter is engaging with the material in a limited and perhaps superficial way, relying too heavily on abstractions and second-hand information. An intensive act of observation requires a level of engagement on the part of reporter that almost necessarily will lead to better reporting. Roberts argues that observation with the goal of 'making your reader see' is 'the essence of great writing and great reporting' because of the way that it forces the reporter to gather and process information (in Warren 2007: 30).

Although observational details can be subject to distortion, there is a kind of 'truth discipline' (Fuller 1996: 18) built into their use. Reporters must avoid the temptation to invent visual details just for the sake of creating a compelling image. A reporter who is challenged on a quote can usually fall back on notes to defend the accuracy of the story and argue the complaint to a standstill. But a reporter who is challenged about a physical fact of description won't find such ambiguity as an ally. In one famous case, the disgraced *New York Times* reporter Jayson Blair invented tobacco fields and cattle pastures to create the ambience that he felt was appropriate for a profile of a rescued prisoner of war returning to her West Virginia home (Blair 2003: B13). The fields and pastures did not exist, and the faked description could have immediately tipped off at least some readers to a flawed report.

Importance of interviews

For all the valuable background that documents can provide, and despite the critical role of direct observation, it is in talking to sources that reporters do their most important work. Human sources can provide confirmation about key details, and can also walk a reporter through an explanation, with digressions as necessary, in a way that a documentary source cannot.

Woodward, perhaps the most acclaimed American reporter of modern times, emphasizes the use of human sources, and works his sources much harder than most. The key to success is 'having many, many good sources – not one or 10 or 40 but hundreds' (*Booknotes* 1991). To make sure that he has his story straight, he engages in extensive cross-checking and rechecking. In some cases he will return to the same source 'a dozen or two times' (ibid.) to nail down an important detail or to clarify a sequence of events.

One of the dangers of working with human sources is that it is very easy to be misled. Some sources may actively seek to mislead, but there are also many sources who may accurately and honestly say something that turns out to be wrong. A reporter needs to cross-check one source against another, and against what is found in documentary and observational research.

Rare is the reporter who is equally skilled in, or equally inclined to use, all three reporting techniques. Thus a by-product of the DOT methodology is that it would make journalists move away from their natural strengths and reconsider how thoroughly they actually understand what they are reporting. Nearly a century ago Lippmann argued:

> You can judge the general reliability of any observer most easily by the estimate he puts upon the reliability of his own report. If you have no facts of your own to check him, the best rough measurement is to wait and see whether he is aware of any limitations in himself [...]. (Lippmann 1920: 83)

But rare is the reporter who provides such an estimate. After all, journalists are trained to report what they know, not what they don't know. If reporters were expected to make explicit their use of documents, observations and talk – and the limitations therein – readers would have an easier time of judging the quality of the effort that went into a report.

'DOT' in practice

If there are any arguments to be made against the use of the DOT protocol, they would likely advance the idea that the approach is impractical to apply or too onerous. But neither argument would hold up, since good journalists are already doing these things. In 1969, investigative journalist Seymour Hersh wrote an article bringing to light the massacre of hundreds of civilians by US forces in and around the Vietnamese hamlet of Mylai, for which he won the 1970 Pulitzer Prize for International Reporting. Writing in the *Saturday Review* in July 1970, Hersh gave a blow-by-blow account of his efforts to nail down the facts of the case in an essay called 'How I Broke the Mylai 4 Story' (Hersh 1970). A review of that essay shows clearly that the blockbuster story was the result of a mixture of documents, observation and talk.

Among the documents that Hersh used was a newspaper clipping from the *New York Times*, and indeed clippings of previously published work are among the most important, and certainly the first, documents that a reporter consults. Clippings provide valuable background information, and also point the reporter to the edge of the news by revealing what has already been written. In Hersh's case, the clipping told him that the Associated Press had moved a story about six weeks earlier reporting that an army officer, First Lieutenant William L. Calley, had been 'charged with murder in the deaths of an unspecified number of civilians in Vietnam' (Associated Press 1969). Perhaps surprisingly, no one until Hersh had sensed that this was a much larger story.

But to get the larger story, Hersh had to get to Calley, which involved a trip to Fort Benning, GA, where the officer was awaiting trial. Hersh turned to other documentary sources once he was there, including the base telephone directory, the register at the bachelor officers' quarters and other military directories at the base. Two key documents that came into play were a slightly out-of-date telephone directory (which unlike the then-current directory included a listing for Calley), and a short personnel sheet that Calley talked a disgruntled GI into purloining from Calley's official file. As in this case, documents are often a good starting point, but they are typically only a starting point. For example, Hersh used a Washington directory to follow up on a tip that Calley's lawyer was named Latimer. The only Latimer in that directory was not the right one, but he pointed Hersh to another lawyer named Latimer, who was based in Salt Lake City and who turned out to be representing Calley.

Calley's lawyer confirmed that the officer was still at Fort Benning, and Hersh recognized that to get an interview he would have to go to the sprawling base and go 'blindly looking for him' (Hersh 1970: 47). Hersh would need to use his powers of observation to track down his subject. Once Hersh learned of the apartment complex where Calley was living, he headed to the site, only to discover that it consisted of 'five two-story buildings, each with about fifty rooms' (1970: 48). Hersh had no choice but to go looking door to door. When he was about to give up for the night, he next went to a nearby parking lot and started flagging down cars to ask their occupants if they knew Bill Calley. His break finally came when he spotted some men working on a car in a distant corner of the parking lot. One of them knew Calley, chatted with Hersh over drinks in his apartment, and ultimately made the introduction just as Hersh was getting ready to walk back to his car and call it a night. Hersh's powers of observation also came into play when he sat down to write the story and used his opening paragraph to create a visual image of the accused mass murderer:

> Lt. William L. Calley Jr., twenty-six, is a mild-mannered, boyish-looking Vietnam combat veteran with the nickname of 'Rusty.' The Army says he deliberately murdered at least 109 Vietnamese civilians during a search-and-destroy mission in March 1968, in a Vietcong stronghold known as 'Pinkville.' (Hersh 1970: 49)

In the end, the key was talking to Calley. In Hersh's words, 'Calley clinched the Mylai story' because it was he who 'confirmed the essential numbers of the story and provided some essential quotes' (Hersh 1970: 49). But before he got to Calley, there were many others he had to talk to, from the original tipster who called the reporter on the phone all the way to the officer who finally connected Hersh to the accused. Hersh estimates that when he first started working the story he 'made at least twenty-five calls a day for two or three days' (1970: 46) until he got a lead on what was going on.

A more recent example of the DOT methodology at work can be found in Alexandra Berzon's article, published 30 March 2008, in the *Las Vegas Sun* under the headline 'Pace Is the New Peril', the first in a series of articles that won the Pulitzer Prize for Public Service in 2009 (Berzon 2008). It reflects the skilful combination of documentation, observation and talk to make a clear and persuasive argument that deadline pressure for contractors to complete new casinos had led to fatal lapses in safety procedures. In the first nine paragraphs, the reader can see evidence of documentation, observation and talk. While the inclusion of all three types of information sources is no guarantee of accuracy or truthfulness, they provide at least an indication of a thorough approach to news-gathering and thus a commitment to impartiality. As discussed more fully in Chapters 10 and 11, the expectations of news audiences are changing in the twenty-first century, but that doesn't mean that news organizations should abandon their traditional tools of information-gathering. Instead, it may be the optimal time to clarify the way that reporters work by explicitly identifying their methods, and in this way underscore how impartiality is key to credible journalism.

Assessment tool

The potential role of the DOT methodology as a practical assessment tool for the credibility and quality of a given news report can be discerned through the analysis of two articles that appeared in the *Post* and the *Times* before the invasion of Iraq. The articles have been cited, with the benefit of hindsight, as examples of the worst kind of journalistic malfeasance (cf. Massing 2004; Rich 2006). The *Post* article, which was written by Walter Pincus with an assist from Woodward, appeared 16 March 2003, under the headline 'U.S. Lacks Specifics on Banned Arms' (Pincus 2003). It has been hailed as the kind of reporting that stood out from the prevailing belief about the inevitability of war, and praised because it called into question the factual basis for launching the war, namely whether Iraq was actively seeking weapons of mass destruction. But it was published deep inside the paper. The other article, which appeared under the byline of Judith Miller in the *New York Times* on 20 December 2001, as 'Iraqi Tells of Renovations at Sites For Chemical and Nuclear Arms', was built upon such a slim base of information that in hindsight it almost seems unbelievable that it was published at all (Miller 2001).

In the one case, the *Times* showcased on its front page an article bolstering the argument that Saddam Hussein possessed weapons of mass destruction. In the other case, the *Post* buried in its main news section an article raising doubts about the existence of those weapons. As events unfolded after the invasion of Iraq, it became clear that the *Times* article was misleading, if not necessarily incorrect, while the *Post* article came closer to reflecting the lack of certainty about Iraq's WMD capabilities. Both the content of the articles and their placement within their respective publications were significant, as doubtful information was given great prominence while information that provided a better basis for evaluation of government actions was downplayed.

Traditionally, editors are vested with the authority to exercise news judgement over an article based on that judgement and signal to readers the importance of a story through its 'play', which consists of such indicators as placement within the paper, the type of headline and the amount of space allotted. By this standard, the troublesome *Times* story enjoyed very strong play. It appeared above the fold on the first page with a two-line, two-column head, before jumping to the B section. It consisted of 1867 words. By contrast, the *Post* article was much shorter, just 1051 words, and appeared deep within the front section, on page A17. Thus it is clear that the *Times* editors believed their story contained a great deal of information that would contribute to reader understanding, while the *Post* editors believed their story had far less significant content than other reports in that day's newspaper.

The application of the DOT methodology as an assessment tool points to exactly the opposite conclusion, namely that the *Post* article had greater and more credible news content than the *Times* article. If editors, or readers, were attuned to the utility of a methodological analysis, the *Times* article would have had less influence than the *Post* article. The main thesis of the *Times* article was that Saddam Hussein had been working to repair production and storage facilities for weapons of mass destruction in violation of international agreements. The *Post* article reported that the situation was far from clear since little in the way of specific information had been turned up about either the quantities or locations of banned weapons. In addition to their different perspectives, the articles reflected different degrees of reliance on the main tools of reporting, as well as relatively little effort either to assess the overall reliability of the reported information based on its provenance, or to show how information from one reporting tool tended to confirm or diminish the information from other tools.

Research into prize-winning journalism has shown that 'information richness' is a mark of superior reporting (Hansen 1990). By this standard, the Pincus article is much stronger than Miller's. Pincus relied on four different documents – which were cited a total of seven times – one minor observational detail and 15 human sources, four of whom were named. Miller's article, despite its much greater length, contained two documentary sources, no observations and ten sources, four of whom were named. If we focus on the two tools that both reporters used, Pincus used 100 per cent more documents and 50 per cent more sources. Furthermore the documents that Pincus used were more substantial. One of Miller's documents was a map that was used to show a landmark car dealership that indicated the approximate location of a purported biological facility. Her other use of documents consisted of a reference to 'copies of contracts' (Miller 2001: B4) that purportedly showed that her main human source had done business with the Iraqi government. Miller did not quote from those contracts or provide specifics about such things as transaction values, the nature of the work performed or time frames. By contrast, Pincus referred to an intelligence report that listed possible weapons sites in Iraq, and quoted from a letter from the former chairman of the Senate Armed Services Committee, a letter from the director of the Central Intelligence Agency, and a report on the Iraq inspection teams that had been fielded by the United Nations Special Commission on Iraq. This last report is particularly significant because it contained specific information about Iraq's weapons of mass destruction, including the quantities that had been destroyed under UN supervision.

But using DOT as an assessment tool involves more than counting the number of sources in different categories; it also invites an examination of how the sources are used. In this case, while one story was certainly more credible than the other, neither reporter did a particularly good job of examining and highlighting the ways in which information derived with different tools may carry more or less weight, or may tend to confirm or diminish the credibility of other kinds of information. Instead, the reporters followed what is the more standard practice of seeking 'convergent validation', what Killenberg describes as 'using a combination of methodologies to examine the same phenomenon' (2009: 32). However, this bias toward validation, sometimes called the 'discipline of verification' (Kovach & Rosenstiel 2001), can be a source of error, particularly when reporters attempt to build a case toward a particular conclusion by emphasizing areas of overlap and consistency, as Miller did. Connecting the DOT implies an opposite approach, using one kind of information to highlight contrasts and inconsistencies until a fuller picture emerges.

At several points in her article, Miller is clearly using one source of information to buttress another source of information, without exploring ways in which the sources may not actually comport with one another. A good example is the use of the contracts she cites to show that her informant had worked for the Iraqi government. By not providing any details about what the contracts covered, she was actually undermining her case that the existence of the contracts provided support for her main thesis: that Saddam Hussein was rebuilding his weapons program. It is also quite possible that the contracts were lacking in supporting details, or that they were not in English and could not be analyzed by her. At other points in her article, she emphasizes that one piece of information is consistent with another piece, glossing over the fact that unrelated phenomena routinely coexist. She quotes a UN official as saying that her source's story is consistent with other reports, and an Australian diplomat as saying that the story is 'plausible' (Miller 2001: B4). After acknowledging, in paragraph 33 of a 35 paragraph story, that there was no way 'to independently verify' her source's account, she goes on to emphasize that her source 'seemed familiar' with relevant facts, and that one of her unnamed sources vouched for the reliability of her key informant (ibid.). She attained the goals of verification and validation, while falling far short of illuminating the truth.

Pincus, on other hand, could be fairly faulted for not going far enough to show how different kinds of information could be used to examine and explore the issue from different perspectives. His point, that the Bush administration either lacked or was unwilling to disclose the kind of detailed information that was once available about Hussein's weapons program, gets lost because of his failure to contrast the precise data available from documents with the lack of precision now coming from human sources within the administration. The very specific numbers from the UN documents on the destruction of Hussein's weapons stockpiles and missiles do not appear until the end of the article, far removed from the headline and the lead, which emphasized the lack of specifics that the Bush administration was providing. Faulting someone for lack of precision does not make a very strong story, which was part of the *Post*'s defence for not displaying the Pincus story prominently. But the story would be stronger if it could be shown that the lack of precision was a dramatic departure from previous practice. That point was not clearly made in the Pincus piece. Attempting to draw a connection between the different pieces of information produced by different methodologies might also have led Pincus to do further reporting, specifically into such things as how the current American accounting of weapons sites differed from, or aligned with, the accounting done by the UN.

Definitional issues

The distinctions that have been drawn here to show the strengths and shortcomings of these two articles can also be shown to help define the essential core of journalism. The lack of definition has been a matter of great consternation among practitioners and scholars, but it remains far from resolution. Perhaps the key dimension to the problem of defining journalism is that while 'core skills are identifiable' (Singer 2003: 144), they are discussed in general terms that encompass a wide range of intentional and casual acts. One of these key skills is 'reporting', but the term remains largely undefined. Newer forms of technology, especially cell phones equipped with keyboards and cameras, mean news reports can be generated by anyone carrying such a device. Reporters who are conscious of their craft should arguably be placed in a different category than those who claim to be journalists but do not follow those craft conventions. But because of the lack of acceptance of a standardized approach to the methodology of journalism, this distinction cannot be reliably made.

Journalists and other observers have been similarly frustrated in distinguishing between reporters who adhere to traditional standards of objectivity and those who appear willing to take part in partisan debate. Raines, a former *New York Times* executive editor, argued that the Fox News Channel has 'overturned standards of fairness and objectivity that have guided American print and broadcast journalists since World War II' (Raines 2010: B3) while most mainstream journalists had turned a blind eye. This may be the result of the way that objectivity, as discussed in Chapter 4, can mean different things to different journalists. When the Obama White House attempted to cut Fox out of a particular news story in apparent retaliation for its partisan news coverage, it set off a revolt within the presidential press corps. A correspondent for a competing network described Fox as 'one of our sister organizations' (Rutenberg 2010). By generally accepted and outwardly observable indicators of journalistic practice, Fox is indistinguishable from other news operations: they field individuals identified as reporters who gather quotes, appear in video footage that is assembled into stories and narrate information before a camera. Although a recognition of a methodology such as DOT is absent, Fox news personalities are entitled to claim the occupation of 'journalist' as much as anyone else who performs the tasks of gathering and disseminating information.

In the face of the technological onslaught that has turned news values and hierarchies on their heads, journalism's vague and sometimes contradictory canons about what constitutes acceptable practice no longer suffice. The profession needs to adopt a disciplined approach – a protocol – to defining what is and what is not acceptable practice, and what is or what is not credible reporting. Rosenstiel has argued that the 'trust me era' is over, and that readers and viewers have adopted the attitude of 'show me' instead (2009). The DOT methodology provides a way for both news producers and news consumers to identify the component parts of a given report, and to assess the degree to which it does or does not measure up.

References

Adam, G. S. (2006), 'Notes Toward a Definition of Journalism', in G. Stuart Adam and Roy Peter Clark (eds), *Journalism: The Democratic Craft*, New York: Oxford University Press, pp. 344–69.

Associated Press (1969), 'Army Accuses Lieutenant in Vietnam Deaths in 1968', *New York Times*, 7 September, p. 38.

——— (2012), 'Facts & Figures', http://www.ap.org/pages/about/about.html. Accessed 24 January 2012.

Barry, D., Barstow, D., Glater, J. D., Liptak, A. and Steinberg, J. (2003), 'Times Reporter Who Resigned Leaves Long Trail of Deception', *New York Times*, 11 May, p. A1.

Berzon, A. (2008), 'Pace Is the New Peril', *Las Vegas Sun*, 30 March, http://www.lasvegassun.com/news/2008/mar/30/construction-deaths/. Accessed 25 April 2010.

Blair, J. (2003), 'Relatives of Missing Soldiers Dread Hearing Worse News', *New York Times*, 27 March, p. B13.

Booknotes (1991), 'Transcript of interview with Bob Woodward for *The Commanders*', http://www.booknotes.org/Transcript/?ProgramID=1057. Accessed 23 July 2009.

Carey, J. W. (2001), 'Lawyers, Voyeurs and Vigilantes', in R. H. Giles and R. W. Snyder (eds), *What's Next: Problems & Prospects of Journalism*, New Brunswick, NJ: Transaction Publishers.

Connery, T. B. (1992), *A Sourcebook of American Literary Journalism: Representative Writers in an Emerging Genre*, Westport, CT: Greenwood Publishing Group.

Deuze, M. (2005), 'What Is Journalism: Professional Identify and Ideology of Journalists Reconsidered', *Journalism*, 6: 4, pp. 442–64.

Elliott, D. (2009), 'Balloon Drama Was a Publicity Stunt, Sheriff Says', *Washington Post*, 19 October, p. A3.

Ettema, J. S. and Glasser, T. L. (1998), *Custodians of Conscience: Investigative Journalism and Public Virtue*, New York: Columbia University Press.

Farhi, P. (2010), 'Lost in the Woods', *American Journalism Review*, March, http://www.ajr.org/article.asp?id=4856. Accessed 26 April 2010.

Fuller, J. (1996), *News Values: Ideas for an Information Age*, Chicago, IL: University of Chicago Press.

Hagen, J. (2012), 'Truth of Consequences', *Texas Monthly*, May, http://www.texasmonthly.com/2012-05-01/feature.php. Accessed 18 April 2012.

Hansen, K. A. (1990), 'Information Richness and Pulitzer Prizes', *Journalism Quarterly*, 67: 4, pp. 930–35.

Hersh, S. M. (1970), 'How I Broke the Mylai 4 Story', *Saturday Review*, 11 July, pp. 46–49.

Gaines, W. C. (2007), *Investigative Journalism: Proven Strategies for Reporting the Story*, Washington DC: CQ Press.

Killenberg, G. M. (2008), *Public Affairs Reporting Now*, Burlington, MA: Focal Press.

Kovach, B. and Rosentiel, T. (2001), *The Elements of Journalism: What Newspeople Should Know and the Public Should Expect*, New York: Crown.

Kurtz, H. (2004), 'The Post on WMDs: An Inside Story', *Washington Post*, 12 August, p. A1.

Lippmann, W. (1920), *Liberty and the News*, New York: Harcourt, Brace & Howe.

Macdougall, C. D. (1938), *Interpretative Reporting*, New York: Macmillan.

Massing, M. (2004), *New They Tell Us: The American Press and Iraq*, New York: New York Review of Books.

Milbank, D. (2009), 'The News Is Broken', *Washington Post*, 20 October, p. A2.

Miller, J. (2001), 'Iraqi Tells of Renovations at Sites for Chemical and Nuclear Arms', *New York Times*, 20 December, p. B4.

Morrison, B. (2004), 'Ex-USA Reporter Faked Major Stories', *USA Today*, 19 March, p. 1A.

New York Times (2004), 'The Times and Iraq', *New York Times*, 26 May, p. A10.

Pember, D. R. and Calvert, C. (2010), *Mass Media Law*, 17th edition, New York: McGraw-Hill.

Pew Research Center for the People & The Press (2009), 'Press Accuracy Rating Hits Two Decade Low', 13 September, http://people-press.org/report/543/. Accessed 20 April 2010.

Pincus, W. (2003), 'U.S. Lacks Specifics on Banned Arms', *Washington Post*, 16 March, p. A17.

Raines, H. (2010), 'Why Don't Honest Journalists Take on Roger Ailes and Fox News?', *Washington Post*, 14 March, p. B3.

Reston, J. (1991), *Deadline*, New York: Random House.

Rich, F. (2006), *The Greatest Story Ever Sold: The Decline and Fall of Truth from 9/11 to Katrina*, New York: Penguin.

Rosenstiel, T. (2009), 'Fighting for Survival: The State of the News Media 2009', Stanford: University of Southern California, 2 September, http://www.youtube.com/watch?v=sJHVhqEZ4PE. Accessed 25 April 2010.

Rutenberg, J. (2010), 'Behind the War Between White House and Fox', *New York Times*, 23 October, http://www.nytimes.com/2009/10/23/us/politics/23fox.html?_r=1. Accessed 11 April 2010.

Schanberg, S. (2005), 'Repairing Journalism', *Village Voice*, 1 November, p. 22.

Schudson, M. (2003), *The Sociology of News*, New York: W.W. Norton.

Schwartz, J. (2002), *Reporting Handbook*, New York: McGraw-Hill.

Shapiro, I. (2010), 'Evaluating Journalism: Towards an assessment framework for the practice of journalism', *Journalism Practice*, 4: 2, pp. 143–62.

Singer, J. (2003), 'Who Are These Guys?', *Journalism*, 4: 2, pp. 139–63.

Smith J. and Butcher, J. (2007), *Essential Reporting: The NCTJ Guide for Trainee Journalists*, London: Sage.

Warren, T. (2007), 'The Inquirer', *Carolina Alumni Review*, September/October, pp. 22–30.

Williams, P. (1978), *Investigative Reporting and Editing*, Englewood Cliffs, NJ: Prentice-Hall.

Note

1 The material in this chapter has been expanded into a university textbook called *Advanced Reporting: Essential Skills for 21st-Century Journalism*. It provides a fuller description of the DOT methodology, and shows how it can be applied in a range of story assignments. It is scheduled for publication in 2014 by Routledge.

Chapter 7

A guilty terrorist suspect? On membership categorization and presuppositions in news texts

Gitte Gravengaard

This chapter demonstrates the constitutive role media discourse plays in defining reality, and the social roles and relations within it. The case analyzed is the media coverage of a Tunisian man accused of planning an assassination of the cartoonist Kurt Westergaard because of his drawing of Muhammad that appeared in the Danish newspaper *Jyllands-Posten* in 2005. By analyzing the membership categorization and presuppositions in these news texts, this study shows how the media and the actors cited in the media construct different identities for the suspect – from 'definitely guilty' to 'probably not guilty'. Thus, two narratives conceptualizing the suspect and reality in two different ways appear in the media texts. The current study is a part of 'The News Week' project, in which Danish media scholars analyze the content of the Danish media in a particular week in 2008.[1]

Every day media and journalists transform occurrences from the world around them into media products and media texts (Molotch & Lester 1974; Fishman 1980). But news stories do not write themselves. They are created in a routinized practice by professional journalists in a particular institutional and cultural setting (Tuchman 1978; Hjarvard 1995 & 2001). Journalists represent, interpret and construct reality in news texts (Grundwald & Rupar 2010).

Journalists and editors construct and select news based on professional norms and routines, and thus provide and selectively construct social knowledge for the public (Fiske & Hartley 1978). Thus, media products do not reflect reality; they construct reality (cf. Bell 1991 & 1994; Fowler 1991; Scanell 1991; Burr 1995; Bell & Garett 1998). As a consequence, media organizations and journalists have the power to edit reality (Lund 1999 & 2002) and to define reality (Lukes 1974) when writing news stories.

By stating that news is 'a window to the world', Tuchman (1978: 1) accentuates the media's important role in society. Lippmann (1922) described how news media influence the 'pictures in our heads' and later the agenda-setting theory (McCombs & Shaw 1972; Dearing & Rogers 1996; McCombs 2004; Coleman et al. 2009) drew attention to the important relationship between the media agenda, the public agenda and the political agenda. The first level of agenda-setting was concerned with what issues the media covered and to what degree, arguing that the media influence what people talk about (B. Cohen 1963). The second level of agenda-setting focuses on how the media describe issues and actors (McCombs, Shaw & Weaver 1997), arguing that the media contribute to the production of meaning in the public domain, thus influencing how people understand these things (cf. McCombs, Lopez-Escobar & Llamas 2000; Kiousis, Bantimaroudis & Ban 1999).

This chapter is primarily concerned with the second level of agenda-setting – with what other researchers have also referred to as 'framing' (Entman 1993 & 2004) – focusing on how an issue appearing on the media agenda is constructed, narrativized and framed, and on what media packages (Gamson & Modigliani 1989) the media discourse offers the public when attempting to understand a given problem, who is responsible for the problem and how the problem can be solved.

News media create mediatized narratives, and therefore to a large extent create the frame within which the public discusses occurrences, contemplates the surrounding world and learns about itself and others (Alexander & Jacobs 1998; Cottle 2006). The news media link us up in an imagined community (Anderson 2006) with other media consumers, and by reading and discussing news stories, we construct ourselves as part of a local, national and global context. Therefore, it is important to perform case studies of how issues and problems are narrativized and framed in the news media.

As described in Chapter 9, pragmatic philosophers have formulated many relevant thoughts on impartiality. How this impartiality is put into practice is the focus of this chapter. The news stories analyzed here are written by journalists who aim at presenting a balanced, accurate and impartial news story (as we also see in Chapter 4). However, this is not as easy as it may seem – as we will also witness in Chapters 10 and 11.

Linguistic analyses of news texts

During the last 30 years, media scholars have studied media language in news stories (Krippendorff 2004; Zelizer 2004). The Glasgow Media Group especially has played an important role in establishing a constructionist view emphasizing that the language in news stories 'imposed a structure of values, social and economic in origin, on whatever it represented; and so inevitably news, like every discourse, constructively patterns that of which it speaks' (Fowler 1991: 4). News texts are not just descriptions of events in the world around us. As all other articulatory processes, news texts are certain ways of forming and conceptualizing reality, social identities and social roles at a linguistic micro-level (Van Dijk 1983, 1987, 1988 & 1991; Fairclough 1989 & 1992).[2]

As a consequence, the point of departure for the current analysis is social constructivism (Burr 1995). The central premise here is that knowledge and world views are socially and historically anchored products of people's ways of categorizing the world. Language is not just a channel mediating facts about a 'real world' – language is a social action that constitutes knowledge, social identities and social relations between people. Discourses always install blind spots because portraying the world in one manner and accentuating particular aspects, simultaneously conceals other aspects of this reality. Therefore, the ambition in this article is to analyze how a particular case about a terrorist suspect is narrativized in the Danish media, and how actors, intentions, relations and consequences are portrayed and constructed here.

Frame and angle

Grunwald and Rupar (2009) refine the notion of frame and subdivide it into two concepts in order to be able to fully explain the process of journalism meaning-making. Grunwald and Rupar use the term 'frame' to describe what a story is about, and the term 'angle' to show how the story is presented; angle is that which 'infuses specific meaning to the text' (Grunwald & Rupar 2009: 8). This definition of angle corresponds to what Pan and Kosicki (2001) refer to as 'the rhetorical structure' reflecting the journalists' stylistic and linguistic choices. The analyses of angle give us knowledge about what a story is about from the journalists' point of view, and how reporters interpret reality. The analysis in this chapter of how meaning is constructed linguistically in news texts demonstrates important differences in how the Danish media represent reality, as well as differences in how the media, the government and other actors interpret reality. Different narratives are constructed by different actors about the same problem and the same actors, thus presenting different maps of meaning (Hall et al. 1978) for the media audience. An analysis of media discourse based on the conceptual framework outlined above, and involving public elite groups with an interest in the discourse, is bound to provide knowledge about the (re) production of society and how this (re)production takes place at a linguistic micro level (Van Dijk 2009).

Following a brief description of the case (presented in the next section), I move on to a review of the linguistic terms 'membership categorization' and 'presuppositions'. Then follows a detailed analysis of the language used by both the media and the actors cited in 'The News Week', the week in which media scholars in Denmark analyze the content of the Danish media (Lund 2000; Lund et al. 2009). 'The News Week' covers a period from Sunday 9 November – Sunday 16 November 2008. All references to dates in this chapter are therefore referring to this period.

The case

The case analyzed in this chapter is connected to the cartoon controversy of 2005, when on 30 September the Danish national daily newspaper *Jyllands-Posten* published twelve cartoons depicting the Prophet Muhammad in response to 'several incidents of self-censorship in Europe caused by widening fears and feelings of intimidation in dealing with issues related to Islam' (Rose 2006).

Three years after this crisis, the Danish Security and Intelligence Service (Politiets Efterretningstjeneste, PET) identified a man, Slim Chafra, suspected of having planned to assassinate one of the cartoonists: Kurt Westergaard. According to the PET, the motive for plotting an assassination attempt was Westergaard's caricature of the Prophet Muhammad with a bomb in his turban in *Jyllands-Posten* in 2005. Chafra came from Tunisia. He was (along with another Tunisian man) arrested in February 2008, administratively expelled from Denmark, and after that was granted tolerated residence in Denmark because the authorities feared he would be tortured if they sent him back to Tunisia. The other Tunisian voluntarily left Denmark in August 2008.

At 22:26 on Saturday 8 November, the webpage of the tabloid newspaper *B.T.*, BT.dk, announced that the suspect actually lived in Århus, Jutland, very close to Westergaard's home and not in the faraway refugee camp Sandholm, North Zealand, as previously thought. In the meantime, Dansk Folkeparti (The Danish People's Party), a right-wing party supporting the Danish centre-right government, was negotiating the Budget with the government.[3] Without any notice, Dansk Folkeparti issued an ultimatum demanding an immediate change to the legislation on tolerated residence to allow for the relocation of the suspect away from Århus close to Westergaard, otherwise, the party would suspend negotiating with the government on the Budget. The government bowed to the ultimatum and the case received huge coverage in the Danish media, turning it into one of the most talked about issues in the 'The News Week' in 2008.

The case of the terrorist suspect fits into the description of 'moral panic' (Hall et al. 1978; Goode & Ben-Yehuda 1994; S. Cohen 2002; Yilmaz 2011), where a person or a group is accused of displaying unacceptable behaviour, and this is seen as a threat to the basic values in the society in which it takes place. Furthermore, we also see that this particular case influences the national legislation (Hall et al. 1978).

This chapter analyzes how impartial the Danish news media were when covering this sensitive conflict in Denmark.

Newspaper articles, TV news and news telegrams

This chapter is an exemplary and text-oriented case study, focusing in detail on how a particular phenomenon is represented, and how reality and the actors in this reality come to be constituted in the language of news texts. Consequently, one should be careful not to draw too many general conclusions from this study. At the same time, a very detailed analysis provides an opportunity to obtain in-depth knowledge about the linguistic construction of a particular case.

The analysis is based on content analyses of newspaper articles, TV news and news telegrams, using the following search words: 'Tunisian', 'the Tunisian case' and 'the changes in the law on tolerated residence'. The corpus was drawn from the following media sources in 'The News Week':

- News articles – in print and on the Internet – from the following newspapers:
  National omnibus newspapers: *Politiken, Berlingske Tidende, Jyllands-Posten*
  National niche newspapers: *Kristeligt Dagblad, Information*
  National tabloids: *B.T., Ekstra Bladet*
  Free newspapers: *Urban, metroXpress, 24timer*

- The national TV news:
  DR1: *TV-Avisen* at 18:30 and 21:00
  TV2: *Nyhederne* at 18:00, 19:00 and 22:00
- All telegrams sent from the national news agency Ritzaus Bureau

The data for the empirical analysis includes 152 newspaper articles (45 print and 108 online), 12 TV stories and 24 telegrams from Ritzau. A close reading of all these news stories made it possible to identify and derive categories used to describe the problem, as well as the actors involved and their relations to each other. In my analysis, I have mainly focused on two linguistic tools used to mediate reality, and thereby important elements of angle in news texts: membership categorization and presuppositions.

This research design does not provide knowledge about the production of these news texts as I merely focus on the media output. In that sense, my position is comparable to that of the Danish media audience who do not have access to experience these events themselves, but have to learn about them from the media. Thus, the analysis explores what knowledge the media audience is offered about this particular case and the actors involved in it in 'The News Week'.

Implicit information in media texts

The media and the actors that are given a voice in the media can, through specific language usage, pass on opinions about people and reality without stating this explicitly, without arguing for these opinions and without indicating they might be presenting debatable knowledge; and without the readers or viewers even noticing this. Therefore, it is important to analyze both membership categorization and presuppositions in media texts. First, I analyze how the media and the actors cited in the media texts categorize the man that the PET suspects had planned to assassinate the cartoonist Westergaard. Second, the presuppositions used by the media and by the actors cited in the media are analyzed. Both linguistic phenomena contain implicit information and this makes them interesting to investigate further.

Membership categorization

The concept of membership categorization was introduced by Sacks (1972a & 1972b) and developed further by Schegloff (2007). Both Sacks and Schegloff focus on how people refer to a given person, on how people do descriptions and on the words chosen for these descriptions. One can choose many different categories for describing a particular person. This person can be a woman, a man, an adult, a child, a Muslim, a Protestant, a Dane, a Swede, a surfer, a diabetic and so on. Attached to these categories are certain understandings and conceptualizations. Thus, a category label (Moermann 1988) is not just a linguistic label. The categories also function as storehouses for the common-sense knowledge people have about how particular people 'are', how they behave, etc. (Schegloff 2007). This knowledge is activated when using references to specific categories. As a consequence, there are important implications when categorizing a person in a specific way. By referring to specific categories, certain aspects of the person's identity are made relevant, and at the same time the categorization can conceal other parts of this person's identity.

Presuppositions

In mediated texts, we also find presuppositions; that is, understandings and opinions emerging implicitly from utterances. What is presupposed in an utterance is the information the sender signals in his or her lexical and syntactic choices, which the recipient must take for granted in order to understand the utterance.

In their theory on presuppositions, Peter Harder and Christian Kock (1976) characterize presuppositions as part of the content passed on by the speaker in a given utterance. Presupposing happens when something is assumed to be taken for granted in an utterance – and when this assumption is accepted by both the speaker and the recipient.

Presuppositions can be found at all levels in the language – from specific semantic features to lexical features and the abstract syntax level. And because the conceptualizations and views presupposed in utterances are not made explicit, the speaker does not have to adduce arguments for these statements – hence the implied and presupposed views and opinions seldom are debated or criticized.

Next, I will analyze how the news media categorize and set out presuppositions about Slim Chafra That the PET suspected had planned to assassinate Westergaard.

The media's language usage

The most frequent categorization of Chafra in the media during 'The News Week' is 'the Tunisian'.[4] In 233 out of 699 references (33 per cent), he is referred to in this way. Thus, this element from the man's identity is the element most frequently accentuated. This categorization underlines his nationality: that he is a foreigner and thus different from the Danes.

The next most frequent categorization of Chafra is related to the pending case concerning PET's suspicions regarding him. Here he is described as: 'The Tunisian who, according to the PET, is under suspicion for having planned to assassinate the cartoonist Kurt Westergaard'. This categorization is found in 15 per cent of all references (106 times out of 699). His nationality is also made relevant in this categorization, but furthermore he is explicitly identified as the person under suspicion by the PET. By accentuating that these are

PET's suspicions, the journalists do not decide on the question of guilt in these utterances. PET suspects him, but he has not been convicted.

In 87 of the membership categorizations (13 per cent of the total), Chafra is described as 'the (terrorist) suspect Tunisian'. This categorization also concerns the accusations against him, and underlines the fact that he is under suspicion of a very serious criminal offence. However, the agent is omitted from these categorizations (Fairclough 1992). The man is a suspect, but it is not stated explicitly who is behind these suspicions. Consequently, the suspicions, to a great extent, are made universal, and one can easily interpret the utterance as if other actors, besides the PET, suspect that Chafra was hatching a plot to assassinate Kurt Westergaard.

In all, 61 per cent of the media's membership categorizations of Chafra point to his nationality and/or PET's accusations against him as the most important elements in his identity. Thus, he is primarily a Tunisian under suspicion in the media.

Some media also use his name, 'Slim Chafra'. This happens 71 times (10 per cent of the total). This is the fourth most frequent way to categorize him. On the surface this language usage seems unmarked, but when analyzing the articles in which the man's name appears, it becomes evident that his name is a high-frequency formulation in articles where the journalists are trying to avoid the categorization of him as a Tunisian under suspicion, and are instead making an effort to describe the person behind this linguistic label.

The most unmarked and neutral categorization of Chafra is when the journalists refer to him as 'the man' or 'the 36-year-old man'.[5] Each of these two categories is employed 5 per cent out of the total references related to him in the corpus. These relatively neutral categories – i.e. gender and age – do not connote nationality or accusations.

Do the plans exist?

Generally speaking, the corpus contains many balanced explications underlining that we are dealing with suspicions that a man has had plans to assassinate Westergaard. Most often the journalists report that it is the PET that suspects him and what they suspect him of – without linguistically implying whether these plans actually exist.

However, some media – especially the national daily *Politiken* – are more critical of PET's suspicions, as is apparent in formulations such as: 'The story about a presumed killing', and 'In February [...] the service (ed. PET) according to themselves prevented a terrorist killing' (*Politiken* 9 November). Here it is clearly emphasized that these are only suspicions, and that they are PET's suspicions. The newspaper and the journalist do not necessarily share these suspicions. It is stressed that one cannot be sure whether the assassination plot was there or not.

In contrast, we see the national tabloid newspaper *B.T.* frequently describing the assassination plans as something that exist or have existed: 'However, nobody knows if the assassination plans concerning him (ed. Westergaard) are abandoned' (*B.T.* 9 November). The utterance presupposes that the plans have actually existed, otherwise it would not be possible to 'abandon' them. The following day on the newspaper's webpage, BT.dk, the suspect is categorized as 'the Tunisian, suspected of being the brains behind the plans to assassinate the cartoonist'. Here it is also presupposed that the assassination plans have been there. This is not relativized, but presented as an indisputable fact: the declarative modus (Fairclough 1989) and the objective modality (Fairclough 1992) result in an utterance being formulated with a high degree of affinity.

Is the suspect guilty?

In most news texts, the media take a balanced and neutral stand towards Chafra vis-à-vis what the PET accuses him of. Most frequently it is stated explicitly that it is the PET that suspects him of planning to assassinate Westergaard: 'Terrorist suspect Tunisian lives close to cartoonist' (Ritzau 9 November); 'The Tunisian suspected of planning the death of Kurt Westergaard lives only 10 minutes away from the cartoonist' (*Berlingske Tidende* 9 November).

However, there are also formulations in the news texts where the journalists' linguistic choices either accentuate that Chafra is only a suspect and not convicted, or where the journalists linguistically construct him as being guilty.

He could be innocent – he has not been convicted

The national daily *Politiken*, in a 9 November article writes: 'Neither of the two Tunisians has ever been interrogated, charged or convicted'. And the national news agency Ritzau writes the same day: 'According to Dansk Folkeparti's leader, the Tunisian – who has never been convicted of anything – should already have been administratively expelled'. Linguistically the man's guilt is relativized in these utterances. By clearly accentuating all the things that have not happened, it is implied that the question of guilt has not yet been ruled on, and that one cannot know for sure whether he is guilty or not. This is not stated explicitly by the journalists, but by underlining that Chafra has not been convicted the reader naturally forms an implicature perceiving this as a relativization – perhaps even as a dissociation from the accusations. This is also apparent in other media.

He is guilty

Simultaneously, other media linguistically construct the suspect as being guilty. In these utterances, there are no relativizations; instead, it is stated with a high degree of affinity that this is a guilty man. This is revealed in both membership categorizations and in the presuppositions concerning him.

For example, the webpage for the national daily *Jyllands-Posten*, JP.dk, runs the following headline on 9 November: 'Westergaard's enemy lives in the neighbourhood'. Categorizing Chafra as Westergaard's enemy presupposes that the man has wanted to harm Westergaard, hence he is guilty. Similar implicatures are found in the membership categorizations published in the national tabloid *Ekstra Bladet*: 'Westergaard's tormentor back in Aarhus' (11 November) while the free daily newspaper *metroXpress*' categorizes him as a 'dangerous neighbour' (10 November).

Additionally, in other cases the presuppositions in the media texts construct Chafra as guilty: 'The man who has threatened Kurt Westergaard' (*metroXpress* 10 November); 'He only lives 10 minutes away from the Muhammed cartoonist whom he wanted to kill' (Ritzau 9 November); 'One of the two Tunisians who planned the death of the Muhammed cartoonist Kurt Westergaard' (JP.dk 9 November). In all these utterances, it is stated with a high degree of affinity and certainty that this man had actually planned to assassinate Westergaard. As a result, he is presented to the reader as guilty.

The construction of the suspect as guilty can be said to conflict with the Danish guidance rules for generally accepted press standards.[6] These rules place strict demands on courtroom reporting and state that 'courtroom reporting has to be objective' and that 'as long as a criminal case is not ruled on or annulled, one may not publish [...] statements declaring that a charged person is guilty'. However, this case is not ordinary courtroom reporting as there has been no trial. The PET had presented their evidence to the Minister of Justice, who subsequently decided to carry out an administrative expulsion of Chafra. Therefore, his case has never been taken to court where a judge could have determined the question of guilt or innocence. In this situation, some media choose to refer to him as guilty whereas other media accentuate that he is only a suspect – and has not been convicted.

In addition to the media's representation of the case and the purported suspect, we can also analyze how other actors cited in the media viewed the issue. These actors are classified into three groups: the government, Dansk Folkeparti and other actors. Politicians and other public actors do not adhere to the same ideal of objectivity balance and impartiality (Skovsgaard 2010) as do journalists. And they do not have the same role as journalists in the public sphere. On the contrary, politicians and other public actors are very much aware of the power of strategic framing (Entman, Matthes & Pellicano 2009) when aiming to strategically affect the media discourse and the public discourse, and hence these people's understanding of a given issue (Benford & Snow 2000). However, both politicians and other public actors play an important role in news texts as they are chosen by the journalists and offered an opportunity to present their perception of reality – and thus framing both problems and the actors involved. As a consequence, they play an important role in the edited reality presented by the media.

The government's use of language

The Danish centre-right government consists of two parties: Venstre (The Liberal Party) and Det Konservative Folkeparti (The Conservative Party). The statements formulated by the government and published in the media texts during 'The News Week' support the PET and their accusations against Chafra. At no time do the government statements relativize the accusations against the suspect, and at no time do the statements emphasize that these are only suspicions and that there is no conviction. On the contrary, in several government statements it is implied that this man is guilty. Furthermore, the statements from the government are to a large extent characterized by generalizations. This applies to the person the PET suspects of plotting to assassinate the cartoonist, and who is on tolerated residence in Denmark, to all persons on tolerated residence in Denmark.

The then Integration Minister and the then Minister for Economic and Business Affairs would often suggest Chafra belonged to the category of 'foreigners on tolerated residence in Denmark'. By emphasizing that the most important element in this man's identity is that he is on tolerated residence, the officials accentuate the whole case: that Chafra is made a suspect by the PET, has been administratively expelled and has now been granted tolerated residence in Denmark. Furthermore, the two ministers generalize by using the plural forms 'foreigners' to all 18 people on tolerated residence in Denmark and lump them together.

The then Minister of Finance, Løkke Rasmussen, in an interview on the national news on *TV2 Nyhederne* on 9 November, categorized Chafra as 'a person who is under suspicion for having been involved in a thought about assassinating Kurt Westergaard, and who is a menace to national security'. In the first part of his statement, Rasmussen emphasizes that we are dealing with 'suspicions', but the affinity with which the second part about national security is formulated constructs the suspect as guilty. It is presented as a fact that this man is a 'menace' and hereby it is presupposed that he is actually guilty of the accusations made by the PET.

The common narrative (Greimas 1966) and representation of reality in the government's statements published in the media are that the suspect is a guilty villain. Furthermore, all the people on tolerated residence in Denmark are also often cast in this role. The PET and the government are the helpers who prevent an assassination, and consequently work together to tighten up the legislation concerning tolerated residence.

Dansk Folkeparti's language usage

Dansk Folkeparti (DF) does not express any doubts concerning the existence of the assassination plans or Chafra's guilt. The only thing DF is not sure of is whether the plans have been abandoned or not. The legal affairs spokesperson Peter Skaarup repeatedly said: 'Nobody knows for sure whether the assassination plans against Kurt Westergaard have actually been abandoned' (Berlingske.dk 8 November).

Dansk Folkaparti's leader, Pia Kjærsgaard, also repeatedly referred to Chafra as guilty. In an interview on *Nyhederne TV2* on 9 November, she stated that she had 'no doubt that this man is guilty' and that she had 'complete confidence' in the PET. One of Kjærsgaard's widely cited membership categorizations is:

As politicians and good citizens, we simply cannot accept that Kurt Westergaard has to live with this insecurity. Constantly there is a possibility that he will meet this man, the

Tunisian, who has assassination plans against him and who is also dangerous. (cited for the first time on *DR TV-Avisen* 9 November)

Besides constructing the suspect as guilty, this formulation implies an antagonistic relationship between 'we' – that is, the 'good citizens' and the politicians who follow the rules and norms of society – and 'this man', the suspect, who obviously does not belong to the group of 'good citizens'. In another statement on the same day, Kjærsgaard told the national news agency Ritzau: 'We must stand together with Kurt Westergaard in this case'. Again, we see an accentuation of the dichotomy: 'we' – the politicians, Westergaard and the good citizens – versus the suspect. Chafra is characterized as being a threat to the community and to the group of good citizens. 'We' is the mass of law-abiding Danish citizens and politicians, who in this case are confronted with a foreign law-breaker who wants to destroy something in the society built by these citizens and politicians. By creating 'something different' (the Tunisian) that is conflict-ridden and alien, Kjærsgaard creates a national 'we' and an imagined national community (Anderson 2006) under threat. She designs an us-them rhetoric, and simultaneously constructs herself as the protector of the threatened national 'we'. In this construction of identities, Denmark functions as the solid and indisputable frame for constructing reality.

On the surface, Dansk Folkeparti's narrative (Greimas 1966) is similar to that of the Danish government: the suspect is the guilty villain and the PET, the government and Dansk Folkeparti are the helpers. But by creating the we-they dichotomies, Kjærsgaard defines and constructs this case as a part of an identity and a national problematic, inflaming cross-cultural tensions and instigating a clash of civilizations narrative (Huntington 1993). All in all, we see several points of resemblance with populism as defined by Yilmaz (2011), presenting an antagonistic division where one camp presents itself as representing the whole (Denmark, the Danes) and simultaneously demonizes the other camp. This demonization of a particular person or group and the division in 'us' and 'them' was also seen during the cartoon controversy in 2005 (Hjarvard 2006; Yilmaz 2011).

The following section presents the alternative and competing narratives and angles as voiced by other public actors.

Language usage of other public actors

Here, it is important to distinguish between Westergaard, who is personally involved in this case, and other actors. In all media interviews carried out during the week selected for the corpus, Westergaard consistently calls the purported suspect 'my potential killer' (18 times) and 'potential terrorist' (four times). Thus, Westergaard expresses his firm belief that Chafra is guilty. He does not talk about 'murder suspect' or 'terrorist suspect', but about 'killer' and 'terrorist'. Westergaard is certain that the plans exist and that the man is guilty, and he does not question the PET's methods, echoing the government's narrative.

However, it is interesting to note that other actors cited in the media, such as lawyers, people from human rights organizations, from the Danish Institute for Human Rights, from the Danish Red Cross, etc., distance themselves from suspicions and guilt in their membership categorization. Instead, they apply a different discursive strategy. They talk about 'people', 'persons' and 'the individual', thereby rendering ethnicity, nationality and the accusations irrelevant. These membership categorizations say nothing about whether the purported suspect is guilty or not, or whether the assassination plans existed. On the contrary, these actors apply very different discourses, namely ethical, juridical and civil rights discourses, referring to the suspect as a person and an individual. Their membership categorizations are different from both the media and the politicians, and they personify and decriminalize the suspect.

The categorizations performed by these other actors often appear in statements that are critical towards the government, the tightening of the law or towards the way the PET has handled the case. Hence, a narrative that differs very much from that of the government and Dansk Folkeparti is created. In most of the statements made by these actors, the villains and the guilty are the PET, and/or the government, and/or the tightening of the law. The people affected by this new law – the suspect and all others on tolerated residence in Denmark – are most often cast as victims, along with the legal rights. The other actors often construct themselves as helpers in these narratives as their aims are to ensure the just treatment of individuals, and to guard the individual against the system. Therefore, their discourse is void of a narrative establishing the conflict (i.e. the Tunisian versus the Danes). Rather, they introduce a narrative that creates a conflict between the Tunisian and the system.

Two narratives

Overall, the linguistic analysis indicates that there are two narratives at play in the media and among the actors cited in the media. These narratives represent two different conceptualizations of reality – and thereby different allocations of roles for the social actors in this reality.

One of the narratives deals with the phenomenon: the Tunisian terrorist suspect who in some cases is referred to as guilty. The other narrative emphasizes the description of the person and the individual, Slim Chafra, who has not yet been convicted. The analysis shows that Chafra is interpolated in different identities, and he is over-determined to a pronounced degree, as different actors construct different identities for him in the media by referring to him in different ways (Laclau & Mouffe 1985).

These two narratives exist simultaneously in the media, and neither of them can be labelled as neutral. Each of them presents a description of reality, and of the roles and relations attached to the actors in this reality. In both we find villains who pose a threat to somebody or something, and we find victims, as well as helpers, who have to protect the victims. The different actors are cast in different roles depending on what narrative a given formulation draws on. In one narrative, the villain is the almost certainly guilty Tunisian – he poses a threat to Westergaard and Denmark; the helpers here are the government, Dansk Folkeparti and the PET. In the second narrative, Chafra is cast as the victim; what is threatened are his civil and legal rights, and the villains are the government, Dansk Folkeparti and the PET, who trample on these rights; the people wanting to help Chafra are lawyers and people from human rights organizations. Whereas the first narrative establishes a conflict between the purported suspect (perhaps guilty) and the Danes, the second narrative establishes a conflict between the individual and the system.

The media are split between these two narratives. The government, Dansk Folkeparti and Kurt Westergaard tie in with the first narrative of the guilty Tunisian, while the people from the human rights organizations and lawyers most often tie in with the second narrative referring to Chafra as an individual with certain rights.

Representing reality

Thus, it does make a difference how one refers to a given person and a given case. The analysis in this chapter demonstrates how language usage imparts perceptions of reality and distributes social roles for the actors in this reality. What might seem to be a rather neutral linguistic choice, for a journalist for instance, can also in many cases tie in with a certain construction of reality. Because the linguistic choices often establish these understandings and perceptions implicitly and indirectly, they are often revealed only when the linguistic utterances and formulations are investigated thoroughly. Both membership categorization and presuppositions used in media texts can threaten the ambition to display balance, fairness, objectivity and impartiality in news texts.

The similarity in the narratives' form also gives rise to the following question: Do these representations of reality do justice to a complex and nuanced reality? By pressing the representations into a relatively fixed narrative format, the nuances and the complexity in this case are toned down. The consequence of the similar narrative structure in the media stories might be that the media's audiences are provided with a representation of reality that lacks subtlety and detail. Only the casting of the fixed roles are in dispute in this discussion of this week's news.

In general, the media coverage of this case is explicitly placed within a national Danish context. Here the journalists identify with the national state, and this is the central frame of reference employed by the media as we have also seen in the Danish media coverage on the war in Iraq (Hjarvard, Kristensen & Ørsten 2004; Jørndrup 2005). This is a phenomenon also known in other countries; both in times of crisis and war (Van Dijk 2009) and in everyday news stories (Billig 1995).

It is not within the scope and limits of a content analysis to analyze to what extent the language usage affects the audience. In this study I have performed detailed analyses of what interpretations of reality and what maps of meaning the media present to the media audience. Further analysis would benefit from focusing on the actual practice in which the news texts are produced in order to gain knowledge of how these news texts are produced.

The analysis of language usage creates an opportunity for journalists to gain a more nuanced insight into their routinized linguistic practice. This makes it possible for the journalists to discuss and reflect upon this knowledge. As we have seen, the linguistic variations and the differences in narratives highlight certain aspects of a problem, while others are underexposed or hidden and consequently encourage certain public perceptions of the world over others (Trew 1979). When this is the case, the mass media exerts a significant influence on shaping the public and political consensus on issues such as the case discussed in this chapter, or issues concerning ethnic minorities in general in Denmark (Gaasholdt & Togeby 1995; Hussain, Yilmaz & O'Connor 1997; Hervik 2002; Hussain 2007). Therefore, it is extremely important that journalists have an awareness of, and reflect upon, their routinized linguistic practice in their media texts. This case underlines that the much sought after norm – impartiality – is a complex and difficult goal to reach in practice.

Acknowledgements

I would like to express sincere gratitude for valuable comments and constructive suggestions from Assistant Professor Leon Barkho, Jönköping University; Professor Anker Brink Lund, Copenhagen Business School; Associate Professors Mark Ørsten and Ida Willig, Roskilde University; and Associate professor Maja Mons Bissenbakker Frederiksen, University of Copenhagen.

References

Alexander, J. C. and Jacobs, R. N. (1998), 'Mass communication, ritual, and civil society', in T. Liebes and J. Curran (eds), *Media, Ritual and Identity*, London: Routledge.

Anderson, B. (2006), *Imagined Communities*, London: Verso.

Bell, A. (1991), *The Language of News Media*, Oxford: Blackwell.

—— (1994), 'Climate of opinion: Public and media discourse on the global environment', *Discourse and Society*, 5, pp. 33–64.

Bell, A. and Garett, P. (1998), *Approaches to Media Discourse*, Oxford: Blackwell.

Benford, R. D. and Snow, D. A. (2000), 'Framing processes and social movements: An overview and assessment', *Annual Review of Sociology*, 26, pp. 611–39.

Billig, M. (1995), *Banal Nationalism*, London: Sage.

Burr, V. (1995), *An Introduction to Social Constructionism*, London: Sage.

Cohen, B. C. (1963), *The Press and Foreign Policy*, Princeton, NJ: Princeton University Press.

Cohen, S. (2002), *Folk Devils and Moral Panics*, New York: Routledge.

Coleman, R., McCombs, M., Shaw, D. and Weaver, D. (2009), 'Agenda setting', in K. Wahl-Jorgensen and T. Harnitzsch (eds), *The Handbook of Journalism Studies*, London: Routledge.

Cottle, S. (2006), 'Mediatized rituals: Beyond manufacturing consent', *Media, Culture & Society*, 28: 3, pp. 411–32.

Dearing, J. W. and Rogers, E. M. (1996), *Agenda-Setting*, London: Sage.

Entman, R. (1993), 'Framing: Toward clarification of a fractured paradigm', *Journal of Communication*, 43, pp. 51–58.

——— (2004), *Projections of Power: Framing news, public opinion, and U.S. foreign policy*, Chicago, IL: University of Chicago Press.

Entman, R., Matthes, J. and Pellicano, L. (2009), 'Nature, Sources, and effects of news framing', in K. Wahl-Jorgensen and T. Harnitzsch (eds), *The Handbook of Journalism Studies*, London: Routledge.

Fairclough, N. (1989), *Language and Power*, London: Longman.

——— (1992), *Discourse and Social Change*, Cambridge: Polity Press.

Fishman, Mark (1980), *Manufacturing the News*, Austin, TX: University of Texas Press.

Fiske, J. and Hartley, J. (1978), *Reading Television*, London: Methuen & Co.

Fowler, R. (1991), *Language in the News*, London: Routledge.

Gamson, W. A. and Modigliani, A. (1989), 'Media discourse and public opinion on nuclear power: A constructionist approach', *Journal of Peace Research*, 2: 1, pp. 64–91.

Gaasholt, Ø. and Togeby, L. (1995), '*I syv sind. Danskernes holdninger til flygtninge og indvandrere*', Århus: Politica.

Goode, E. and Ben-Yehuda, N. (1994), *Moral Panics: The Social Construction of Deviance*, Cambridge: Cambridge University Press.

Greimas, A. J. (1974), *Strukturel semantik*, København: Borgen. First published 1966.

Grundwald, E. and Rupar, V. (2009), 'Journalism curiosity and story-telling frame', *Journalism Practice*, 3, pp. 1–12.

——— (2010), 'Capturing meaning-making in journalism', *Journalistica*, 2, pp. 28–48.

Hall, S., Crithcer, C., Jefferson, T., Clarke, J. and Roberts, B. (1978), *Policing the Crisis: Mugging, the state, and law and order*, London: Macmillan.

Harder, P. and Kock, C. (1976), *The Theory of Presupposition Failure*, København: Akademisk Forlag.

Hervik, P. (2002), *Mediernes muslimer. En antropologisk undersøgelse af mediernes dækning af religioner i Danmark*, Copenhagen: Board of Ethnic Equality.

Hjarvard, S. (1995), *Nyhedsmediernes rolle i det politiske demokrati*, Copenhagen: Medieudredningen.

——— (2001), 'Politik som mediemontage. Om mediernes forandring af den politiske kommunikation', in Andersen et al. (eds), *Den demokratiske udfordring*, København: Hans Reitzels Forlag.

——— (2006), 'Religion og politik i mediernes offentlighed', in L. Christoffersen (ed.), *Gudebilleder: Ytringsfrihed og religion i en globaliseret verden*, København: Tiderne Skifter.

Hjarvard, S., Kristensen, N. N. and Ørsten, M. (2004), *Mediernes dækning af invasionen af Irak 2003*, Copenhagen: Modinet.

Huntington, S. P. (1993), 'The Clash of Civilizations', *Foreign Affairs*, 72: 3, pp. 22–49.

Hussain, M. (2007), 'The cartoons controversy and the Danish press', *Quaderns del CAC*, 27, pp. 47–58.

Hussain, M., Yilmaz, F. and O'Connor, T. (1997), *Medierne, minoriteterne og majoriteten – en undersøgelse af nyhedsmedier og den folkelige diskurs*, Copenhagen: Board of Ethnic Equality.

Jørndrup, H. (2005), *Midt i en krigstid*, Odense: Syddansk Universitet.

Kiousis, S., Bantimaroudis, P. and Ban, H. (1999), 'Candidate image attributes: Experiments on the substantive dimension of second-level agenda-setting', *Communication Research*, 26: 4, pp. 414–28.

Krippendorff, K. (2004), *Content analysis: An introduction to its methodology*, Thousands Oaks, CA: Sage.

Laclau, E. and Mouffe, C. (1985), *Hegemony and Socialist Strategy*, London: Verso.

Lippmann, W. (1922), *Public Opinion*, New York: Free Press.

Lukes, S. (1974), *Power: A radical view*, London: Macmillan.

Lund, A. B. (1999), 'Journalister i det redigerede samfund', *Politica*, 31, pp. 133–46.

——— (ed.) (2000), *Først med det sidste. En nyhedsuge i Danmark*, Aarhus: Ajour.

——— (2002), *Den redigerende magt – nyhedsinstitutionens politiske indflydelse*, Gylling: Aarhus Universitetsforlag.

Lund, A. B., Willig, I. and Ørsten, M. (eds) (2009), *Hvor kommer nyhederne fra?*, Aarhus: Ajour.

McCombs, Maxwell (2004), *Setting the Agenda: The mass media and public opinion*, Cambridge: Polity Press.

McCombs, M. E., Lopez-Escobar, E. and Llamas, J. P. (2000), 'Setting the agenda of attributes in the 1996 Spanish general election', *Journal of Communication*, 50: 2, pp. 77–92.

McCombs, M. E. and Shaw, D. L. (1992), 'The Agenda-Setting Function of the Mass media', *Public Opinion Quarterly*, 36: 2, pp. 176–87. First published 1972.

McCombs, M. E., Shaw, D. L. and Weaver, D. (eds) (1997), *Communication and Democracy: Exploring the intellectual frontiers in agenda-setting theory*, Mahwah, NJ: Lawrence Erlbaum.

Moermann, M. (1988), *Talking Culture: Ethnography and conversation analysis*, Philadelphia, PA: University of Pennsylvania Press.

Molotch, H. and Lester, M. (1974), 'News as purposive behaviour: On the strategic use of routine events, accidents and scandals', *American Sociological Review*, 39, pp. 101–12.

Pan, Z. and Kosicki, G. (2001), 'Framing as strategic action in public liberation', in S. D. Reese, O. Gandy and A. Grant (eds), *Framing Public Life*, Mahwah, NJ: Lawrence Erlbaum.

Rose, Flemming (2006), 'Why I published those cartoons', *Washington Post*, 19 February.

Sacks, H. (1972a), 'An initial investigation of the usability of conversational data for doing sociology', in D. N. Sudnow (ed.), *Studies in Social Interaction*, New York: Free Press, pp. 31–74.

——— (1972b), 'On the analyzability of stories by children', in J. J. Gumperz and D. Hymes (eds), *Directions in Sociolinguistics: The ethnography of communication*, New York: Holt, Rinehart & Winston, pp. 325–45.

Scanell, P. (ed.) (1991), *Broadcast Talk*, London: Sage.

Schegloff, E. A. (2007), 'A tutorial on membership categorization', *Journal of Pragmatics*, 39, pp. 462–82.

Skovsgaard, Morten (2010), *The Danish Journalist*, Odense: Department of Political Science, Center for Journalism, University of Southern Denmark.

Trew, T. (1979), 'What the papers say: Linguistic variation and ideological difference', in R. Fowler, B. Hodge, G. Kress and T. Trew (eds), *Language and Control*, London: Routledge.

Tuchman, G. (1978), *Making News: A Study in the Construction of Reality*, New York: The Free Press.

Van Dijk, T. (1983), 'Discourse Analysis: Its Development and application to the structure of news', *Journal of Communication*, 33: 1, pp. 22–43.

———— (1987), *Communicating Prejudice: Ethnic prejudice in thought and talk*, London: Sage.

———— (1988), *News Analysis*, Hillsdale, NJ: Lawrence Erlbaum.

———— (1991), *Racism and the Press*, New York: Routledge.

———— (2009), 'News, Discourse, and Ideology', in K. Wahl-Jorgensen and T. Harnitzsch (eds), *The Handbook of Journalism Studies*, London: Routledge.

Yilmaz, F. (2011), 'The Politics of the Danish cartoon affair: Hegemonic intervention by the extreme right', *Communication Studies*, 62: 1, pp. 5–22.

Zelizer, B. (2004), *Taking Journalism Seriously: Journalism and the academy*, London: Sage.

Notes

1   'The News Week' project covers a period from Sunday 9 November – Sunday 16 November 2008 (Lund 2000 & 2002; Lund, Willig & Ørsten 2009).

2   For an overview, see Van Dijk (2009).

3   The Danish centre-right government consists of two parties: Venstre (The Liberal Party) and Det Konservative Folkeparti (The Conservative Party).

4   All quotations is this chapter are my translations of the Danish news texts.

5   The media disagree regarding the man's age; some say '36 years old', some say '37 years old'.

6   http://www.pressenaevnet.dk/Love-og-regler/Regler-for-god-presseskik.aspx

Chapter 8

Impartiality and autonomy: Preconditions for journalism in weak states

Jöran Hök

The autonomous role of Swedish journalists has been won after centuries of bitter struggle since the first laws on liberties for the printed press were legislated in 1766. Sweden is well repudiated for this professional culture, which implies an independent and impartial social role for mass media, free from state censorship, and open to investigative reporting and critical debate; in other words, autonomous media able to sustain impartial reporting.

Efforts to create a similar position for the media in post-conflict or transition states are countered by strong political and economic forces, by a path dependency of older rules and norms, and also by lack of professionalism and investigative resources. In these states there is limited legal protection of critical journalism and a lack of a civil society that places demands on those in power to act as a counter-force against oppression and arbitrariness in the community.

In several states, especially those who previously lacked democratic mass media, there has emerged a plethora of new media which are independent in form but not in content. They are not functioning as correctives to power, and offer no room for impartial journalism. Instead, they have become a megaphone for special interests. The question is why this development has taken place and which strategies internal and external actors apply to change the situation.

Currently there are extensive studies of journalism in war, conflict and change phases. But there is very limited research on the development of journalism in subsequent periods. This chapter addresses the points of departure for future research on the conditions for journalism in states after crisis, open conflict and substantial social transitions. Studies in states such as Afghanistan and Kosovo demonstrate that international actors, companies and aid agencies have acted inconsistently and ended up in the role-conflicts which have frustrated efforts to create autonomous and impartial journalism.

Introduction

The focus of this chapter is preconditions for journalistic autonomy in weak states. The message is: without autonomy it is not possible for journalists to work impartially.

The chapter is built around four assumptions:

1. History shows that the road to an autonomous journalist profession is long and winding, which has been the case in Sweden, as well as in most other western European countries, and in North America.
2. It is not easy to export journalism to states in transition from authoritarian rule to democracy. Efforts in this direction have been hindered by a number of strong structural and situational obstacles.
3. To make things even worse, attempts to promote democracy-building via support to independent journalism in these states have been half-hearted and not very successful.
4. For this strategy to be a success, several goal-conflicts are to be overcome, and strong pressure is needed from internal as well as external forces – mainly local civil society and international actors.

The long road to autonomy

What is meant by an autonomous social position for journalism? The concept is analytical and mostly used in research. Journalists seldom label themselves as 'autonomous'; if asked, a journalist in our part of the world would probably describe herself as 'independent', 'impartial' and 'objective'. These labels can be seen as parts of fundamental professional aspirations, although everyone is well aware of the difficulties to be totally independent, impartial or objective.

A profession is autonomous when it has a high degree of recognized and legalized independence. Lawyers, medical doctors and specialized engineers are often mentioned as examples of autonomous professions. Journalists are often labelled as a semi-profession as there is no licensing that creates unique access to the craft (Hallin & Mancini 2004; Kovach & Rosenstiel 2007). We can distinguish between external autonomy and internal autonomy: external autonomy is reached when journalists have been liberated from censorship and extensive control by the political power elite; with internal autonomy, the editorial staff can work independently of media company owners or the economy department, but the individual journalist also has space for initiative and possesses a high degree of integrity.

The time-span of reaching external as well as internal autonomy can be long, as is shown by the Swedish example. The Swedish parliament adopted a Freedom of the Press Law in the late 1700s, the first of its kind in the world. It was followed by more than 50 years of stubborn struggle between autocracy (monarchy) and the journalists, before consensus was reached for external press autonomy, followed by a period of more than 100 years of dominance of partisan journalism. The political parties owned or were closely affiliated to the newspapers. News journalism was more or less openly framed by party politics, and seen as important tools to reach and control public opinion (Hadenius, Weibull & Wadbring 2008; Gustafsson & Rydén 2010).

The breakthrough for both external and internal autonomy of journalists in Sweden was closely connected to the gradual growth of consensus for the idea of independent and impartial reporting. This implies that journalism as a craft serves the public, truthfully mirroring or objectively describing events and processes, and thereby making it possible for citizens to take part in democracy. Proponents of the profession often emphasize that skilled reporters are in a better position than other information professions to conduct impartial and critical reviewing of matters in society. The reason is that they are not biased by their taskmasters; they are only in the service of their main clients – the public (Kovacs & Rosenstiel 2007).

The concept of impartiality was stated early on in the internal charter for Swedish press, radio and television adopted by the industry representatives in the middle of the 1950s: 'Strive to give people who are criticized in a news report opportunity to respond to criticism. Try also to reflect the views of all parties' (Swedish Journalist Union 2011).

The victory for this professional set of ideas, this professional ideology, was slow in coming and was not totally accepted until in the 1960s. The reason for this had to do with extensive changes in society and in the media landscape. Loyalties to political parties loosened during the 1950s, while the new journalism ideology was heavily influenced by developments in North American and British mass media, and transmitted by television news from international cable networks. Furthermore, the winning ideology was definitely precipitated by state journalism schools that were started in the 1960s in the two largest cities, Stockholm and Gothenburg.

Broadcasting news was presented as impartial; radio news as early as 1937. Swedish radio became a corporatist monopoly of British design, and private companies did not get licenses until the 1990s. Television followed the same pattern, changing only when the satellite broadcasts could bypass the law by broadcasting from abroad (Hadenius, Weibull & Wadbring 2008). But during the 1940s and 1950s, critical journalism was more exception than rule. Power holders were treated with great respect, and examples of investigative journalism were rare. All this changed during a decade, not least in news journalism on television. Some leading reporters introduced critical interviewing in the 1960s, which was seen as an ideal by the rapidly growing and mainly younger journalist generation. Self-confidence grew, as did the status of journalistic work.

To be impartial was seen as being independent in relation to the state as well as to corporate boards and interest groups. Michael Schudson has described how this ideology replaced partisan journalism in the North American press. An important conclusion of his review is that the objectivist ideology prevailed as a result of a number of converging factors, among them:

- changes in the political landscape;
- changes in reporting techniques (mainly more interviews);
- changes in professional identity and ethical codes (Schudson 2001).

Professionally, it was victorious during the second half of the twentieth century. It was 'the emergence of a skeptical, critical, and aggressive accountability journalism dedicated not to partisan triumph but to a sense of public service that is in many respects a product of the 1960s and after' (Schudson 2011).

This breakthrough had to do with a professionalization of the craft, the opening up of the political scene – not least because of the impact of television – as well as the strong financial backing brought about by high revenues from advertising (Schudson 2011). The same development was seen in Sweden. During these years, Swedish political parties agreed that journalism should be free to act as a third state in addition to the judicial and legislative power. This was even established in a number of statements (1975 & 1994) by the political parties represented in parliament. During the 1970s, this was reinforced when newspapers started to receive substantial state financial assistance (taxpayers' money) with the intention to secure alternative voices all over the country (Hadenius, Weibull & Wadbring 2008; Gustafsson & Rydén 2010).

Obstacles to exporting autonomous journalism

Swedish journalists, as well as other journalists in Western Europe and North America, experience today a period of media insecurity which is reconstructing the profession to some extent. But at the same time, Swedish authorities, the journalism unions and other actors are involved in development efforts in transition states (sometimes called 'new democracies') and post-conflict states.

Although both concepts are disputed, they are used here to give an acceptable positional picture of the regions or states in focus of the study. In political science, a distinction is made between post-conflict states on one side and transition states on another. The main difference is that the former group often lack functioning state apparatus, while the latter group is in a better position to rebuild authorities. In the group of post-conflict states there is a distinction made between (1) fragile states, (2) crisis states and (3) failed states (Putzel & Van der Zwaan 2006).

Many transition states can be considered as post-conflict states as they have gone through, or are still strongly influenced by, an international or regional conflict. This is the case in former East European countries such as Poland, Hungary and the former Czechoslovakia, states which were hampered in their democratic aspiration by Soviet military force. Several countries in Asia and Africa are still affected by strong internal tensions severely affecting the media sector; for instance Sri Lanka and the South African Republic.

What is the motivation behind the efforts to export journalism? It is a belief that is fundamentally based on the experiences of media autonomy in Sweden and other states in Western Europe and the United States:

Democracy support is an important factor in promoting freedom of expression and freedom of the press. Support for journalistic activities, publishing, free media and access to the Internet and mobile telephony are all important tools for creating conditions in which people can freely seek and impart information. [...] Independent, critical media are essential to freedom of expression and form an important part of the watchdog functions that distinguish a democratic society. Free, independent media help ensure greater exchange of correct information, improved opportunities for public debate and the exchange of political views and ideas. This can in turn help reduce the risk of conflict and corruption. Moreover, free media have a long-term effect on norms, values and attitudes, as well as on the growth and development of a democratic culture. Journalists are among the most important actors for democratization [...]. (Swedish Foreign Department 2010)

The same objectives are also used by other official development agencies, such as the United Nations, the British development agency DFID, and the Swedish International Development Cooperation Agency (Sida), as well as by many voluntary organizations and consultant groups involved in programs to develop free and fair media arrangements in many states in Africa, Latin America, Asia and former Eastern bloc. A recent report to OECD/DAC notes:

The purpose of support to media within democratic governance varies significantly across agencies. For some, it is explicitly focused on (and results therefore measured against) enhancing domestic accountability, improving service delivery, mitigating risks of violence (e.g. around elections) and other governance objectives. For others, it is shaped by a broader set of goals designed to promote political freedom, human rights and democracy. For most, a combination of objectives is apparent. (Arnold & Odugbemi 2011)

Efforts to create sustainable conditions for autonomous journalism in post-conflict or transition states are countered by strong political and economic forces. The democracy watch organization Freedom House recently made the following alarming statement based upon an annual survey of media independence in 196 countries:

After two decades of progress, press freedom is in decline in almost every part of the world. Only 15 percent of the world's citizens live in countries that enjoy a free press. In the rest of the world, governments as well as non-state actors control the viewpoints that reach citizens and brutally repress independent voices who aim to promote accountability, good governance, and economic development [...]. (Freedom House 2011)

In a comment in its latest report, a spokesperson for the organization writes: 'one in six people live in countries where coverage of political news is robust, the safety of journalists is guaranteed, state intrusion in media affairs is minimal, and the press is not subject to onerous legal or economic pressures' (Karlekar 2011). Freedom House made an assessment of 196 countries and territories during 2010: 68 states (35%) were rated 'free', 65 (33%) were rated 'partly free', and 63 (32%) were rated 'not free'. This can be compared with 2009: 69 free, 64 partly free, 63 not free (ibid.).

There are a few signs in another direction – for instance connection to the rapid changes in Northern Africa – in a few African countries (Niger, Guinea-Conakry, Kenya, Senegal, Zimbabwe), and also in some states in former Eastern Europe (Moldova, Georgia and Kyrgyzstan). But in general the trend is negative. Why? Karlekar points to five main causes:

1. State regulatory frameworks are used as key method to control media and limit space for independent media, especially broadcasting. Russia and Venezuela are mentioned among a range of states who try to hinder or suspend broadcasting.
2. Comprehensive resources are used to control social media and the Internet. Among the techniques are: blocking of satellite television (Egypt and Iran), blocking of Facebook (Pakistan briefly) and Facebook being made unavailable (China, Syria, and Vietnam). Increased censorship of the Internet in South Korea and Thailand.
3. Growing suppression of press freedom by non-state forces. For example, by the drug mafia in Mexico and in Guinea-Bissau.
4. Violence and physical harassment towards journalists forcing them into self-censorship or exile. Some of the most risky countries for reporters in 2012 were Honduras, Indonesia, Iraq, Mexico and Pakistan. According to Freedom House 'the failure to punish or even seriously investigate crimes against journalists has reached scandalous proportions'.
5. Threats to media freedom in established democracies, for instance in South Africa and Hungary (new restrictive media legislation). (Karlekar 2011)

In general, institutional problems are reinforced by instability within the states. Journalists have to face a harsh social environment with certain common structural characteristics, among them deep-rooted ethnical divides, weak democratic institutions and lack of legal regulations, poor governance, and corruption and criminality.

The problems must be taken into consideration when preconditions for media autonomy are researched. In accordance with Hallin and Mancini (2004), it is fruitful to emphasize four other factors that influence external autonomy:

1. the role of government;
2. the degree of political governance (political parallelism);
3. the development of media markets;
4. the degree of professionalization.

I would like to add two other societal factors that are of utmost interest: the first is the development of civil society; the other is the impact from the international community. Civil society means social networks, organizations and institutions made up of citizens outside the state and private sphere. The international community consists of democratic states, and also transnational institutions working worldwide, for instance the United Nations.

Table 1: Crucial factors for external autonomy.

Role of government	Weak governance; lack of legal protection for independent journalism
Political governance	Often strong political parallelism; mass media used to promote political power
Media market development	Few companies; weak funding; problems with distribution
Professionalization	Low level of journalism education; weak relation to research institutes; absent or weak journalist union
Civil society	Few checks on mass media
International actors	Few actors; uncoordinated, few sustainable activities

To try to overcome some of the problems, several international donors, among them the United Nations, have committed themselves to support mass media enterprises and journalism. This is part of the development strategy to create stability by promoting democracy, which is sometimes followed by actions in the form of information intervention.

The fragility of information intervention

What motivates an information intervention? What is its strength or weakness? In what ways have different intervening actors contributed to independent and impartial journalism?

It is only recently that democracy-building and media support have been adopted by state leaders, institutions and organizations as central to state reconstruction. During the two decades following the Second World War, stability was the key concept for state-building in war-torn states, as well as in former colonial areas (cf. Hayman & Manning 2009).

During the Cold War, support went to actors and governments that favoured hegemonic power on each side. Stability was chosen before democracy, although lip service was paid to the latter. This strategy promoted state leadership of a long row of autocrats, military regimes, one-party states, racist governments and even kleptocratic rulers – all sworn enemies of impartial journalism.

In the 1990s, after the demolition of the Iron Curtain, democracy became a leading concept in international relations, especially for donors. Now the ranking of stability and democracy changed. Among intervening actors and donor states active in Bosnia, Afghanistan, Kosovo and Iraq democratic state-building was seen as a prerequisite for stability, not the other way round. Human rights became central to international support.

The changing promotion of human rights had far-reaching consequences for many international actors, among them the United Nations. The UN Charter has not been altered, but has been interpreted differently (Barber 2009). Principles of sovereignty and non-intervention were called into question, partly as a result of the dark experiences in Bosnia (Srebrenica) and in Rwanda 1994.

Although not being the central matter, the role of mass media was highlighted in a negative sense. In Rwanda and Bosnia, radio stations and newspapers were used as propaganda tools to stir up ethnic violence. The invading forces had these bad examples in mind when they created ethical rules for mass media agencies in Kosovo, and Rwanda and Bosnia were also in the mind of the American administration when it planned for post-Taliban Afghanistan.

It is important to point at the double-edged role of mass media in conflict situations. The credo of quality journalism is a mass media that functions as arena for an informed citizenry. But different actors want to use the media for their purposes; as a forum for directed information often presented as 'strategic communication'. This type of mass media is useful for stability strategies. Even if not often stated, it is (at least) not promoting critical, debating and investigative journalism.

Recently, intervening international actors have used mass media channels as a tool for directed information. Information interventions in states like Bosnia, Afghanistan, Iraq and Kosovo are described as parts of humanitarian intervention. In these interventions, citizen rights, not the rights of states or state leaders, were emphasized. The concept of 'human security' challenged the state sovereignty norm (Hettne & Odén 2002). A growing number of international actors stated that if a government could not protect citizens, then international society has the right to intervene. Information intervention strategies are a vital part of the responsibility to protect legitimized humanitarian intervention (Barnett 1995; Mingst 2008).

Information intervention is aimed at (1) countering disinformation from hostile actors (enemies or unwanted regimes); and (2) informing citizens about the purpose of international actions. The goals can be achieved by using direct channels, often carried out by information units, but also by using indirect channels: community information, non-governmental organizations (NGOs) and mass media. The Swedish Foreign Department recently stated:

> In the case of *post-conflict countries* and *new democracies*, it is particularly important to include a diversity of interests. Media that listen and communicate interests can have a conflict-prevention effect in these countries. Tensions between different interest groups will be less if the latter are given the opportunity to express their views; critical media provide some guarantee against attacks against individuals and minorities. Local media can also help reduce isolation in rural areas. (Swedish Foreign Department 2010)

This leads to a central issue of media policy and media ethics: Can journalism be completely liberalized in weak states? Is there not a risk that we may get strongly biased journalism that counteracts stability and encourages ethnic tensions?

This question must be answered on a case by case basis. In fragile or crisis states the aim is to create stability and security by ensuring a legitimate state organization. Efforts to create independent media are complicated as the media then may be used to destabilize the fragile governmental bodies, including the judicial system. A well-reputed research team gathered by the London School of Economics to discuss strategies in fragile states pointed out that media support in those states needs to 'contribute to specific aspects of state formation, delivery of services, reduction of violence, enhancement of economic activities, strengthen accountability and create increased legitimacy of the political process' (Putzel & Van der Zvaan 2006).

How far press freedom can range in fragile states is a delicate issue and not easy to solve. Often it is proposed that a regulation designed to combat hate and slander must be resolved through some type of press ombudsman, or if necessary, a UN body (Putzel & Van der Zvaan 2006). How donors are acting here is of great importance, so that press control does not institutionalize partiality.

Analyzing donor behaviour in international intervention, Thompson and Price (2002) identify four approaches for donor media support:

1. The first one is use of established international media from intervening states, as was Done before the NATO attack on Serbia in 1999, for instance by regular radio programs Produced by the BBC.
2. The second approach is about establishing international media enterprises within the area. This was positively tested in Cambodia during the 1990s, as the country lacked free media input. But the same concept did not work in Croatia as the new Croatian leadership 'easily thwarted the UN's attempt to disseminate well-meaning but simplistic propaganda for peace' (Thompson & Price 2002).
3. The third approach is about creating local media capacity, which has been tested in a range of countries: Congo, Liberia, Burundi, Rwanda, the Central African Republic, Sierra Leone and Sri Lanka.
4. The fourth is supporting existing local media, as was done in both Kosovo and Afghanistan.

Are there any of these strategies which can be preferable? Thompson and Price conclude that the last approach has several advantages:

Local journalists working for local media in conflict zones earn credibility more easily than outlets set up by the UN or NATO. The purpose of strengthening indigenous media outlet is not only to boost specific kinds of content, but to build professional media that can outlast the intervention that sponsors them and hence stengthens the public sphere and civil society of the target state. Constructing a network independent of the international community would also help to build a pluralist infrastructure, an informed electorate and a heritage of non-partisan information. (Thompson & Price 2002)

Goal conflicts to be overcome in achieving autonomy

When supporting local media, international actors, in cooperation with their local partners, have to cope with several goal conflicts. Goal incompatibilities are different in various areas due to what constitutes the specific social conflict formation, but there are some common features.

At least three goal conflicts can be identified that restrain support for mass media enterprises in post-conflict states. The first has to do with allocation of resources; the balance between international and local capabilities. The risk is that too little attention is paid to resources among the local actors. The second goal conflict has to do with differences between security and development strategies, between short-term military intervention and long-term democracy-building. The risk is that this contravenes the goal of stable peace and sustainable development (Hök 2009 & 2010). The third goal conflict has to do with role-sharing between different professional groups. Militaries and civilians have historically had very different roles, but during recent expeditions the military has taken on many civilian tasks. Borders between the professions can be blurred, and this creates a difficulty in distinguishing military and civilian actors. Several officials in international organizations have opposed the role-sharing with different arguments. Some hold that militaries should stick to their conventional duties, others that the cooperation makes work more risky for aid workers (Barnett & Weiss 2008).

The military has introduced media support as a part of its communication strategy, creating an accountability dilemma. It could be defended by the argument that in crisis states, and during short periods, there is no other resource-strong actor to inform the public. However, the problem is that criticism of the intervening parties may be prevented or suppressed. There is a difference of being information officers and being journalists.

There is a need for strong pressure from civil society and the international community to support autonomous media in post-conflict and transition states. If not, state leadership or other powerful forces will swallow the media arena and use it for their own interests. The outcome will be the opposite of impartial, i.e. biased media. This has also to do with the delicate balance between stability and development. There is always a risk for international actors to favour stability, leading to more military actions and a more closed communication strategy.

This is reinforced during times of financial crises. Development aid activities to promote free media get a smaller amount of the budget. The risk is then that the media companies fall into the hands of vested interests, power groups, external powers or local political parties. Both these tendencies have been visible in Afghanistan and Kosovo, and also in transition states like Moldova. The outcome is what has sometimes been labelled 'protocol journalism'. Journalists are reporting what the authorities tell them, nearly in the same way as a secretary reports a meeting in a protocol. The authorities are seldom questioned and investigative journalism nearly invisible (Limani 2004; Van Zweeden 2007; Barker 2008; Andresen 2009; Taylor 2009).

Conclusions and suggestions for further research

The Swedish example shows that the time span of reaching external, as well as internal, autonomy for journalists can be long. The emergence of independent journalism that is 'dedicated not to partisan triumph but to a sense of public service' (Schudson 2011: 227) is a phenomenon not more than 50–60 years old in Anglo-Saxon journalism and Sweden. It was winning as it had a strong sense of craftsmanship combined with pride of its social mission; it was explicitly authorized by the authorities; and it was supported by a strong financial position of the leading media companies and the state. Finally, it could use an opening-up of the political scene.

Swedish development aid authorities, the journalist unions and other actors are involved in media development efforts in transition states and post-conflict states. The motivation is the belief that it can bring changes in direction of democratization of these societies based on the experiences in Sweden, as well as other states in Western Europe and the United States.

But many interconnected structural problems are making the export of autonomous journalism difficult. As is shown by case studies in states like Afghanistan and Kosovo, mass media is often used to promote political power (strong political parallelism); media companies are financially weak and seldom supported by tax money; there is limited civil society pressure for the spirit of public service media; and international efforts to support independent journalism still suffer from short-sightedness and lack of sustainable coordinated efforts.

Several goal conflicts can be identified that restrain such support to mass media enterprises in post-conflict states. Some of these conflicts have been pointed at in this chapter with examples from information interventions by the UN and other international forces.

Many of these problems are also present in transition states in former Eastern bloc. The result has been an absence of autonomous journalism, as state leaders and other powerful forces have swallowed the media outlets and are using them for their own partisan interests. The outcome has been the opposite to impartial (i.e. biased) media that acts according to the vested interest of the usurper.

The development has certainly been different in different countries, and research about conditions for autonomous journalism in these countries therefore requires invasive studies in each area. It is important to stress the necessity to use multilevel analysis. Preconditions can not only be studied in relation to legislation or media owners, it must also be put into a larger context where local (civil society) and international actor efforts are taken into consideration.

This research is highly motivated as there is still no overall picture of the conditions for journalism in post-conflict and transition states, and also few studies on international efforts to support autonomous journalism.

References

Andresen, Kenneth (2009), 'Producing "protocol news" in Kosovo's public broadcaster: journalism in a transition risk society', *Conflict and Communication Online*, 8: 2.

Arnold, Anne-Katrin and Odugbemi, Sina (2011), 'International Support to Media Development: Context, Evidence, Challenges and Possible Strategic Principles', in Media Assistance Today, *Joint WBI/Internews/BBC World Service Trust/OECD-DAC-Govnet Seminar on Trends in Accountability*, Paris, 6–8 June.

Barber, Martin (2009), 'Humanitarian crises and peace operations', *Conflict, Security & Development*, 9: 3, pp. 387–409.

Barker, Michael J. (2008), 'Democracy or Polyarcy? US-funded media developments in Afghanistan and Iraq post 9/11', *Media, Culture and Society*, 30: 1, pp. 109–30.

Barnett, Michael (1995), 'The new UN politics of peace: from juridical sovereignty to empirical sovereignty', *Global Governance*, 1: 1, pp. 79–97.

Barnett, Michael and Weiss, Thomas (2008), *Humanitarianism in Question: Politics, Power, Ethics*, New York: Cornell University Press.

Cottle, Simon (2006), *Mediatized Conflict*, Berkshire: Open University Press.

Giddens, Anthony (1999), *Runaway World*, London: Profile.

Gustafsson, Karl Erik and Rydén, Per (2010), *A History of the Press in Sweden*, Gothenburg: Nordicom.

Hadenius, Stig, Weibull, Lennart and Wadbring, Ingela (2008), *Massmedier – press, radio och TV i den digitala åldern/Mass media – press, radio and television in the digital age*, Stockholm: Ekerlids.

Hallin, Daniel and Mancini, Paolo (2004), *Comparing Media Systems*, Cambridge & New York: Cambridge University Press

Hayman, Rachel and Manning, Carrie (2009), 'Fostering stability or democracy? Aid for democracy promotion in post-conflict countries', *American Political Studies Association*, Toronto, Canada.

Hettne, Björn and Odén, Bertil (2002), 'Global Governance in the 21th Century, Swedish Foreign Ministry Expert Group on Development Issues', *Egdi Study*, 2: 2, Stockholm: Almqvist & Wiksell.

Hök, Jöran (2009), 'Public service in danger: Perspectives for journalism in a fragile state: the case of Afghanistan', *The Future of Journalism*, Cardiff University, 9–10 September.

—————— (2010), 'International intervention, democracy promotion and goal conflicts in Kosovo and Afghanistan', *ECPR European Consortium for Political Research: Standing group on international relations (SGIR) working group 13 – 'Challenges of Democracy Promotion'*, Stockholm, 9–11 September.

Howard, Ross (2003), 'International Media Assistance, a review of donor activities and the lessons learned', Amsterdam: Netherlands Institute of International Relations.

Irex (2011), www.irex.org.

Karlekar, Karin (2011), 'Press Freedom in 2010: Signs of change amid repression', *Freedom House*, http://www.freedomhouse.org/template.cfm?page=350&ana_page=382&year=2011. Accessed 15 Nobember 2010.

Kovach, Bill and Rosenstiel, Tom (2007), *The Elements of Journalism: What news people should know and the public should expect*, 2nd edition, New York: Three Rivers Press.

Limani, Sahadete (2004), 'Paradigms of the relationship between civil society and media in Kosovo', in Orlin Spasov (ed.), *Quality Press in Southeast Europe*, Sofia, Bulgaria: South East Media Centre.

Mingst, Karen (2008), *Essentials of International Relations*, New York & London: W.W. Norton.

Nohrstedt, Stig-Arne (2009), 'New War Journalism: Trends and Challenges', *Nordicom Review*, 30: 1, pp. 95–112.

Putzel, James and van der Zwaan, Joost (2006), *Why Templates for Media Development do not Work in Crisis States*, London: London School of Economics Crisis States Research Centre.

Scholte, Jan Aart (2005), *Globalization – a critical introduction*, 2nd edition, London: Palgrave.

Schudson, Michael (2001), 'The objectivity norm in American journalism', *Journalism Studies*, 2: 2, pp. 149–70.

―――― (2010), 'News in Crisis in the United States: Panic – and Beyond', in David Levy and Rasmus Klein Nielsen (eds), *The Changing Business of Journalism and its Implications for Democracy*, Oxford: University of Oxford & Reuters Institute for the Study of Journalism.

Swedish Foreign Department (2010), *Freedom from Oppression: Government Communication on Swedish Democracy Support*, article 08.077, 26 September, http://www.government.se/content/1/c6/11/62/71/5013cca7.pdf. Accessed 21 August 2010.

Swedish Journalist Union (SJF) (2011), 'Spelregler för press.,radio och TV'/'Ethic rules for press, radio and television', *Journalist Forbundet*, www.sjf.se.

Taylor, Maureen (2008), 'Protocol journalism as a framework for understanding public relations-media relationships in Kosovo', *Public Relations Review*, 35: 1, pp. 23–30.

Thompson, Mark and Price, Monroe (2003), 'Intervention, Media and Human Rights', *Survival*, 45: 1, pp. 183–202.

Van Zweeden, Cees (2007), 'The state of the media in Kosovo', *Helsinki Monitor*, 18: 2, pp. 138–49.

Voltmer, Katrin (2008), 'Comparing media systems in new democracies: East meets South meets West', *Central European Journal of Communication*, 1: 1, pp. 23–40.

Zogani, Avni (2010), 'Lack of funds suffocate investigative journalism in Kosovo', *Scoop, Kosovo*, 22 July.

Chapter 9

Towards a pragmatic view of impartiality

Leon Barkho

This chapter examines some of the major lines of thought of pragmatic philosophers like Dewey, James, Peirce, Putnam and Habermas, and relates them to issues of impartiality in news and current affairs. The chapter also draws on Hannah Arendt and her deliberations of politics and discourse. It starts by laying down the basic concepts these thinkers have used in their attempt to explain the social reality of our modern world, and the reasons they have provided for how and why we have drastically failed to solve the crises facing us. It shows how important and relevant their concepts can be to unravel the mystifications surrounding today's political and media discourse, and how useful they can be to news and current affairs scholars and practitioners concerned with issues of impartiality and objectivity. It analyzes a few samples of political discourse in light of the key concepts these thinkers present, and examines their discursive and social categorizations in terms of impartiality and objectivity criteria. Relying on media representations of current crises, the chapter shows how the discursive and social patterns we use exacerbate conditions, drive opposing parties further apart, and hinder dialogue and compromise.

Introduction

Whether individuals or societies, we usually make big claims to democracy, tolerance and civility. Rarely do we pay attention to the fact that our discourses and actions, when based on a social world of binary divisions, of entrenched camps of good and bad or good and evil, are a major threat to our own way of life and that of others. We mostly consume the type of discourse that deepens this divide and provides little opportunity for open dialogue and debate. The opposition between what is benign and malignant, what is black and white, what is positive and negative and what is good and evil is no longer confined to centuries-old conflict between the 'Christian' West and the 'Muslim' East. Today, these divisions have come to undermine even the societies living under the umbrella of the same religion or sharing the same history, culture and tradition, as the violence that currently engulfs several Arab and Muslim states testifies. Today, the perpetrators of violence of all hues and colours, as we shall see, draw on ideological, historical, religious and sectarian divisions to justify not only their violent actions, but discourses tainted with hatred and rancour, and intended to humiliate the other. This kind of world, according to pragmatic thinkers like Dewey, Peirce, Putnam and James, breeds uncertainty and fear, prompting human beings to resort to 'moral absolutes' that are deeply rooted in their history, culture and religious upbringing. In times like these, people glorify their absolutes, seeking solace in their beliefs that help them sometimes to even justify acts of violence (cf. Arendt 1965; Habermas 1973; James 1977; Dewey 1981; Peirce 1992; Putnam 2002).

Bernstein (1976, 2005 & 2010) is perhaps the philosopher who has done more than any other present-day thinker to inform us about the major lines of thought of these pragmatic philosophers, and how relevant their writings are to our current world and the crises it confronts. To my knowledge, and despite the impact pragmatist philosophers like Dewey, James, Peirce, Putman and Rotary have had in North America, Europe and elsewhere, and the significance of their writings for current deliberations on politics, democracy and education, their thoughts have largely been overlooked in media studies with a focus on impartiality and critical discourse. These studies have shown more interest in the writings of Habermas, but they have mainly focused on his theories of communication and largely ignored his pragmatic side, which makes him the closest European philosopher to American pragmatic thinkers. And although the writings of Hannah Arendt are a must for any investigation into actions and discourses involving hatred, violence, abuse, massacres and evil, to my knowledge her deliberations of these issues and the language used to represent them have largely gone unnoticed in studies of impartiality in news and current affairs.

Theoretical background

Basic notions

There are four major lines of thought that can be derived from the writings of these thinkers (Putman 1994: 152). The first relates to fallibilism in the sense that there is no 'metaphysical guarantee' that our viewpoints, stands and even beliefs as represented in our actions and discourse 'will never need revision'. The second, even more important thesis is that there is no fundamental dichotomy between 'facts' and 'values', a notion which runs contrary to the perception of objective and impartial observer capable of telling 'it as it is'. The third is the thesis that 'practice is primary in philosophy'; what matters is not the rigor and sophistication of our theories and methodologies, but how they are translated into action and their consequences. Finally, the agreement that the binary categorizations and dichotomies that divide not only social sciences but our social world into camps of positive/negative, benign/ malignant, good/bad, good/evil, etc., are not 'absolutes', and it is legitimate to have them questioned, challenged and resisted.

These four principles constitute the 'way of thinking' for prominent American pragmatic philosophers, and they are loudly echoed in the writings of Arendt and Habermas. Together, these thinkers react strongly against rigid dichotomies of good and bad and categorizations of positive/benign and negative/malignant, not only in the actions that we take but also in the language we use. On the basis of these four lines of thinking, they all share a faith in the role of consultation, of debate, of persuasion in the formation of actions and communication, and a disbelief in the infallibility of what we stand for in terms of our cultural and religious convictions, as well as our way of life. They all endorse open dialogue and communication involving all actors from different and opposing sectors. They all see democracy in terms of 'inclusiveness' where everyone has a voice, rather than in terms of 'exclusiveness' where it is 'my' and 'our' voice that counts. 'Exclusiveness' segregates and separates moral values, convictions and cultural views of others. It is the opposite of cultural pluralism and contrary to democratic principles which stress the need that the rights of those with opposing and different cultural views are to be respected and protected (cf. Arendt 1965; Habermas 1973; James 1977; Dewey 1981; Peirce 1992; Putnam 2002).

Either/or epistemologies

These pragmatic thinkers react strongly against epistemological divisions and moral justifications based on Descartes' (1979) 'either/or' views, and the fact that our actions and discourses must be such and such. In their deliberations and explications of our world, they see either/or dichotomies as a threat to our existence. Our stands, beliefs, actions and discourses, according to these philosophers, should always be open for criticism, and we should always be ready to correct ourselves following dialogue with different actors from different sectors. For these thinkers, it is debate that constitutes 'the very essence of political life' (Arendt 1977: 241). They urge all of us to listen carefully to those challenging, criticizing and resisting our ideas and actions.

But what is happening in our world is the opposite. Most of our actions and discourses, as the cases examined in this chapter show, emanate from stands, ideologies and beliefs we see as 'absolute facts' not possible to revise or change. Dividing the world into forces of good and evil, and taking our beliefs – particularly our religious convictions – to be absolutely correct to the extent of justifying our resort to violence (Bernstein 2005), is not only impractical, but a threat to our civilization. Our world today is turning into 'galaxies' of binary and opposing certainties, and absolutes based mainly on our own religious, moral, political, ideological and cultural convictions and justifications. If we knew or were made aware that there are no absolute facts, we might not have resorted to violence in forcing our values; and those questioning, challenging or even resisting them should not have feared retaliation or punishment. But we frequently resort to violent actions and 'distorted' discourses to impose our values and our way of life because we believe, or are made to believe, that our actions and discourses are 'white' and actions and discourses of those opposing us are 'black'. Samantha Power, criticizing the division of our world into 'benign-and-malignant' binaries, writes: '[S]heltering behind black-and-white characterizations is not only questionable for moral or epistemological reasons. It poses a practical problem because it blinds us from understanding and thus undermines our long term ability to prevent and surmount what we don't know and most fear' (2004: 37). And for those hiding behind the infallibility of their religious and cultural values and convictions, Schlesinger has the following warning: 'There are no more dangerous people on earth than those who believe they are executing the will of the Almighty. It is this conviction that drives on terrorists to murder the infidel' (2004: 116).

The role of language

One other fundamental element bringing these scholars together is their emphasis on the vital role language plays in our modern age. They maintain that language not only reflects our actions in the world, it prompts us to carry those actions through its capacity that preserves almost intact our religious texts, their interpretations, as well as our culture, traditions, etc. In Habermasian terms, language 'objectifies' communicative actions through the discourses employed to represent them. When critically examined, we shall see that the language we use to relay the crises of our world through news demonstrates our way of life because, as Habermas says, the meaning of 'social norms [...] is objectified in ordinary language of communication' (1973: 92). According to Habermas, we shape and determine what we are not only through our deeds, but also through our communicative action. Language, more than anything else, shows what traces of our history can still haunt and imprison us. Our actions shape and are shaped by the language we use. There are certain purposes and intentions behind our actions, whether good or bad, and these are immersed in our histories, cultures and religions and inserted into discourse, consciously or unconsciously, in different ways. It is important and fundamental to understand the language the sides to a conflict use if we are to understand their actions. It is likewise important and fundamental to know why and how observers relaying communication actions select certain discursive and social patterns at the expense of others.

The role of practice

The last major idea bringing these thinkers together is 'practice'. These thinkers agree that practice, a term almost equivalent to Arendt's 'action', is important for human relations, particularly at times of crises and stark clash of mentalities, religions and ideologies. At the same time they see language as constituted by practice and vice versa. Hannah Arendt has probably done more than any other philosopher in unpacking the practice of evil in our modern age. Most of Arendt's work concerns the Nazi horrors of the twentieth century, but her writings can have a lot of relation to what constitutes evil and bad in all ages, and I find them relevant to unravel central journalistic concepts like impartiality. Arendt says evil takes place when someone or some institution sees other people (opponents, different ethnic, religious or sectarian groups, etc.) as unnecessary and superfluous. The Nazis considered Jews, gypsies, homosexuals and other groups superfluous, and being superfluous meant that they had no rights – either human or judicial – and were therefore worthy of being exterminated: 'The aim of an arbitrary system is to destroy the civil rights of the whole population, who ultimately become just as the outlawed in their own county as the stateless and the homeless. The destruction of man's rights, the killing of the juridical person in him, is a prerequisite for dominating him entirely' (Arendt 1968: 451). Arendt's view of how 'an arbitrary system' can destroy the human rights of 'the whole population' can be extended to cover 'the linguistic rights' which populations and groups are entitled to. The denial of human rights is normally accompanied by a denial of the discourses of those opposing or resisting our values. The way 'an arbitrary system' makes a population 'homeless' and 'outlawed', even in its 'own country', the same system works to distort and constrain its language and discourse.

Method of the study

This chapter applies some of the basic lines of thought of prominent American pragmatist philosophers as outlined in the preceding section. To operationalize these concepts, the analysis leans on Habermas and his theory of communicative action and language, and the importance of open dialogue with actors from different sectors. The theory is neither objective nor subjective. It is a linguistic process that is intersubjective, whose operationalization requires a system of 'a self-critical community of inquirers'. To assess and substantiate these thinkers' thoughts, the study applies Habermas' notion that human beings do not determine what they are only through their actions. The social reality of individuals and groups can also be determined through their communicative actions and language. Therefore, for a critical analysis of 'ordinary language' to have an emancipatory function, it should not start from a pre-ordained position. Its target should be the unravelling and explaining of the meanings, purposes and motives of actions by different actors (Habermas 1973). A critical inquiry that takes the views of all actors into consideration will tell whether language results in distortive/non-distortive or constrained/non-constrained communication (Bernstein 1976).

Besides Habermas, the critical analysis below draws on Hannah Arendt's notions, particularly those related to language and its role in rendering human beings opposing our way of life not only judicially superfluous, but also linguistically unnecessary. Like Habermas, Arendt relates human action to language and communication: 'Action and speech are so closely related because the primordial and the specifically human act must at the same time contain the answer to the question asked of every newcomer: who are you? This disclosure of who somebody is, is implicit in both his words and deeds' (Arendt 1958: 178). At times of major crises and violence, groups or individuals seeking 'total domination' strive to strip those they see as 'evil' or those they think pose a threat to their rule of their rights as human beings (Arendt 1968). Violence does not only breed torture, killing and destruction;

it generates a narrative and a discourse which makes the other not only morally, but also linguistically unnecessary. The dominated and humiliated groups are transformed 'into something less fully human' (Bernstein 2005: 7).

The analysis below demonstrates how the major lines of thought of these philosophers can be operationalized to assess the discursive and social representations of current conflicts and crises of our world, taking the events in Syria and their coverage by Arab and international media as major examples. News samples from the BBC, two major Arabic media players – Al Jazeera and Al Arabiya – as well as some samples of western media discursive representations of Arabs and Muslims, are critically analyzed in light of the concerns pragmatist philosophers raise about the current state of our world. These philosophers' major lines of thinking are summarized below in the form of six research questions:

1. How can we transform the concepts and notions presented above into empirical tools to assess the impartiality and objectivity of news and current affairs?
2. What type of justifications do we make to advance our claims about things being right or wrong?
3. Are our justifications for what is right or wrong morally or religiously based?
4. How and why do we make other people and groups discursively 'superfluous and unnecessary'?
5. Do the media resort to open debate and dialogue to challenge propositions the sides to a conflict put forward to buttress their views?
6. Are the media consistent in their representation of different conflicts in the world?

Analysis

The conflict in Syria has been the bloodiest of the events known as the 'Arab Spring'. At the time of writing, more than 70,000 people were reported to have been killed, massive damage has been inflicted on major urban centres, and hundreds of thousands of people were said to have been either displaced or forced to flee the country. There have been horrendous tales of human rights violations, including massacres of hundreds of civilians, among them children. The events in this country have received more attention from both Arab and international media than any other conflict that has been associated with the 'Arab Spring' due to the duration of time it has been going on and the resulting human suffering.

The analysis here does not start with an attitude because issues of 'right' and 'wrong,' as pragmatist philosophers tell us, are debatable. It is not the job of an analyst to start by insisting that 'the fault lies exclusively on one side' (Dobbs 2012). The aim is not to give ad hoc explanations of the cases that are discursively and socially investigated in this chapter, but to build a theory that describes, explains and predicts at least part of the social reality of how, and why, the events chosen for analysis are covered the way they are by different media in a logically consistent and interrelated manner (Shoemaker, Tankard & Lasorsa 2004; Shoemaker & Vos 2009). Thus, the major target of a critical analysis or study should be to explain what we or our socieites may see as 'evil'. Explaining and interpreting 'evil' does not mean endorsing it. (See Chapters 5 and 7).

Let us first start by analyzing three pieces on the events in Syria; one from each of the all-news Arabic channels of Al Arabiya (2012) and Al Jazeera (2012), and the third from the BBC (2012). The Arabic stories are rendered into English by the author. Due to considerations of space, only the paragraphs concerning deaths resulting from violence or 'massacre' are cited and analyzed.[1]

Massacre in al-Khalidiya neighborhood in Homs as a result of the regime's ferocious shelling

The Syrian Information Center has said that the city of Rustin was bombed with a new kind of shells which are difficult to identify.

The number of those killed in Syria yesterday rose to 180, among them 75 in the city of Aleppo which has been witnessing fierce bombing by the regime's army.

According to local revolutionary coordination committees there are children and civilians among the dead. They were killed following the shelling of a bakery in Bab neighborhood by the regime's forces.

The Union for the Coordination of the Revolution [...] has released videos showing the capture of a weapons depot belonging to the regime's army in Aleppo [...] at a time the regime's forces continued their shelling of Damascus suburbs with heavy artillery. (Al Arabiya 2012)

173 killed and shelling continues in Syria

The Syrian Network for Human Rights has said that 173 people were killed yesterday (Friday) most of them in Homs, Damascus and its suburbs and Aleppo as shelling of several districts in Aleppo and Damascus continued.

The local coordination committees said 40 people were killed on Friday in Damascus and its suburbs, 36 in Aleppo, 30 in Daraa among them 8 burned bodies which were found in the district of Nowi, 30 in Homs, 10 of them were found in the district of Balaba, 12 in Adleb, 5 in Deir al-Zoor and 4 in Hama among them a woman and a baby.

The General Commission for the Syrian Revolution said that 16 bodies in civilian clothes were butchered by knives in the ranches of al-Shfouniya in Doma in Damascus suburbs.

Activists said 12 people were killed in the villages of Shalakh and Maaralbeet in Adleb suburbs as a result of shelling by the regime's army.

Activists released pictures on the website of the Syrian Revolution showing bodies under debris some of them of children and women. Activists said a great number of houses have thoroughly been destroyed. (Al Jazeera 2012a)

Syria activists 'find 60 bodies in Damascus suburb'
At least 60 bodies have been found in a suburb of Damascus, activists say, following what the opposition described as a 'massacre' by government forces.

A poor-quality video posted online showed what appeared to be the charred remains of dozens of people, many with their hands tied behind their backs.

Activists said the bodies were found on Thursday at a rubbish dump outside Qatana, south-west of the capital.

The death toll included the 60 reportedly found at Qatana. Activists said they were still trying to find out who the victims in Qatana were and what happened.

They believed government forces had executed the victims before setting their bodies alight, they said.

It is impossible to verify the activists' reports of the alleged massacre, as international media cannot report freely in Syria. (BBC 2012b)

Which journalism is 'right'?

Critical analyses, particularly based on language and discourse, consume time and space, even if they are restricted to the major discursive properties of a few sentences from one single text. A discursive analysis leaning on an intersubjective linguistic process, as Habermas (1973) and Arendt (1977) tell us, requires taking into account the positions and stands of different actors from different sectors, and still it has to remind readers that the analysis itself might be as fallible as the attitudes and mentalities it criticizes (Putnam 1994). Such analysis might be even more time and space-consuming. Bearing all these considerations in mind, I will try to be as concise as possible, focusing on the major critical highlights in the three texts above.

Al Jazeera Arabic and Al Arabiya are supposed to be rivals, discursively and socially. In fact the former was set up in 2003 by the royalty in Saudi Arabia to offset the influence, and more specifically the exposure, by the latter of what goes on in the secretive kingdom of Saudi Arabia. A few years after Al Arabiya's launch, the Qatari-owned Al Jazeera, which came into being in 1996, had to tone down its criticism of Saudi monarchy. The Qatari and Saudi royals, in a meeting in 2007, agreed to halt attacking each other's monarchical systems not only through their pan-Arab news channels– their most influential media tools – but across their media empires (Worth 2008). Between them, the two monarchies own or control most pan-Arab media (Hammond 2007). Their differences regarding other issues persisted, but the tit-for-tat media vitriolic targeting each other's monarchical systems came to an end. They and their media have had their differences over the events known as the 'Arab Spring' in Egypt, Tunisia and Libya, but they see the events in both Syria and Bahrain almost eye to eye. Both countries and their media have thrown their weight behind the rebellion in Syria, but are glossing over the peaceful demonstrations in Bahrain (BBC 2012c; Hashem 2012).

A simple critical analysis of the texts above would substantiate that both Al Arabiya and Al Jazeera see the events in Syria from almost one discursive and social perspective. The language of the disparate Syrian opposition groups and organizations is transmuted or reproduced as if it were the final news output; in other words, as if it had gone through editing, vetting and gatekeeping processes, which communicative events are subjected to before they become news. A close discursive investigation would reveal that Al Arabiya and Al Jazeera's pieces are unauthenticated and almost impossible to verify. Note the contrast between the headline in Al Arabiya and the content of the story. The scene of the 'massacre' in the headline is 'al-Khalidiya' but there is no mention of the site or district in the story. There are three different sources in the story all belonging to the Syrian opposition: The Syrian Information Center; Local Revolutionary Coordination Committees; and the Union for the Coordination of the Revolution. There is no indication of any form of independent confirmation of the claims by the three opposition groups, and no sign of how the broadcaster obtained the content, which is not its own. The broadcaster even fails to substantiate the word 'massacre' in the headline, or 'ferocious shelling'.

Al Jazeera's piece is even more problematic. The figures of the dead do not tally. In the headline it says '173 killed'. In the body of the story the figures are not only much higher than that, but are misleading. The sourcing, though unverified, is a mess. There are five different sources, each providing different casualty figures and different content. The broadcaster solely relies on opposition groups and activists: the Syrian Network for Human Rights, the Local Coordination Committees, the General Commission for the Syrian Revolution – and two groups of activists. Like Al Arabiya, what these groups feed Al Jazeera with is taken for granted. Although there is no way to verify what they say, both channels raise not a single doubt about the authenticity of the material. The amateur videos these groups provide are broadcast on-air, and their statements are issued online with no reference to their authentication or provenance. There are no warnings to audiences about how they obtain their user-generated content (UGC), which makes up the bulk of their coverage of the rebellion in Syria. Issues about UGC's provenance, authentication and representation through warnings on-air, or in writing that the content received cannot be independently confirmed, are crucial not only for impartiality and objectivity, but for transparency, inquiry and open debate (Habermas 1973; Arendt 1977). But such caveats are nowhere to be seen in the coverage by both Al Arabiya and Al Jazeera of the events in Syria.

The text by the BBC is discursively and socially different from Al Arabiya's or Al Jazeera's. First, there are enough warnings and caveats about the authenticity and provenance of the

UGC the broadcaster is turning into news. Audiences can tell not only how the BBC received the content, but what it represents and how it should be treated by them. Note the use of inverted commas in the headline, and the lead to show that the word 'massacre' is not the BBC's. The inverted commas tell readers in writing that the BBC has no way of confirming that a 'massacre' has taken place. On-air, the same term would either be given a different intonation or preceded by a discursive caveat like 'the purported or alleged massacre, what they (UGC) said was or what the activists described as a massacre'. The BBC is keen to describe for its audiences not only the provenance, but also the quality of the UGC: 'A poor-quality video posted online showed *what appeared to be* the charred remains [...]' (my emphasis). The attribution of the UGC is consistent throughout 'activists'. In fact, the BBC is not satisfied with just one caveat about provenance; it throws in one full paragraph at the end as a last warning to audiences that this is UGC and not BBC content: 'It is impossible to verify the activists' reports of the alleged massacre, as the international media cannot report freely in Syria'. All the precautionary measures the BBC undertakes, discursively and socially, about UGC's provenance – through punctuation and the use of special linguistic expressions in its verbal representation of the conflict – for the sake of impartiality are not to be found in the Arabic channels' representation of the events in Syria. The channels see their discursive patterns, mainly based on religious, sectarian and political convictions, as absolutely correct and justifiable (Bernstein 2005). (See Chapter 11 for details on how Reuters sources and verifies UGC).

Interactivity

Interactivity is today a major characteristic of human communication, and it assumes additional significance in the media (McQuail 2005). In the world of news and current affairs, it mainly relates to users' responses to a story, as major media today give their readers the opportunity to express their views vis-à-vis the theme(s) the story presents. An investigation of the users' responses and initiatives can tell a great deal not only about viewership, but also about the orientation and inclination of both the source and sender.

A cursory examination of Al Arabiya and Al Jazeera's news content on the events in Syria would show that Syria coverage generates more responses from users than any other communicative event the channels have broadcast on the 'Arab Spring'. A critical analysis of users' responses or comments tells volumes of how and why the two channels end up issuing stories like the two samples mentioned above.

Evidence of both Arabic channels turning a blind eye to issues of objectivity and impartiality in covering the events in Syria is not confined to their news content. Their siding with the rebel or opposition side in the conflict discursively and socially emanates from centuries of religious and sectarian schism between the two main branches of Islam: the Shiite (a form of which is represented by the Syrian President Bashar al-Assad and his minority Alawite sect in Syria) and the Sunni (the sect of majority Muslims of which the immensely rich royalties of Saudi Arabia and Qatar claim to be the guardians).

Al Jazeera Live, a sister channel of Al Jazeera Arabic, allows viewers to send in messages which are screened as subtitles. Here are a few examples spotted during intermittent viewing of the channel in December 2011: 'My brethren in Syria recite the Surah of Ya Seen'; 'Bashar have mercy on your people and do not kill them'; 'thanks to Syria's revolutionaries you, Assad, are doomed'; 'salute to every member of the (Syrian) Free Army'; 'to Homs, muarat al-Nuaman, we are with you until death'; 'march, march in support of Homs people'; 'God have mercy on the martyrs of the occupied Nuwa' (cf. Ismael 2011). The messages reveal two major threats of thought that are steering the course of events in the Muslim world in general, and Arab countries in particular. Firstly, excessive reliance on the Muslim Holy Book, the Koran – written more than fourteen centuries ago – to justify not only violent actions and abuses, but also 'distortive' discourses (Bernstein 1976). Note 'the Surah of Ya Seen', a Koranic Chapter of 83 verses, which in essence is a dialogue between believers and disbelievers who are described as people entertaining 'evil omens […] *Al-Mujrimoon* [criminals, polytheists, sinners and disbelievers in the Islamic Montheism] […] *Musrifoon* [those transgressing all bounds by committing all kinds of great sins and disobeying Allah]' (Koran 36: 20–58). The binary division of bad and evil is obvious. The Syrian President Assad and those supporting him are 'the disbelievers', while those opposing them are 'the believers'. The discursive analysis provides evidence that the broadcasters hide behind the discursive and social infallibility of the religious, sectarian and cultural values and convictions their sponsors and financiers propagate (Schlesinger 2004).

The second threat, like the first, draws on historical 'fact' to justify retaliation and reprisals on the part of one side of the conflict. Note the expression 'to Homs, *muarat al-Nuaman*, we are with you until death'. The emphasized name refers to a Sunni saint and a follower of the Prophet Muhammad, which attaches added religious significance to Homs, the scene of some of the most ferocious fighting throughout the conflict. Similarly, the message, 'God have mercy on the martyrs of the occupied Nuwa', reverberates with sectarian incitement. It describes the Syrian town of Nuwa as 'occupied' by forces loyal to the Syrian government, and those killed in the struggle for its 'liberation' as 'martyrs', a term Islam reserves for those who fall in defence of the faith.

It is hard to believe that a network like Al Jazeera with international reach would allow comments like these appearing on its screens. There are parallels and commonalities between the actions taking place in Syria and the discourses employed by the Arabic broadcasters because, as Habermas (1973) points out, actions are objectified in the language we use to communicate an event. Material like this should not have been allowed in accordance with the network's slogan of 'opinion and the other opinion' and its own ethical code (Al Jazeera 2010) or house rules (Al Jazeera 2012a). But in the case of Syria, codes and rules do not hold, because for Al Jazeera and its financiers, the Qatari royals, rebel groups are 'the believers', 'the good', 'the oppressed' and 'the victimized' and Assad, his army and his supporters are 'the disbelievers', 'the evil', 'the oppressors' and the 'victimizers'. The social and discursive binaries and dichotomies of good and bad and of black and white which pragmatist philosophers strongly reject are not hard to detect. (cf. Arendt 1965; Habermas 1973; James 1977; Dewey 1981; Peirce 1992; Putnam 2002).

Syria-related stories usually generate most interactivity in both Arabic channels. In Al Arabiya, a Syria online story normally attracts more than 500 comments. Here are a few samples selected from six stories published in the first six days of September 2012:

1. Let NileSat stop the transmission of Rawafidh channels which [...] disseminate Majosi Shiisim [...] and do not forget the channel of the party of Allat [...].
2. [...] the Hulagu of Syria, the blood-succor, the vampire, who has killed 70,000 people so far [...].
3. The Alawites are a threat to the whole world for their deeply rooted rancor and hatred. They are terrorist by nature and terrorism is found in their genes. Everyone who posts a comment in support of Assad is an Alawite.
4. The Hitler of the Arabs, the butcher and son of a butcher, the dean of criminals, this F(B)ashar the donkey is going to exterminate the whole nation [...].
5. This Satanic and demonic devil Aub Lualua [UN Syria envoy Lakhdar Brahimi] is going to produce from his box the principle of banning weapons from all sides. This is the first blow to the blessed revolution by this traitor so that no one will spot the demonic devils of the Red Cross Commission move under the umbrella of humanitarian assistance
6. The Nasiriya are the people of mockery and treachery.
7. The man [Bashar al-Assad] does not know how to pray and the Prophet has said, 'The covenant between you and me is the prayer, the one who does not pray is an infidel.' And now you come and say that we brand whoever we want an infidel. Not everyone we want but those who the Prophet has told us about [...].
8. Fouad al-Hashem in al-Watan daily has affirmed that Maher al-Assad [brother of Syrian President Bashar] has made a vow to Qassem Sulaiman, the commander of the Iranian revolutionary al-Quds Corps that he will not let a single Sunni family in Syria breathe (Oxygen). We say to this lunatic criminal we shall smash your skull with the boots of the valiant free army (the rebels), the depraved man you are.
9. [...] the gangs of the terrorist Bashar al-Assad, the leader of al-Nasiriya terrorists [...] the feast is to have the terrorist Bashar al-Assad the leader of Nasiriya terrorists executed in the Square of Marja in Damascus. This will be the greatest of days and we shall turn it into a national holiday for all the Syrians [...].
10. This is what Ibn Taymiyya made note of and warned us against regarding these Nasiriya and Alwiya hundreds of years ago and we today see that substantiated in their actions.

These comments might have little meaning for those not versed in the Arab and Muslim history, religion and culture. But for Arabs and Muslims they are immersed in history, tradition, Koranic and Hadith (sayings of the Prophet Muhammad) references and Koranic scholars' interpretations, which for many Sunni Muslims are as sacred as the 'holy' text. The major theme behind comments like these is incitement, defamation and abuse, all geared towards proving through religious and historical 'fact' that the Syrian president, his sect (the Alawites who are about 10 per cent of Syria's population) and those supporting them fall in the category of infidels, or enemies of God and Islam. The comments are deliberately provocative. There is clear binary categorization here with the Sunni Muslims representing 'the white, the good, the positive, the benign' side of the conflict, and the Shiite Muslims (with the Alawite branch being an offshoot) representing 'the black, the evil, the negative and the malignant' side.

Note, for instance, the term *Rawafidh* in first comment, which is religiously abusive and tantamount to a swear word because it is specifically used to humiliate Muslim Shiites and show them as depraved human beings who have strayed away from the true path of Islam; hence *Rawafidh* or 'rejectionists'. Similarly, terms like '*Majosi Shiism*' in (1) and *Nasiriya* (6, 9 and 10) are deployed by 'radical' Sunnis to brand Shiites and relegate them to infidels. Other references to history and religion rendering Shiites and Alawites not only 'less human' but totally unnecessary include the mention of *Ibn Taimiyya* (10), a thirteenth-century Muslim theologian considered the linchpin of extremist Muslim thought (Waller 2006) and whose teachings, for radical Sunnis, particularly for al-Qaeda operatives, affiliates and members, are as revered as the verses of the Koran. This scholar, who *Le Monde diplomatique* described as 'a great theoretician of Jihad' (Antonin & de Miramon 2012) is the one who promulgated among Sunni Muslims that Shiites are people without religion, who believe in superstitions, spread lies and are as evil as other infidels, among them Christians and Jews. Ibn Taimiyya's jurisprudence is tantamount to the teachings of the Prophet for the branch of Islam prevalent in both Qatar, and particularly in Saudi Arabia (Ibn Taimiyya 1975). The resort to religious discursive patterns prevalent in the Middle Ages to undermine the linguistic and human rights of others is a reminder of Arendt's (1977) thesis that violence and evil prosper when someone, a group or an institution sees opponents as superfluous and unnecessary in language and action.

Let us now examine the comment in (5). It is critical, but in an abusive and defamatory manner, of the UN's envoy to Syria, Lakhdar Brahimi, and the International Committee of the Red Cross. Both are branded 'demonic evils' and Brahimi is called 'traitor' and compared to Abu Lualua, a Muslim Persian (*Majosi*) who the Sunni Muslims condemn for treachery for his killing of one of the Caliphs succeeding the Prophet in the seventh century. Bashar is called 'the leader of Nasiriya terrorists' and 'lunatic criminal', and the Lebanese Shiite Hezbollah or Hizb Allah (party of God) is discursively relabelled into 'Hizb Allat' (party of *Allat*), an idol and symbol of paganism which the Prophet ordered torn to pieces because *Allat* and its supporters 'follow naught but conjecture' (Koran 53: 19–23). The connotations are clear with discursive representations not only distorting and constraining the other, but rendering them superfluous and less fully human (Arendt 1958; Berstein 1976). There are other swear words as in (4), where Bashar is called 'Fashar,' an indecent expression in Arabic. There are references to other publications, as in (8), which despite their malignant nature, the author was unable to verify.

This binary interactive discourse of good and evil is not only a characteristic of these two pan-Arab channels. It has crept into most media financed by the royalties of Qatar and Saudi Arabia. While Al Jazeera posts a code of ethics and some terms and conditions for posting comments in Arabic – though not adhered to in the case of Syria – there is no such material on Al Arabiya's website. There are no instructions on how users should behave before posting a comment. There are no warnings about the existence of any defamation laws that will protect individuals or organizations from attacks on their reputation, and whether such attacks may result in prosecution. It is not clear whether the broadcasters resort to any form of moderation before posting, apart of course from deleting comments from users on the other side of the fence of the conflict since not a single anti-Sunni Islam remark was spotted in the hundreds of comments selected for analysis. All religious and sectarian groups have a depository of absolutes that is discursively and socially contrary to their opponents' convictions and beliefs, but are we allowed to broadcast or write them in a public forum seen by tens of millions of people, as the viewership and ratings of both channels testify (Campbell 2011). The presence of a decent form of moderation would have failed many of the comments above. Some of them are swear words and culturally and religiously offensive, and are used to harass, humiliate and threaten the other. Compare Al Arabiya, and even Al Jazeera for that matter, with the extensive house rules and their terms and conditions to which the BBC alerts users and draws their attention before posting a comment (BBC 2012a).

Words as armaments

The short texts analyzed above exhibit some salient discursive features besides their binary nature of good/evil characterization. The initiators of this type of discourse render nameless those who in their eyes represent 'evil', their humanity unreasoning and unjustified, despite the fallibility of the ideas their language carries and despite the fact of being righteous from only one viewpoint (c.f. Arendt 1965; James; 1977; Dewey 1981; Peirce 1992). When repeated by influential broadcasters with a wide reach like Al Arabiya and Al Jazeera they cause a lot of damage. Violent political rhetoric is as harmful as violence itself (*New York Times* 2011).

But is this type of discourse confined to the Arab media? It seems that in our binary world, it is sometimes hard to cope with the coinages, neologisms and nonce words that represent the other malignantly and negatively. Examine the following terms that have crept into Western media in the aftermath of September 11: axis of evil; Islamic fanatics; enemy combatants; chauvinistic Islam; jihadists; Islamists; Muslim fascists; extremists; militants; terrorists; insurgents; master-bombers; homicide bombers; Islamofascism, etc. Many of these labels are frequently used in western media to categorize Arabs and Muslims. But there are three important issues to remember here. First, these labels are not innocent coinages, neologisms and nonce words (that is we deny 'the other' its own linguistic rights at the same time as we keep our own linguistic rights intact). Second, we reserve these negative labels to groups with whom we are in conflict. Third, and most importantly, labelling in this way is no help to start an open debate or a moral inquiry that is necessary for democracy and reconciliation. Bernstein warns against such labelling: 'Simply *labeling* something or some person as evil is *not* moral inquiry. For all the emotional appeal of this labeling, it obscures and distorts our choices' (2005: 57).

And note the use by the US military of what appears to be agreeable and inoffensive linguistic terms, or benign discursive representations, to justify their torture of detainees:

special renditions; mild, non-injurious physical contact; stress position; sleep management; illegal combatants; black sites; refined interrogation techniques; extraordinary rendition (Henley 2007). The media adopts euphemisms like these most of the time without challenge or questioning: 'The newspaper said that a special hearing would be then held in Iraq to determine whether the detainees should be released, held as POWs or declared illegal combatants' (BBC 2003); '[…] he was subjected to extraordinary rendition on behalf of the United States, and sent to Thailand' (Nordland 2011). (See Chapter 3 for details on how NATO manipulates information in warfare).

Selection of language is today part of combat, with some media adopting language not only to humiliate but also to make others appear 'less human'. In their *Washington Post* op-ed 'Terrorism as a Virus', Stares and Yacoubian call for the use of an 'ideological antidote' (2005: 58) as part of measures, among them language, in the global war on 'Islamist militancy' (ibid.). The West and its media, as is the case with the Arab and Muslim media, employ language to introduce what can be described as 'preventive discourse'. Like preventive medicine, preventive discourse is a discursive discipline focusing on keeping our language (our bodies) healthy, void of the discursive traces (diseases) prevalent in the language of those opposing or resisting our way of life. While barriers to guard against diseases are necessary and vital in medicine, such walls or 'discursive barriers' are a threat to human communication (Power 2004; Schlesinger 2004). However, representing those who challenge, oppose or resist our views and way of life as 'viruses', or 'bacteria' ready to attack our way of life, is not confined to the discursive level. It is translated into action. That is what policy leaders like Haass (2005) call for: 'So if terrorism is not a war, how should we understand it? Perhaps as a disease. There are steps that can be taken to eradicate or neutralize specific viruses or bacteria'. And this health/sickness binary is no longer restricted to the clash between the 'Christian' West and 'Muslim' East. It has crept into pro-Sunni Muslim discourse of pan-Arab news channels like Al Jazeera and Al Arabiya in their representation of the events in Syria.

Words do matter in any conflict in the world. It is the approach that differs. In the Middle East, the discursive emphasis is on religious convictions and historical events. In the West, the approach to humiliate and undermine the other starts first by rejecting the 'enemy' language and second by inventing new coinages that are as deadly as 'viruses' and 'bacteria'. Urging the US and its allies to launch a linguistic offensive alongside the military forays to combat 'Islamic militancy', Waller (2006) writes: 'In the "war of ideas," words matter. By accepting the enemy's terminology and adopting its definitions as our own, we cease fighting on our terms and place our ideas at the enemy's disposal.'

Discussion and implications

Do we make other individuals, groups, or populations superfluous in news discourse? We do when we discursively undermine human beings who are different from us through labels and malignant discursive and social representations (Bernstein 2005). This is the first step that usually precedes the denial of other human rights (Arendt 1965 & 1977). In conflicts and wars, language assumes additional power, with certain vocabularies becoming part of the battlefield gear. This 'linguistic offensive' is launched to undermine, humiliate and diminish the other as a tactic to justify the resort to violent action. The launch of a 'linguistic offensive', unlike a military attack, takes a little effort and not much money. The binary distinctions, whether discursive or social, accompany the crises and conflicts afflicting our world. In the war in Iraq, anyone challenging or resisting the US occupation was discursively represented as 'superfluous' (Bernstein 2005; Barkho 2010). The Arabic channels have turned President Bashar al-Assad, his sect and his supporters into something like 'demons', discursively 'evil', and consequently unnecessary and superfluous. Of course Assad is not a nice man, but are the Arabic channels telling 'it as it is' or they are telling it as their Sunni Muslim benefactors and financiers want them to tell it? Would these channels issue stories about human rights violations in Saudi Arabia and Qatar? Are not these two channels reflecting their own countries' foreign policy? Are not the two 'absolute monarchies' through their influential news channels promoting 'freedom' and 'democracy' in Syria 'without having any democratic legitimacy of their own'? Would they show the 'black', 'unhealthy', 'negative', 'malignant', and 'evil' side of the groups fighting Assad? (cf. Allmeling 2012; Amado & de Miramon 2012; Fisk 2012; Ketz 2012; Qassemi 2012). Language matters in representing conflicts and clash of mentalities. The intentional choice of vitriolic and violent rhetoric, whether conscious or unconscious, funny or serious, hurts and causes a lot of pain and breeds more violence.

Making others discursively superfluous or humanly less significant (Arendt 1965) is a task that the media know better than any other profession. This has been the practice in the so-called 'War on Terror' in which forces of 'good', fight the forces of 'evil' via invasions of whole countries, the launching of unmanned aerial attacks, and other military and violent measures. But nowhere has it been so ostensible as in the coverage of Syria and its uprising, and particularly by the Muslim Sunni-dominated media. The samples analyzed in this study are good discursive representations of 'absolute' convictions and beliefs which we use to represent those who are 'bad' from our viewpoint, and in the construction of which we mainly rely on our own prejudices, histories, religions and sects. Once absolutes are introduced into 'the political realm', Arendt warns, they spell 'doom to everyone' (1963: 79).

Pragmatist philosophers would react strongly against this type of discourse, which sees our own way of life to be superior to others. Dewey (1930), for instance, teaches us that it is wrong to impose what we believe is 'good' and 'right' on others because they are different from us or challenge and resist our views. Crises, divisions and conflicts exacerbate when corporations like multilingual and global media giants want us, or compel us through their discourse to see communicative events their own way. The analysis demonstrates the fears these thinkers express about our own ideas and way of life turning into ideologies – absolute ideologies – to the extent that we justify a discourse meant to subdue those holding opposing ideas and pursuing a different way of life. Their advice, which seems to have gone unheeded, is that 'ideas should never become ideologies' (Menad 2001: 31). For the Arabic broadcasters, not only centuries old convictions and schisms driving Muslim communities and sects apart are still valid, but their linguistic representations are being turned into absolutes to justify both communication and action. This is contrary to William James' pluralistic universe, in which no idea, interpretation, stand, moral value or even philosophy remains the same throughout history (James 1977).

The analysis shows how news discourse can be deployed not only to turn others superfluous, but also to have them discursively assimilated in the name of 'liberation', 'democracy' and 'emancipation' to make them 'the same' like us. Assimilation through communication and action has traditionally been confined to the clash of civilizations and mentalities, mainly between the 'Christian' West vis-à-vis the Muslim East. This process of assimilation is called 'ontological imperialism' by Emmanuel Levinas (cited in Spanos 2000: 216). However, it has currently swept, and with horrendous consequences, the ranks of the multifarious Islamic groups fighting each other under the banner of their own religious interpretations.

The samples analyzed in the study demonstrate how generalizations in which a widely disparate phenomena like culture, religion or a sect within the same religion is represented negatively, and how the nuances of negative labelling are extended to include all those sharing the same values. Representations like these lead to what I call 'discourse of fusion', where members of a culture or religion, even if they number more than 1.3 billion – in the case of Muslims – are lumped together. Although 17 of the 19 hijackers responsible for the atrocities of September 11 were Saudis and all of them Sunnis, and although al-Qaeda recruits are Sunnis, this type of discourse of fusion now makes many relate the group and its violent actions to Iran, a country governed by a Shiite theocracy, which in the eyes of the Saudi and al-Qaeda branch of Islam is blasphemous. Had we engaged in a critical enquiry as Harbermas, Peirce and Dewey ask us to, we would have discovered that Shiites, more than any other group, including the US, have been the target of al-Qaeda terror whether in Iraq, Pakistan, Syria or elsewhere. The notion of 'discourse of fusion' blinds Al Jazeera and Al Arabiya from detecting any negative or malignant practice by the Sunni-dominated rebel groups, to the extent that both channels frown on all evidence in the western media of al-Qaeda operatives and groups infiltrating the rebel ranks (cf. Amado & de Miramon 2012; Fitzgerald 2012; Husain 2012). In the same vein, western policy-makers do not see al-Qaeda in Syria in the same 'evil' perspective as in Afghanistan, Iraq, Yemen, Somalia, Mali or Pakistan, where the slightest suspicion of the presence of al-Qaeda 'militants', even in rugged mountains, prompts deployment of military force, mainly by unmanned aircraft.

Conclusion

The discussion above has provided some answers to the questions and the issues this study wanted to tackle. This section rounds up the chapter with a brief summary of its major findings, and suggestions for future work:

- The events known as the 'Arab Spring', and particularly the one in Syria, have generated a genre of religion-based discourse and partisanship on the part of major media players in the Arab and Muslim world. Its binary and dual discursive character of good and evil is a reflection of our post September 11 world (Bernstein 2005). But the Arab Spring, and specifically the events in Syria, has shown that this binary categorization is no longer related to 'Christianity' and western 'Christian' beliefs, and values facing Islam and Islamic 'evil'. In Syria we have co-religionists resorting to religious semantics and rhetoric to discriminate between faithful/infidel, believer/disbeliever, with us/against us, our martyrs/their dead and heaven/hell. We are face to face with an ideology that justifies violence by reliance on discursive tactics on the basis of our own convictions.

- We forget that once we have applied negative discursive representations to describe others who are culturally, religiously, denominationally or politically different from us, we are closing the door for dialogue and communication, and using our own prejudices and partialities as a criterion. We are partial because we refrain from labelling our own people, our own decisions and our own actions in the same manner, even if they are an exact replica of what happens in the camp of those opposing us.

- The measure of justification and morality, particularly for the Arabic broadcasters of Al Jazeera and Al Arabiya, is religion, and specifically the brand that is practiced by the monarchies supporting them. We are in the twenty-first century, but it seems that many of us have learned nothing from Kant, who tells us that it is wrong to use our religious notions and convictions as a measure for our morality. He notes that 'morality does not need religion at all' (Kant 1960: 6). Nonetheless, appeals to religion, and sometimes interpretations deeply rooted in history, are being used to justify slanted discourses as well as violent actions, some of them with horrific consequences.

- We can rely on Kant and his view of morality to assess whether a piece of news is impartial or not. It is a sign of bias to lean on religious notions and convictions to justify communication and action based on labelling someone or something as bad or evil. Appealing to religious and historical 'facts' in promoting communication, as Al Jazeera and Al Arabiya do in their coverage of Syria, breaches the basic elements of impartiality and objectivity in news and current affairs. It becomes news with a purpose, a motive and an agenda.

- One other good measure of impartiality to apply in communicative circumstances like these is consistency or universality (see Chapter 1). It is important to examine whether Al Arabiya and Al Jazeera apply the same consistency in their coverage of Syria to their coverage of Iraq, for instance, or the reporting of other events in the Middle East or elsewhere. This is an area of research that needs to be explored.

- Another good suggestion for future research is a critical analysis on the lines outlined here of the coverage of the war in Libya, in which western military force was extensively used to change the course of the Arab Spring events in that country. The analysis can examine how western media, particularly British and French news outlets, covered the war, since the two countries were directly involved in the fight, and then have the analysis compared and paralleled with Al Jazeera Arabic and Al Arabiya's coverage. Both Saudi Arabia and Qatar were also heavily involved in the Libyan Arab Spring.

References

Al Arabiya (2012), 'Massacre in al-Khalidiya neighborhood in Homs as a result of the regime's ferocious shelling', 11 August, http://www.alarabiya.net/articles/2012/08/11/231578.html. Accessed 30 August 2012.

Al Jazeera (2010), 'Al Jazeera Code of Ethics', http://www.aljazeera.com/aboutus/2006/11/20085 25185733692771.html. Accessed 3 September 2012.

—— (2012a), 'Terms and Conditions', http://yourmedia.aljazeera.net/terms. Accessed 3 September 2012.

—— (2012b), '173 killed and shelling continues in Syria', 18 August, http://www.aljazeera.net/news/pages/8e1556b9-f2d5-4b0e-915b-927723e772dc. Accessed 30 August 2012.

Allmeling, Anne (2012), 'Suliman: "Al Jazeera plays the piper, but Qatar calls the tune"', *Deutsche Welle*, 24 December, http://www.dw.de/suliman-al-jazeera-plays-the-piper-but-qatar-calls-the-tune/a-16477490. Acces sed 1 February 2013.

Amado, Antonin and de Miramon, Marck (2012), 'Syria's propaganda war', *Le Monde diplomatique*, 2 September, http://mondediplo.com/2012/09/02syria. Accessed 15 August 2012.

Arendt, Hannah (1958), *The Human Condition*, Chicago, IL: University of Chicago Press.

—— (1965), *Eichmann in Jerusalem: A Report on the Banality of Evil*, 2nd edition, New York: Viking Press.

—— (1968), *The Origins of Totalitarianism*, revised 3rd edition, New York: Harcourt Brace Jovanovich.

—— (1977), *Between Past and Future*, New York: Penguin Books.

Barkho, Leon (2010), *News from the BBC, CNN, and Al-Jazeera: How the three broadcasters cover the Middle East*, Cresskill, NJ: Hampton Press.

BBC (2003), 'Iraq detainees "not going to Cuba"', *BBC News*, 1 April, http://news.bbc.co.uk/2/hi/middle_east/2905479.stm. Accessed 5 September 2012.

—— (2012a), 'House Rules', http://www.bbc.co.uk/blogs/moderation.shtml#house. Accessed 9 September 2012.

—— (2012b), 'Syria activists "find 60 bodies in Damascus suburb"', *BBC News*, 17 August, http://www.bbc.co.uk/news/world-middle-east-19293304. Accessed 30 August 2012.

—— (2012c), 'Al Jazeera website defaced by pro-Syrian hackers', *BBC News*, 5 September, http://www.bbc.com/news/technology-19488739. Accessed 8 September 2012.

Bernstein, Richard J. (1979), *The Restructuring of Social and Political Theory*, London: Methuen.

—— (2005), *The Abuse of Evil: The Corruption of Politics and Religion since 9/11*, Cambridge: Polity Press.

—— (2010), *The Pragmatic Turn*, Cambridge: Polity Press.

Campbell, Matthew (2011), 'Al Jazeera Enrages Dictators, Wins Global Viewers With coverage of Unrest', *Bloomberg*, 25 February, http://www.bloomberg.com/news/2011-02-25/al-jazeera-enrages-dictators-wins-global-viewers-with-coverage-of-unrest.html. Accessed 11 September 2012.

Descartes, R. (1979), *The Philosophical Works of Descartes* (ed. by. E. Haldane and G. R. T. Ross), 2 vols, Cambridge: Cambridge University Press.

Dewey, John (1981), *The Philosophy of John Dewey,* (ed. John J. McDermott), Chicago, IL: University of Chicago Press.

Dobbs, Michael (2012), 'To explain evil is not to justify it', *Foreign Policy*, 30 August, http://dobbs.foreignpolicy.com/posts/2012/08/30/to_explain_evil_is_not_to_justify_it. Accessed 2 September 2012.

Fisk, Robert (2012), 'Syria's road from jihad to prison', *The Independent*, 2 September, http://www.independent.co.uk/voices/commentators/fisk/robert-fisk-syrias-road-from-jihad-to-prison-8100749.html. Accessed 5 December 2012.

Fitzgerald, Mary (2012), 'The Syrian Rebels' Libyan Weapons', *Foreign Policy Magazine*, 9 August, http://www.foreignpolicy.com/articles/2012/08/09/the_syrian_rebels_libyan_weapon. Accessed 15 September 2012.

Haass, Richard (2005), *The Opportunity: America's Moment to Alter History's Course*, New York: PublicAffairs.

Habermas, Jürgen (1973), *Theory and Practice* (trans. John Vietel), Boston, MA: Beacon Press.

Hammond, A. (2007), 'Saudi Arabia's empire: Keeping the masses at home', *Arab Media & Society*, 3 (Fall), http://www.arabmediasociety.com/?article=420. Accessed 3 September 2012.

Hashem, Ali (2012), 'The Arab spring has shaken Arab TV's credibility', *The Guardian*, 3 April, http://www.guardian.co.uk/commentisfree/2012/apr/03/arab-spring-arab-tv-credibility. Accessed 12 September 2012.

Henley, Jon (2007), 'A glossary of US military torture euphemisms', *The Guardian*, 13 December, http://www.guardian.co.uk/world/2007/dec/13/usa.humanrights. Accessed 3 September 2012.

Husain, Ed (2012), 'Al-Qaeda's Specter in Syria', *Council on Foreign Relations*, 6 August, http://www.cfr.org/syria/al-qaedas-specter-syria/p28782. Accessed 23 August 2012.

Ibn Taimiyya (1975), *Minhaj al-Sunna al-Nabaiya/The Pathway of as-Sunnah an-Nabawiyyah – sayings and deeds of the Prophet* (ed. by Mohammed Salem), Cairo: Al-Qurtuba Establishment.

Ismael, Mohammed (2011), 'Al Jazeera Live issues messages of incitement turning itself into a party to the conflict', *Almanar*, 27 December, http://www.almanar.com.lb/adetails.php?fromval=1&cid=41&frid=41&eid=156276. Accessed 18 March 2012.

James, William (1977), *The Writings of William James* (ed. by John McDermott), Chicago: University of Chicago Press.

Kant, Immanuel (1960), *Education*, Ann Arbor, MI: University of Michigan Press.

Ketz, Sammy (2012), 'War of words on the streets of Syria's Aleppo', *Your Middle East*, 8 September, http://www.yourmiddleeast.com/news/war-of-words-on-the-streets-of-syrias-aleppo_9375. Accessed 10 September 2012.

Koran (n.d.), 'Chapter 36, Surah Ya Seen', http://www.iqrasearch.com/surah-yaseen-translation.html. Accessed 6 September 2012.

Koran (n.d.), 'Chapter 53, Surah Al-Najm', http://www.alislam.org/quran/search2/showChapter.php?ch=53&verse=21. Accessed 9 September 2012.

Koran (n.d.), 'Surah Al-Najm, 53: 19–23', http://www.holyquran.net/cgi-bin/prepare.pl?ch=53. Accessed 16 September 2012.

McQuail, Denis (2005), *McQuail's Mass Communication Theory*, London: Sage.

Menad, Louis (2001), *The Metaphysical Club: A Story of Ideas in America*, New York: Farrar, Straus and Giroux.

New York Times (2011a), 'Lock and Load Politics and Blood Libel', 14 January, http://schott.blogs.nytimes.com/2011/01/14/lock-and-load-politics-blood-libel/. Accessed 8 September 2012.

Nordland, Rod (2011b), 'In Libya, Former Enemy Is Recast in Role of Ally', *New York Times*, 1 September, http://www.nytimes.com/2011/09/02/world/africa/02islamist.html?pagewanted=all. Accessed 9 December 2012.

Peirce, Charles S. (1992), *The Essential Peirce* (ed. by Nathan Houser and Christian Kloesel), vol.1, Bloomington, IN: Indiana University Press.

Power, Samantha (2004), 'Hannah Arendt's Lesson', *New York Review of Books*, 29 April, http://www.nybooks.com/articles/archives/2004/apr/29/the-lesson-of-hannah-arendt/?pagination=false. Accessed 10 September 2012.

Putnam, Hillary (1994), *Words and Life* (ed. by James Conant), Cambridge, MA: Harvard University Press.

—— (2002), *The Collapse of the Fact/Value Dichotomy and other Essays*, Cambridge, MA: Harvard University Press.

Qassemi, Sultan al (2012), 'Breaking the Arab News: Egypt made al Jazeera – and Syria's destroying it' *Foreign Policy*, 2 August, http://www.foreignpolicy.com/articles/2012/08/02/breaking_the_arab_news. Accessed 25 August 2012.

Schlesinger, Arthur M. (2004), *War and the American Presidency*, New York: W. W. Norton.

Shoemaker, P. J., Tankard, J. W. and Lasorsa, D. L. (2004), *How to Build Social Science Theories*, Thousand Oaks, CA: Sage.

Shoemaker, Pamela J. and Vos, T. P. (2009), *Gatekeeping Theory*, New York & London: Routledge.

Spanos, William V. (2000), *America's Shadow: An Anatomy of Empire*, Minneapolis, MN: University of Minnesota Press.

Stares, Paul and Yacoubian, Mona (2005), 'Terrorism as Virus', *Washington Post*, 22 August, http://www.washingtonpost.com/wp-dyn/content/article/2005/08/22/AR2005082201109.html. Accessed 10 September 2012.

Waller, J. Michael (2006), 'Making Jihad Work for America', *The Journal of International Security Affairs*, 10 (Spring), http://www.securityaffairs.org/issues/2006/10/waller.php. Accessed 28 August 2012.

Worth, Robert F. (2008), 'Al Jazeera no longer nips at Saudis', *New York Times*, 4 January, http://www.nytimes.com/2008/01/04/world/africa/04iht-04jazeera.9019066.html?pagewanted=all. Accessed 21 August 2012.

Note

1   Full versions are accessible from URLs in the reference list.

PART III

Practicalities

Chapter 10

Issues of impartiality in news and current affairs – some practical considerations

Kevin Marsh

The BBC's earliest interpretations of impartiality were very simple. They did not require any elaboration so long as the public discourse appeared bipolar: There was the government on the one hand and the opposition on the other; there was capital, there was labour. But by the turn of this century, the BBC found itself in a position in which it became extremely difficult for its editors to apply and practice impartiality as before. Dramatic changes and transformations within British society and the world at large prompted the BBC to come up with new defining values for impartiality. This chapter traces how the BBC developed its own standards and practices of impartiality in news and current affairs in the decades since its establishment in 1922.

Introduction

In June 2001, soon after Tony Blair won his second term as British prime minister, he faced an important question: whether or not to push his reluctant Chancellor of the Exchequer, Gordon Brown, to declare that Britain was ready to join the European single currency and to call a referendum on swapping the sterling for the euro.

The ruling New Labour party was split – not in one direction but in many. Chancellor Gordon Brown was opposed to joining the euro at all. The 'five economic tests' he'd set to decide whether the British economy was ready for the euro were generally seen as impossible to pass.

But there were divisions, too, amongst those who, like Prime Minister Blair, were euro enthusiasts. Some wanted an early referendum, irrespective of Chancellor Brown's 'five economic tests'. Others thought there was no need for a referendum even though Prime Minister Blair had promised one – let's lead the country into the euro when the time is right. Yet others thought he should take his time – not rush, but still promise a referendum when the time was right.

I was the editor of the influential BBC radio program *The World This Weekend* – a program that had a reputation for detailed analysis of political issues and public policy. And I decided to examine the different arguments and voices that Prime Minister Blair was listening to; voices of those inside his party, and of advisors who wanted to swap the sterling for the euro but had differing views on timing and on the referendum.

When the piece was broadcast, a member of the British House of Lords, who was the leading voice advocating Britain withdrawal from the EU, complained that it was not impartial. He said the program contained no voice that was anti-euro or anti-EU.

The highest court in the BBC, the Board of Governors, upheld the complaint. I should have included an anti-euro voice, even though there was no chance whatsoever of such a voice influencing the prime minister in any way whatsoever.

Impartiality a complex issue

It was a classic example of how the BBC's defining value of impartiality had, by the turn of this century, become so complex and differentially understood that even the BBC Governors didn't quite understand it and found it difficult to apply in practice.

Impartiality was complex enough in 2001, but in the decade since then, the media landscape has become yet more complex, societies and the public discourse have become more diverse, and challenges to the notion of impartiality have come from every direction; philosophical, cultural, societal. There is no shortage of media students and critics ready to argue that impartiality is as impossible as it is outdated.

For a working journalist, especially one in the BBC, the theoretical discussion is not very helpful. It is essential to have some kind of understanding of what impartiality could – and perhaps even should – look like in practice, even if it is a struggle to define it rigorously in theory.

Practical impartiality is not as impossible as theoreticians would argue. It is true that it should be seen as an aspiration rather than a measurable goal. That it is a collection of characteristics rather than a formal definition. And that it will change over time.

It is also true that in the chaotic, churning media landscape in which we now operate, values such as impartiality – however described or characterized – could be, and are, emerging as important markers that distinguish deliberate acts of serious journalism from the noise out on the web.

Early interpretations of impartiality

BBC impartiality which, for good or ill, is well understood as one of the global news organization's defining aspirations, began life not as a voluntary value or aspiration, but as a legal requirement: in 1922, John Reith's British Broadcasting Company – later to become Corporation – was allowed by the government to broadcast on this new thing, the radio spectrum.

There were many reasons for the requirement. The BBC had a monopoly of the very limited airwaves – and continued to have for over 30 years. And the government, even then, was wary of the power of a medium that could intrude into every home.

It was a requirement that was ill-defined, simply because in the 1920s it didn't seem to need any elaboration. Society, and therefore the public discourse, appeared bipolar. There was government, there was opposition. There was capital, there was labour. There were the pit owners, there were the miners. British society was at its most deferential and it's least diverse. Almost everyone living in Britain at the time was Judeo-Christian, white and had English as their first language. And when the BBC began global broadcasting in 1936, the name gave a clue as to its value system: the BBC Empire Service. Values didn't seem to need an explanation.

1926 general strike

Even so, within four years the BBC faced its first major test of impartiality: the general strike of 1926. Coal mine-owners had tried to force on their workforce a cut in pay and an increase in hours. The mining unions called a strike and the Trades Union Congress (TUC) had called all other union members out in support.

The Conservative Chancellor of the Exchequer, Winston Churchill, saw the importance of the media in the strike, and started a government newspaper, *The British Gazette*. He also tried to put pressure on the BBC to become a government mouthpiece. He even tried to commandeer it.

Reith resisted. He knew that any appearance of supporting one side or the other, any loss of impartiality and independence, could be fatal to his young enterprise. And while he won the argument over commandeering the BBC, he also maintained impartiality by the unsatisfactory method of keeping the argument substantially off the air. He argued that the BBC had reported Conservative, Labour and trade union perspectives in the crisis impartially. And there is much truth in that. But he had also refused airtime to the Labour Party and TUC leader – as well as the Archbishop of Canterbury.

It may have been an imperfect application of impartiality, even in an age when such ideas appeared to need no elaboration, but it demonstrated something else too; that in the real, practical world, impartiality cannot exist without the independence of the journalist. It established an important precedent; that in the determination of impartiality, it is the broadcaster or the news organization – accountable for its decisions to its audience – that is the final determiner, not governments or power.

Inevitably, it is in the reporting of conflict that impartiality is most strenuously tested. It is also the subgenre of journalism where we can best see how impartiality in practice has mutated over the past 70 years or so.

The Second World War

Within 20 years of the BBC's foundation, it found itself reporting a conflict that all of Europe had hoped would never happen, while at the same time fearing its inevitability: the Second European and, eventually, World War. It was the conflict that for two generations, long after the conflict had ended, defined the BBC in the public mind.

The Second World War, unlike the First and subsequent wars in which the UK has played a role, was a war of national survival. A war fought at home as violently and destructively as it was fought abroad – even though the UK was never invaded or occupied.

The BBC's role in such a war was never in question. Its purpose was to sustain a population fighting on to victory. The BBC's entertainment soothed and calmed a people under pressures they had never known – food shortages as well as nightly aerial bombardments. Its news reporters stood alongside men at arms. Sharing their danger, in uniform, with honorary ranks, under the command of the military and prepared to shape or delay the truth – though not lie – in the interests of national victory.

The Suez Canal crisis

Some of the same attitudes continued into the early wars of 'peace', whether the late colonial interventions in Kenya or Malaya – that reached back to old imperial mindsets – or the multinational intervention in Korea – that reached forwards to a new one. But it was the 1957 Suez campaign, and the BBC's perception of its impartiality in reporting that, which broke the continuity.

The Suez Canal campaign divided Britain. Egypt's President Nasser had nationalized the Anglo-French Suez Canal Company; to overturn that, British and French troops had been dropped into the Suez Canal zone with a view to occupying it and reasserting control.

But there was little appetite for war. The official parliamentary Opposition was against it, and the BBC took the view that it was obliged to reflect that division. Unlike 1926, the BBC tried to ensure broadly equal access to its airwaves – and when the prime minister had appeared on radio and TV to put his case, the BBC offered similar airtime to the leader of the Opposition. The government was incensed and, once again, threatened takeover or punishment. Their anger was exacerbated still further by the BBC's refusal to remove reporting of the divisions in British opinion from its broadcasts to the Middle East.

It was a short crisis lasting just three days. The prime minister was humiliated, and BBC impartiality and independence remained intact. It was, however, just the beginning.

Northern Ireland

In 1969, British troops were sent to restore civil order in Northern Ireland. For the BBC, it raised a wholly new question: what was the role of a 'national' broadcaster in a part of the United Kingdom where at least 35 per cent of the population did not see themselves as part of that nation – not by choice, at any rate?

In reporting this story between 1969 – the date British troops were first deployed to support the civil power – and 1998 – when the Good Friday Agreement offered an end to conflict – the BBC had to report a complex web of contentious issues, many of whose arguments overlapped and intersected. And it could not assume that the communities it was reporting into in Northern Ireland had the same views of their own histories.

It was possible, for example, to support the continued presence of Northern Ireland within the United Kingdom – broadly, the Unionist position – while still agreeing that the Catholic population did not enjoy, in reality, full civil rights. It was possible to support the military intervention while opposing the internment of terrorist suspects. In other words, the conflict in Northern Ireland was an important example of how the previous, unspoken and assumed bipolarity of the idea of impartiality no longer pertained. It was no longer a simple question of a united Ireland or not; troops in or troops out.

It raised, too, the question of impartiality in the reporting of lethal action, on the one hand by the state in support of the status quo or political resolution, on the other by those proclaiming loyalty to another state or resolution by violence.

This complexity of differential audiences, intersecting axes of difference and debate and perceptions of lethal activity – and all within the United Kingdom – challenged the notion of impartiality in a way nothing previously had. One BBC director general in the early years of the 'Troubles' – the BBC never called it a 'war' – made it clear his journalists would offer no impartial treatment of the forces of law and order and those of criminality and terror. But it became clear as we approached the possibilities of resolution, the reconciliation of political differences and the rehabilitation of former 'terrorists' as leading politicians that the director general's clarity was no longer of any practical use.

'Terrorists'

Indeed, the very use of terms such as 'terrorist' became difficult because of the judgment inherent in them and the broadening perception, particularly amongst the BBC global audiences, that they defined a prior judgment that was incompatible with impartiality. And by the early 2000s, the BBC decided that in most cases, the word 'terrorist' shouldn't be used, certainly in broadcasts to outside the UK. Instead, neutral terminology describing the action itself should be preferred. So, terms such as 'bombers', 'suicide bombers', 'gunmen' and 'hostage-takers', etc. became the norm.

But of course, while that was a practical formula in global broadcasting it was impractical domestically. When suicide bombers struck in London in July 2005, the BBC, like all other news organizations in the UK, called the attacks 'terrorism'. It would have been a massive misreading of the public mood to do any other.

Bipolar or multipolar

By this time, it was clear to everyone that the old assumed bipolar model of impartiality was no longer applicable. The UK population was more diverse than previously; notions of citizenship and of national and religious affiliation were more complex; the age of 'post-modern' defence and security policy had involved the country's armed forces in an apparently continuous sequence of overseas interventions – in Sierra Leone, Kosovo, Afghanistan and Iraq – each one of which was hotly debated and required political justification. There was no question of the whole, or even most, of the UK population supporting without questioning such interventions. And those who did support or oppose were likely to do so for a wide range of reasons. There was no simple 'yes/no' question arching over the many arguments.

What was true of conflict was true of other areas of public policy. The post-war consensus on propositions such as healthcare, education, housing provision, public ownership and so on had fallen away. The political debate over the social settlement no longer focused on simple questions of public versus private, low tax versus high spend. Questions of means and quality came to dominate, while at the same time the question of state or private provision became blurred.

The TUC had lost much of their political power, and after Britain had dropped its exclusion from the EU Social Chapter in 1997, it became more focused; on-dialogue with employers, public and private, and less agents of bipolar confrontation. Party support at elections had become much less class-based and much less tribal.

And, of course, there was Europe. What had once been a simple 'in or out' debate, beautifully bipolar, was now crisscrossed with dozens of intersecting arguments on different planes about Stability and Growth Pacts, borders, vetoes and qualified majority voting.

'From Seesaw to Wagon Wheel'

For the BBC, this meant having to make a closer and more explicit examination of the idea of impartiality if it was to continue to hold it as one of its core journalistic values. That came in a 2007 paper, commissioned by the BBC Governors and inherited by the BBC Trust when that became the corporation's governing body. The paper, 'From Seesaw to Wagon Wheel', was written by a former BBC producer John Bridcut, and it set out to precisely map the changes in British society, public life and discourse that meant the old bipolar idea – the 'seesaw' – had to be replaced by a concept of multiple axes of debate, rather like the many spokes of a wagon wheel.

'From Seesaw to Wagon Wheel', while a carefully argued, conscientious account both of the issues and of a possible way of addressing them, failed to gain significant traction in the BBC at the level of the newsroom or the individual journalists within it. It tried very hard to be a practical model – but in a sense, the issues were too complex and required too numerous and too nuanced understandings ever to be fully adopted as a practical handbook.

It did, however, provide a number of key concepts that became the foundation stones of teaching, through the BBC College of Journalism, for all the corporation's 7500 or so journalists. The College tried to capture the main ideas like this:

Impartiality is in large measure a mindset. It is a mindset that:

- initially, sets out to look for the facts and opinions relevant to a particular story without any bias or preconceptions;
- gathers the facts and opinions that those involved in the story see as significant and relevant;
- considers and weighs those facts and opinions to come to a judgment, without bias or preconception, as to where the axis of debate lies and which are the important arguments on that axis.

Impartiality versus objectivity

It also enables BBC journalists to draw the distinction between impartiality – as the BBC intended to mean and apply it – and other similar concepts: objectivity, neutrality, fairness, lack of bias and balance. It reinforced what had been clear for some time: that there was no obvious and assumed bipolar opposition of arguments or fact selection on any major question; there were many 'axes of debate'. It also established the idea that an impartial journalist could still weigh the evidence and make informed and evidence-based judgments, and that impartiality was achieved over time, not in every report – particularly important in live and continuous news reporting where the 'truth' is still emerging.

Those distinctions between 'impartiality' and other, apparently similar, terms is important. They are often used interchangeably – even in the BBC. Indeed, you are still more likely to hear a BBC editor or journalist talk about 'balancing' a piece than about 'making it impartial' – an indicator of the difficulty in giving a subtle understanding of the idea any real traction.

Impartiality contains elements of all of those terms, such as 'fairness' and 'balance', but is not the same as all of them. Objectivity is famously impossible either to define, describe or achieve. Even before we begin to speak, our gender, ethnic group and appearance prevents us from being truly 'objective' – and once we open our mouths, the possibility of objectivity recedes even further. Even if we try to define it, there is a paradox. A classic attempt to define objectivity is that 'no statement is true from every possible standpoint'. That definition is itself a paradox: to make it true, you would have to add 'except this one'. In other words, the definition of objectivity cannot itself be objective.

'Passive journalism'

'Objectivity' and 'neutrality' imply passive journalism. They imply an attempt to view the world without weighing the evidence you find there – holding up a mirror to reality. For the 'objective' or 'neutral' journalist, that would mean reporting all – or as many as practicable – possible facts and interpretations of those facts without making any observation of their truth or their relationship with each other. A journalist who is truly 'objective' or 'neutral' arriving at the scene of what is self-evidently a massacre would have to report what the relevant sides say, with equal weight and no judgment, based on what he or she can see for themselves.

When, in 1991, the veteran BBC correspondent Sir Charles Wheeler arrived in northern Iraq, he was confronted by what was – as far as he could establish – a massacre of Kurdish people carried out by Saddam Hussein. 'Neutrality' would have meant describing what he saw as 'objectively' as possible, and giving the Iraqi denials the same weight as the evidence of his own eyes and ears. Wheeler called it a massacre and did so 'impartially'.

'Balance' and 'fairness' are also often used interchangeably with 'impartiality' but, once again, are not the same. 'Impartiality' almost always contains elements of both – but the concept of 'balance' implies equality of treatment regardless of the importance of any fact or argument; 'fairness' implies that all relevant facts and arguments get a 'fair hearing'.

The MMR scandal

This sounds reasonable until you consider an example such as the notorious 'MMR scandal'. That affair concerned a British government health policy which was to give all young children, soon after they were born, a combined 'triple-vaccine' to give immunity to three childhood diseases; measles, mumps and rubella. In the 1990s, a single doctor – Andrew Wakefield, a surgeon who specialized in liver and digestive medicine but had no specific expertise in paediatric medicine nor immunology – hypothesized that there may be a link between the 'triple-vaccine' and autism. He had no research evidence to support this hypothesis – though he was able to demonstrate one link in the hypothetical chain – and indeed conceded in a published paper that any link he could find was not causal.

The British press picked up the story and ran strongly with it. Mothers of autistic children came forward and shared their stories – tearfully – with TV audiences almost daily. Dr Wakefield became a media celebrity.

But there was a problem. The press – and the BBC – had reported this debate over several years, as if it were a debate amongst equals. Debates would include a 'mainstream' doctor as well as Dr Wakefield – and usually a crying mother. Except this was not a fifty-fifty debate: the mass of medical opinion – 99.999% of doctors who were experts in the field – held that the MMR vaccine was not linked to autism, yet that view was represented less than 50% of the time. Dr Wakefield's views were both unsupported and unproven.

It was clear with hindsight that we journalists should have treated Dr Wakefield as the maverick he was. That he, along with the mothers, crying babies and lawyers who represented his hypothesis, should not have received half the airtime in a debate in which his hypothesis was untested and a minority view. However, such was the power of the emotion we broadcasters and journalists attached to his side of the argument that the number of children receiving the 'triple-vaccine' dipped below the critical proportion of the population to keep immunity to the diseases high. Real public damage was done.

A better interpretation of impartiality would have been to make a judgment about the relative weight of the arguments and treat them accordingly; to give the maverick doctor with an unproven, harmful thesis much, much less exposure than mainstream, proven medical opinion and practice; and to avoid adding power to that minority argument with high emotion.

Impartiality is a process

Impartiality, though, is more of a process than it is an outcome. The important thing is that the journalism is done impartially: that evidence is viewed and weighed; that missing evidence along a particular axis of debate is sought; that diverse voices are heard; that, over time, all the significant voices along all the significant axes are heard – but weighed to reflect their overall significance to the debate.

Which leads in to the final consideration: the process of impartial journalism cannot be completed in isolation from the other values of ethical journalism – truth and verification; independence; the public interest and accountability especially.

The essence of the practical approach to impartiality is that it is an ever-present aspiration. And like all aspirations, while it is unlikely ever to be fully achieved, it remains in place, a driver to behaviours and a measure of honest intent. Accountability to audiences means that you, the journalist, are constantly alive to the necessity to explain to your audience why you took the decision you took. Why that framing and not this one? Why that set of facts and not these? Why those views and not these? Alive, too, to the likelihood that your judgment may sometimes be wrong, and that your audience is also there to critique your work; a critique you may sometimes have to concede is better than your original effort.

With the other values, it is clear that 'impartial' journalism that is untruthful or dealing in unverified facts is an ethical contradiction. Impartiality self-evidently requires you to use facts you have verified and arguments that do not contain untruths. In interrogative journalism – interviewing – challenging a speaker's version of the facts is a key element both of verification and impartiality; similarly with independence. As the BBC discovered in 1926, independence and impartiality go hand in hand. No journalist can claim truly to be impartial if he or she is pressured to tell the story in a particular way, or include speakers selected by someone else, usually by power.

The former Irish Prime Minister, the late Dr Garret Fitzgerald used to ask of his country's rapidly growing economy 'it works in practice… but does it work in theory?' It is a similar question we can ask ourselves – if we care to – about impartiality. Though, as with the Irish economy, it may not matter if we fail to generate a good theory while perpetuating good practice. And in the constant struggle we journalists have now to differentiate what we do from all the communication and sharing of news, some of it calling itself 'journalism' in some qualified form – 'accidental', 'citizen', 'informal', 'pro-am', etc. – perpetuating that good practice may be absolutely what's required. It may well be that the aspiration to be impartial is precisely one of the characteristics we now require to validate our deliberate acts of bearing witness and reporting as true 'journalism'. And that the difficulties others find in defining it should be an opportunity to us journalists to discover practical, daily interpretations of that essential journalistic aspiration.

Chapter 11

What are the new rules for reporting, sourcing, verifying, editing and publishing a social media world?

Eric Auchard

Reuters has developed its own standards of impartiality. A global and multilingual news agency, Reuters highly values issues like independence and components such as fairness, balance, transparency, consistency and disinterestedness – the elements that have characterized its news and current affairs coverage for decades. With the advent of the digital age, the agency has been revising its coverage rules, experimenting broadly, and holding training courses and in-house discussions on how to extend its objectivity guidelines to embrace the exponential growth in input from social media. Eric Auchard of Reuters sheds light on the agency's endeavour to set up its own objectivity rules in dealing with our social media world.

Introduction

Rather than dwelling on the word 'impartiality', Reuters breaks down what it means into more specific concepts like accuracy, balance, even-handedness, distance and context as its yardstick for the coverage of news and current affairs. Our journalistic guidelines rely on many similar words and phrases like fairness, 'freedom from bias' and 'striving for balance'. These principles of independence go back 160 years to our founding. But, if you read the history more closely, our freedom from government-funding and interference by the British government dates to the 1950s, specifically to our coverage of the Suez crisis, when Reuters pursued an independent line from the government. Going back further, to the 1920s, we had refused to use the word 'terrorism' as a synonym for attacks by militant opponents of governments, though it often is loosely used that way by other news organizations. We upheld that principle through Ireland, India and in Palestine, even when the King David Hotel was blown up in 1946 and many British soldiers died, and on through the many colonial struggles that followed. After September 11, Reuters came under sustained attack from conservative bloggers for acting as some sort of a fifth column working on behalf of jihadists. Debates over just that one hot-button word are just one example of the ongoing struggle we face living up to standards of impartiality.

News and technology

I went to journalism school in the early 1990s thinking I was going to write about politics, but quickly found my way into the burgeoning field of technology news. I came to the subject with more background than many journalists, having worked for start-ups and a venture capital firm before becoming a journalist. But before I dive into the main subject, I want to highlight something about technology news that informs my views on social media.

One of the problems I have run into in covering technology news over the years was how traditional journalistic notions of objectivity have produced a profound disconnect between observers and their subjects. I watched my competitors and colleagues trying to 'stand back' from the topic, and let the PR spokesmen and executives they interviewed explain to them what was going on. Objectivity too often meant complete ignorance of technical matters and an over-reliance on these sources to translate what was happening. This journalistic aloofness became increasingly apparent as the story moved from being about big, abstract systems and mainframe computers to consumer technologies, which people had to interact with and web services that everyone could see. I found you actually needed to play with the stuff, and you needed to engage in the technology and actually understand what you were writing about. Many of my competitors remained aloof. I found this to be a constant competitive advantage over traditional journalists. I am from that world of traditional journalism that struggles to remain objective. But I strongly believe the journalist's primary role is to foster debate and to challenge assumptions rather than remain aloof from the messy business of finding out what is new and different and important.

News and innovation

In 2011, Reuters gave me the job of doing something called 'editorial innovation'. Innovation means a lot of different things to different people. For me, it is just an opportunity to build tools for my fellow journalists to do their jobs. This role, and my previous reporting experience, informs what I have to say about the changes brought on by technology, new media, social media, democratic media, or all the various terms that we can use to describe the changes sweeping news reporting. There are dozens of tools that I could highlight: Facebook, LinkedIn, Google, and a variety of video, picture, collaboration and production tools.

But none of these other tools and services comes close to the impact that Twitter is having on the role of journalists. I argue that the Twittersphere has an outsized impact on journalism compared to some other forms of social media, even though some of the other formats probably have an equal or greater effect on consumers and society at large.

From a reporting perspective, Twitter made its impact first felt in technology circles, then politics, entertainment, sports and an ever-expanding number of realms. It's very hard to ignore Twitter when covering the news on almost any subject these days.

And yet I must qualify this broad statement and say it holds true in some parts of the world, but not necessarily everywhere. Factors like access to the Internet, government censorship and wealth are at play. Certainly, my assertion about its broad impact is true in much of the English-speaking world, as well as many other cultures and regions. I study this on an empirical basis as I help local journalists around the world develop monitoring tools to track breaking news online, wherever it occurs. But this is not so in China, for instance, where Twitter is frequently blocked by the government. There, the undisputed emperor of social media is Weibo, the Twitter-like social network service run by Sina.com, whose growth has dwarfed that of Twitter. Depending on the type of story, Twitter's impact is often vast (but not always global, I would like to stress).

Twitter and news

Today, Twitter has become an important forum for breaking news; arguably the most important. As a variety of researchers have noted, Twitter's impact does not necessarily stem from what is said directly on Twitter, but rather its role as a megaphone that amplifies information that first appears in many other places, online and offline, in newspapers and TV and radio broadcasts, government agencies or elsewhere.

Twitter importance to general news subjects is widely recognized, but its impact on financial news is less well understood, although increasingly important.

I am not here to advocate the supremacy of social media. I am simply describing what we as Reuters journalists are trying to do to embrace the trend and incorporate its functions into our reporting. To the extent that Twitter brings together informed opinion, subject matter expertise and smart news aggregation – not just idle chitter-chatter about what one had for lunch today – it is a must-watch source for news of all sorts. It is a new way of fostering democratic debate and involvement. As journalists, we need to figure how to incorporate social media into all the normal news feeds, databases and other sources we rely upon to keep abreast of breaking news. We have sometimes been slow to integrate efficient ways of watching social media into our normal work routines. At times, it makes news organizations look stiff, resistant and ignorant about what is already widely known via social media. This does not reflect an opposition between journalism and social media. It is just that we have been slow off the mark. This is changing fast, however, as the following examples show.

Twitter and markets

Let's take the example of Eric Burroughs, Reuters' Asian markets editor, who works in Hong Kong. He manages a team of reporters across the region, whose job is to track the flows of monies into stocks, bonds and other markets. For many years, covering financial markets involved a reporter hearing a rumour from a trader that 'something is going on', or to spot some dramatic spike in a financial chart and find out what was behind the move. Everyone available would know to hit the phones to call sources as fast as they could to find out whatever rumour might be moving the market. That was the classic way that such reporting has been done for decades. What Eric, my colleague, found after being involved in various chat rooms and then getting very interested in social media is that a lot of those rumours were out there on Twitter for hours, sometimes even days, before they were reflected in market movements. The failure to look at Twitter and pay attention to where rumours with a potential to drive markets first surface is, in financial reporting terms, akin to ignoring breaking news and just writing stories when you feel like it. Ignore Twitter and you miss a lot of news.

Eric found that we and other news organizations were often quoting traders telling us what was going on when, in many cases, all these traders were doing was passing on to us information that was already there on Twitter. Sometimes the news was simply highlighting a story from Reuters somewhere else in the world, or from a competitor such as Bloomberg or Dow Jones. Social media can function like an echo chamber in such situations: so-called 'market rumours' are just hours- or days-old stories recirculating in the Twittersphere. Just as it is true, in my view, that no one should be writing a news story these days that does not do at least as good of a job as Wikipedia does in explaining the 'who' or 'what' about a particular subject, I do not think anyone should be covering breaking news without staying on top of what has already been said about the topic on Twitter and other widely available new media outlets. Whether or not we as journalists accept what has been said is true or not, there is no denying that social networks can at least inform where we look next for the news.

Industry coverage and Twitter

Reuters airspace correspondent Tim Hepher provides another example of how useful Twitter can be for news reporting. Tim is based in Paris and he runs a Twitter feed called @ ReutersAero.[1] As of early 2011, he has developed a following of about 8000 people, including everyone from aviation CEOs to industry trade magazines, media competitors, etc. He has attracted a variety of local 'plane spotters' who are really into the geeky aspects of any specific plane or model. Every time there is a major event, for example, the launching of new plane models, his following takes off to a new level.

I am going to list a few things of what Tim has found particularly useful about Twitter. He uses it to flush out news and try new reporting approaches. He has developed a style that is almost like radio reporting. When he goes out to cover an event and is waiting for the real news to start, he sets the scene with a handful of nice, descriptive colour that would not fit normally into our main story. It is also far easier with Twitter and all the social media to incorporate multimedia links in our stories – camera phone pictures, various hyperlinks, documents, audio recordings, etc. It is a dirty little secret, perhaps, but Reuters is a big player in wholesale television video, photographs and graphics, both in general news and financial markets. But we produce all of these things separately, and often do not have easy ways of bundling them together in unified packages. Social media gives reporters a handy shortcut for creating multimedia packages on the fly.

Connecting the services Reuters provides was part of the inspiration that moved us into blogging nearly a decade ago when blogs were hot. And this is why we have been so interested in using social media, particularly Twitter, where the action has now moved. As our aviation correspondent watches companies and other sources breaking news on Twitter, he has had to adapt. Although most of what he sees is what we would call 'secondary news', Tim says he finds it useful for staying on top of the flow of general industry discussion, and, from time to time, to spot breaking news developments before they have become mainstream.

Another example is from our Detroit autos team. They use Twitter to track the various parties they are following, from the industry leaders to the corporate PR people to the trade unions, as well as some auto trade press. For their purposes, Twitter has been less valuable than Facebook. The difference is that Twitter is where people link the things that are already out there in the world, whereas Facebook is, of course, more about personal conversation. A lot of the discussions that are happening in groups on Facebook still happen in the open. As a journalist you can go and join these groups and see what happens, to find out what normally would have been held in closed-halls discussions. Covering the last round of Chrysler labour-management talks, the team were basically able to go in to the various union groups on Facebook and watch the debate play out. Oftentimes, the members were tearing the leadership of the unions apart over their negotiating positions, discussions that would have been impossible to monitor via conventional means because it would have required running around to all those union halls in city after city – an almost physical impossibility for such a dispersed story.

Reuters pix and Twitter

Reuters' photographers are probably the agency's biggest consumers of Twitter. They use it for all kind of things. Probably their biggest success, as of late, was when a jet engine fell off a Qantas airline aircraft. Somehow a German tourist turned on his phone and started tweeting about it, and our photographers picked up on it and were able to figure out who the person was not from his Twitter feed, but from his Facebook profile. They e-mailed him and managed to meet with him and got all the pictures and videos of the engine falling off, which he had shot out the window with his consumer camera phone. When you hear a report on the news from local media that a bomb has been blown up in Pakistan, it is critical that you actually figure out where the explosion happened. Identifying the location or the scene of disaster helps notifying the freelance photographers who can get there quickly. Twitter, and various ways of watching Twitter like TweetDeck, have become a primary tool for this.

Impartiality and news-based social media

Transparency and making intelligent connections is what's at work here. In the past we would have held back identifying many of the sources we use to report our stories. This is still true on certain types of sensitive stories. But increasingly, we are looking at ways to be able to let our sources become people that have voices themselves. Readers can then go ahead and follow and see for themselves. Why is it that we interview a source for 15 or 30 minutes for a story, and then only one or two quotes appear? This in no way captures the source's wider thinking on the subject. These days, we have the opportunity to quote the source and then, simply through hyperlinking to their social media profile, readers can explore more deeply what the source has to say. They can even start a conversation directly with them (if the source is willing to do that). It's also possible for the reporter to publish extended transcripts of any particular interview for readers who want to dig deeper into the source's thinking. It's not efficient to do this all the time, but the opportunity to more richly tell stories in this way is at hand.

Independence and social media

Reuters has been experimenting with all sorts of methods of incorporating social media into news, and debating the issues it raises in terms of objectivity or impartiality. I guess the biggest concern for journalists is verification: how to avoid the many traps – fake stories, fake profiles, unattributed information treated as facts – and so on and so on...

It's dawned on most attention-seeking journalists that Twitter is a great way to build your byline – your personal brand. And while it is a great thing to get yourself more widely known and to create a name for yourself, I think there are many more reasons, in terms of reporting and the quality of the resulting journalism, for using Twitter. One of the most important is just to find new sources, as well as to be more aware of what your current sources are saying and doing. I would say that the contemporary way journalists start reporting is to take a quick glance at a source's Twitter feed to find out what they are saying, where they are and whether they might be busy before they call or e-mail that source. All of these changing ways of producing journalism are becoming more real over time, requiring us to adapt our approaches and reporting tools.

It is surprising, when one stops to consider these changes, to see so many people taking such an open approach to what they are doing and saying on Twitter, relative to the traditional way that we as wire service journalists worked to uncover 'the news'. This openness is a two-way street. Journalists now often bypass the public relations spokesman and PR handlers for a lot of the celebrities and officials we cover, and go straight to the source. This has all kinds of interesting consequences. Perhaps most importantly, the roles of various actors making news are up for grabs. Journalists now have to worry about their sources scooping them. Embargoes – the mutual agreement not to publish a story before an agreed time – now has to be applied to the sources and analysts we used to call before the news was news. Many of our specialist readers have become smart sources and pundits themselves, further inverting the tidy hierarchy of relationships that once separated news-makers, news producers and their audiences.

Twitter is a great tip-off service. But I wish to underscore that Reuters does not report most things we read directly from Twitter. We use it to understand the direction of the debate, what our competitors are saying, interesting bits of context provided by smart news watchers, etc. Then we go out and we collaborate these things ourselves, using a lot of traditional tools, other digital tools, the many proprietary databases we can access, etc. Then we report it ourselves, with attribution to any original sources. Having said that, as journalists become more familiar with the personalities they follow on Twitter, we become more comfortable quoting known personalities directly off Twitter.

Retweeting!

Then again, we are having a strong, continuing debate within our organization about the notion of retweeting, and where our responsibilities lie in terms of fact-checking stories as they emerge on Twitter. Retweeting means taking somebody else's tweet and republishing it to your own network of followers. When you retweet, there is always a lurking question around whether you are endorsing the remark or simply acting as a neutral messenger. In the traditional way of reporting, we would fully attribute what somebody was saying and what forum they were saying it in to make the context clear; something hard to do, but by no means impossible, in short-form microblogging. Reuters' journalists and editors are looking to define the lines between what is acceptable to be retweeted immediately, and what is not and must be verified ourselves, through further research with established sources. Immediate retweets would be things reported by key competitors or sources who are well-known to our reporters.

Sources

In terms of finding new sources, Twitter has become a great forum for finding outspoken and demonstrably well-informed contacts. It offers a much bigger set of sources than a reporter might ever keep in a Rolodex. Twitter lists provide a constant reminder of who is important to track and follow. They give journalists an opportunity to identify new viewpoints. Many of these people have emerged as interesting commentators on a specialized subject based solely on their social media track records. Finding new sources, identifying them and then developing relationships with them offline is very important to digital journalists. Social media makes all of this source-building work hugely more efficient, although it remains rarely the whole story behind the reporting of major news stories.

Challenges

One of the issues we have seen playing out again and again, and that we will keep struggling with, is the confusion which a lot of our journalists have between their conventional sources of information and new forms of input. At Reuters, we have dozens of established feeds and databases and screens we have to watch and monitor to cover the news. It's hard to stay on top of all this information, even before you throw social media into the mix.

Social media has been around at least as long as the first e-mail-based chat rooms, and long before that if count various offline analogies. But its impact on journalism has exploded since the advent of blogs more than a decade ago, and in the profusion of social networks since then. At first, only a limited set of journalist geeks were interested in utilizing these new media for reporting, and even then, it took a back seat to normal work routines. As social media became more important as a reporting tool, a tension arose over where busy journalists should pay the most attention. Where once social media was treated as an extra, an add-on, a nice-to-have, that's no longer the case. Increasingly, Twitter and other social media platforms have become incorporated into the normal workflows of journalists at Reuters. Twitter becomes a way of spotting trends which we can use alongside our arsenal of more sophisticated professional reporting tools and databases to verify. The apparent dichotomy between these reporting approaches dissolves quickly as reporters figure out how to make these approaches work together.

Yet many journalists still find it hard to strike the right tone as journalists on social media. There is a conversational, open-ended quality to many good Twitter posts that runs counter to much of our training in telling the story straight. There is always a learning curve that journalists new to the format need to play around with before they figure what works and what falls flat. And it is very easy to become co-opted into the easy, opinionated tone of many bloggers and tweeters. There is a social media persona that relies on snarky irony and a cutting kind of humour and omniscient voice that I believe does not work at all in any journalism that aspires to the goal of impartiality.

As a journalist at Reuters, the closest comparable format is what we call a 'bright', a breezily written item that reveals some humorous oddity of human experience. The best writers do this with an effortless-looking light touch that can be very funny without crossing some sort of line into mockery. This is an art, and not every writer can do it. That's okay because we have room for quite a variety of different types of reporters, writers and story formats at Reuters. We don't expect every one of our journalists to tweet, in the sense of regularly publishing. But increasingly, we do expect them to pay attention to what's going on Twitter and other social media.

More pressingly, we are working hard to get our people not to forget that they are Reuters journalists, morning, noon and night, on the job and off. I find myself repeating this mantra all the time: just be a journalist, remember to be a journalist; you do not stop being a journalist when you leave the office at the end of the day; 24 hours a day you have a responsibility to observe our codes and remain on your toes as journalists. In an instant, you can sacrifice any claim to being an independent, impartial journalist if you adopt the lazy Twitter persona of the casual tweeter.

These are complicated questions, which get us into the difficult realm of what rights journalists should have to have their own points of view. I do believe that it is important to articulate the principle of what it is we are doing and why we are doing it, and reminding my colleagues that what we do as journalists actually involves some professional trade-offs. Your ability to cover multiple sides of an argument depends on both the perception and the reality that you are fair and impartial about who and what you cover, and how you write about them. Nothing in the 'Twitter Age' has rescinded these classic journalistic tensions.

The danger of professional journalists loosely expressed their personal opinions has another twist in our global news organization. An otherwise highly professional journalist who is careful never to inject personal opinions into their reporting or social media comments can still get into hot water if they casually air their personal opinions on subjects which they do not report about. As citizens, as everyday people, as human beings, it's understandable to sometimes want to express dismay at events happening half a world away. The problem for Reuters journalists is that we are a part of a global news operation. So casually expressing views about politics or world events in other places can be extremely dangerous for our journalists on the frontlines in many places. It's hard to separate these casual personal views from those of our organization and the Reuters brand. So we ask our journalists to stick to what they know, to dive deeply into the subjects and controversies that they cover, but to steer clear of casual comments on controversies they do not cover first hand.

Social media guidelines

We have maintained guidelines for how Reuters journalists use social media for some time now, but we are currently reworking them. Some of the latest that I thought I would read out to you comes from our ethics editor, Alex Freedman, who recently joined us from the *Wall Street Journal*. She talks about the principle of open-mindedness and enlightened scepticism. We expect our journalists to reach conclusions through reporting, but they will also have to be intellectually disciplined to keep any conclusions they arrive at open to further reporting, other perspectives and different conclusions. Impartiality is impossible to demonstrate in every 140-character tweet one may post. But maintaining this posture is critical to our credibility and reputation as journalists.

At Reuters, we rely on what we call the 'second set of eyes' rule. Reuters' journalists have it drilled into them that we never publish anything in isolation; that one always sends what they produce through an editor first. In practice, this can be as simple as asking a colleague to look over your shoulder when you are publishing something – that colleague is acting as an editor in such circumstances – 'the second set of eyes' – and shoulders responsibility for any mistakes that may occur. The rule is used to reduce the number of mindless mistakes, typos, misspellings and dropped words individuals commonly make. But it is absolutely vital we apply this rule to avert more egregious mistakes, especially when we stray into controversial territory.

This has always been difficult when reporting from the field under real-time deadlines and has become all the more so with the constant connectedness of smartphones. We are constantly trying to figure out how we can adapt these rules to new situations.

In the context of Twitter it is fundamentally impossible to have a second set of eyes on individuals tweeting. Yet we do have the rule that if you find yourself heading into controversial territory, you need to recognize that and pause and talk to a colleague, editor or manager before you tweet. If you are slow off the mark with your tweet and someone beats you, that's okay; that is sometimes necessary. It boils down to reminding our journalists to not just absorb the ethics of whatever is popular on Twitter and social media, and to retain their journalistic voice and principles. What we are really asking them is just to retain their professional, journalistic sense of themselves in any forum they enter.

More issues

There is a lot of work to be done even in regard to the things that I have just described. There are surely many assertions here that as an organization of 3000-plus journalists, we will have a hard time living up to at all times. Many of these topics remain interesting and complicated questions that we are still getting our heads around as an organization. I talked about what material we can retweet and whether we should be fact-checking it first. Is there some way of attributing retweets within Twitter that makes it more clear what the source and quality of the information is? We need clearer retweeting policies so our journalists know what sorts of information we can quickly pass along and what we stop to verify.

What does it mean that among the people I follow on Twitter is (Anders Behring) Breivik[2] (accused of killing 77 people in two attacks in Norway). There is a simple explanation: when the story broke in July 2011, a lot of the information available about him was actually through his well-manicured, rather narcissistic social media profiles that he had set up himself ahead of the event. So to get his manifesto, to get pictures of him, to find out his relationships I had to 'follow' him on Twitter and 'friend' him on Facebook, so of course I am connected to him. Can that be construed as an endorsement? Of course, if you appreciate that I am working as a Reuters' journalist, does that explain it? That simple logic doesn't work for anyone with an axe to grind against me or Reuters. Over time, and with lots and lots of sources, is it paranoid to wonder whether the assorted collection of extremists I follow won't be used as evidence to show some kind of bias or favouritism or skewed thinking on my part? I open myself to attack and, I have found previously, such attacks can become highly personalized. It is the nature of the medium and the openness of social media networks; something, I suppose, journalists need to develop a thick skin to protect against.

Source security

What about ethical issues related to the pursuing or chasing of sources on Twitter? What happens when we get into a legal situation that could expose a key source? There are all kinds of landmines, all kinds of complexities. It is no longer the type of problem that one might have when everyone is trying out a new social media with a following of 50 people. I have 7000 sources in my phone and at some point almost all those 7000 sources will be on some sort of social media. Using rudimentary digital detective work you can probably deduce some of the connections I have with various sources. So we are looking at the issue of source security and how we protect our sources in this open landscape where everything is more or less traceable.

Balancing act

Then there is the simplest issue of balance within short-form tweets. It's very rare for a single tweet to encapsulate a full story, let alone the different sides of an argument. Is it enough to ask that journalists be judged by the fullness of their Twitter feed? Are short disclaimers inserted in one's Twitter profile enough? How is Twitter changing the notion of the fair exchange of ideas? One direction we are heading in is to deconstruct the traditional inverted pyramid style of traditional wire service journalism, in which the most important facts are stuffed up high in the story and less important paragraphs follow, which was once vital in enabling newspaper editors to cut the story from the bottom to fit constantly changing page layouts.

Can we rebuild the notion of the story or blog, tweet by tweet, where we tweet and counter tweet? Another possible format is that, as journalists, we just invite all our sources into a live blog and let them tweet and counter-tweet – and we just become the moderators of the live debate. That's already happening across a range of breaking news events we cover. But these are obviously issues that threaten and challenge traditional forms of presenting the news in a fair and balanced fashion.

There are similar issues related to the 'friending' of people on Facebook and or 'liking' an organization you want to monitor, or joining a 'cause' to learn more about their plans. Do these actions mean that you, the journalist, actually like or favour the people you report about, or are you just trying to get in contact with that person or group for reporting purposes? The example I used earlier about our Detroit reporting team: they had to like the union locals to join the discussion. It is a strange marketing gimmick of Facebook. We are trying to educate people and journalists that they should really not be out liking social media profiles arbitrarily. But if they need to go and get to the bottom of a story, they may do so, cautiously and uncloaked, always making clear they are from Reuters and working as a journalist. The issue of drawing a line between the professional responsibilities of journalists and their civil rights is not easy to solve in a world fascinated by social media, and at a time when people are becoming more intimately connected with friends, family, old school buddies and random members of their audience.

Notes

1   https://twitter.com/ReutersAero
2   https://twitter.com/AndersBBreivik

List of contributors

Eric Auchard is editorial innovation director for Reuters, based in London. He manages dozens of projects to transform how a network of more than 3000 journalists covers the news, both in terms of editorial practices and technical capabilities. Educated at the University of California at Berkeley, Auchard's job has been to encourage and develop ideas that improve how journalists work, putting into practice what he has learned by talking to smart people for 16 years as a technology reporter at Reuters. Previously, he worked as chief technology correspondent, columnist and editor for the global news organization. From 1993, Eric covered the rise of companies ranging from Netscape, to Cisco, Nokia, Google, Skype, Facebook and Twitter. As a sidelight, he has built many websites used inside Reuters to help journalists around the world collaborate. He sat on Reuters' internal venture board for funding innovative businesses from 2005 to 2007.

Leon Barkho is associate professor in media and communication science and manager of Media Content Practices and Effects Program at Sweden's Jonkoping University. He holds a master's degree in applied linguistics, and a doctorate in media and communication science. Previously, he held positions at Reuters news agency as bureau chief and was a staff writer at the Associated Press. A specialist in journalism and discourse, he is the author of *News From The BBC, CNN, And Al-Jazeera: How The Three Broadcasters Cover The Middle East*, and his research has been published in the *International Journal of Business Studies, Journalism Studies, Journal of Pragmatics, Studies in Language and Capitalism, Journal of Arab and Muslim Media Research*, and the *American Communication Journal*.

Dr Stephen Cushion is a senior lecturer at the Cardiff School of Journalism, Media and Cultural Studies, Cardiff University. He has sole authored *The Democratic Value of News: Why Public Service Media Matter* (Palgrave, 2012) and *Television Journalism* (Sage, 2012), and is co-editor (with Justin Lewis) of the edited collection, *The Rise of 24-Hour News Television: Global Perspectives* (Peter Lang, 2010). He has also published many book chapters which have broadly engaged with debates about the relationship between media, politics, democracy and citizenship, as well as in a wide range of international peer reviewed journals including *Journalism Studies, Journalism: Theory, Practice and Criticism, Journalism Practice, Journal of Public Affairs, Representation, Javnost: The Public, Cyfrwng: Media Wales Journal, Young: Nordic Journal of Youth Research, Journal of Youth Studies* and *Media & Jornalismo*.

Gitte Gravengaard (Ph.D.) is associate professor at the Department of Scandinavian Studies and Linguistics at the University of Copenhagen. She has written several articles and a book on professional practice and professional self-understanding among journalists. Furthermore, in several articles and papers she has argued that combining media sociology with linguistic analysis and conversation analysis is one of the most fruitful ways in which to study professional practice, professional self-understanding and professional identity

Jöran Hök is a senior lecturer at Södertörn University, the second University of Stockholm, founded in 1996. He was for more than ten years editor-in-chief of the Swedish development magazine *OmVärlden* (1998–2009), lecturer and research fellow at Gothenburg University's Peace and Development Research Institute and Department for Journalism and Mass Communication (1986–98), and lecturer at Stockholm University's Department for Journalism, Media and Communication (2007–09).

Dr Eva Kingsepp is a media and communication scholar, specialising in the uses of history and memory in popular culture. She is currently a postdoc researcher at Stockholm University's Department of History and senior lecturer at the Department of Media Studies and the section for Middle Eastern and North African Studies.

Miles Maguire is a professor of journalism at the University of Wisconsin Oshkosh, where he teaches writing, editing and reporting. He was the founding editor of the Oshkosh Community News Network, a non-profit online news organization whose work was cited as a notable innovation in journalism in the Knight-Batten Awards. More recently, Maguire has focused his research on two interrelated areas – quality standards for news organizations and reporting methods. An associate editor of *Literary Journalism Studies*, he is working on a biography of Thomas Whiteside, a writer for *The New Yorker* whose articles were credited with bringing a halt to the use of Agent Orange by the US military.

Kevin Marsh spent 33 years at the BBC. Joining the corporation as a news trainee in 1978, he was made editor of PM in August 1989, and then moved to edit *The World At One* in 1993, before bringing the programs together under a single editorship in 1996. In 1998, he developed and launched Radio 4's Broadcasting House. In addition to editing *The World At One*, *The World This Weekend*, PM and Broadcasting House, he produced numerous specials for Radio 4 and has won numerous Sony Awards. He became editor of the BBC College of Journalism in February 2006. One of his first tasks was to establish an online presence for the college, which was launched officially in January 2007. He is currently a visiting fellow at Bournemouth University Media School and director and founder of OffspinMedia. He is a regular contributor for the UK's *Press Gazette*.

Rune Ottosen (b.1950) is professor in journalism at Oslo and Akershus University College of Applied Sciences. He has written extensively on press history and media coverage of war and conflicts. He is co-editor with Stig Arne Nohrstedt of several books, the latest, *Global War – Local Views: Media Images of the Iraq War*. In 2008, Ottosen published *VG, Saddam og vi. Et kritisk blikk på nyhetsdekning av kriger og konflikter*. In 2010 he was one of the editors and co-author of the four volume Norwegian press history, *Norsk Presses historie (1767–2010)*.

Morten Skovsgaard (Ph.D.) in an assistant professor at the Center for Journalism/ Department of Political Science at the University of Southern Denmark. He wrote his Ph.D. dissertation on the professional norms, values and autonomy of Danish journalists. His research interests are journalism and political communication, particularly on journalists' professional ideals, their practice, and the effects of their products on the audience. He has published in books such as *The Global Journalists in the 21th Century* (2012), and journals such as *Journalism, Journalism Studies* and *Journalism Practice*.